Practical Ruby Gems

David Berube

Practical Ruby Gems

Copyright © 2007 by David Berube

ISBN-13 (pbk): 978-1-59059-811-5

ISBN-10 (pbk): 1-59059-811-3

Printed and bound in the United States of America 9 8 7 6 5 4 3 2 1

Lead Editor: Jason Gilmore
Technical Reviewer: Yan Pritzker
Editorial Board: Steve Anglin, Ewan Buckingham, Gary Cornell, Jason Gilmore, Jonathan Gennick, Jonathan Hassell, James Huddleston, Chris Mills, Matthew Moodie, Jeff Pepper, Paul Sarknas, Dominic Shakeshaft, Jim Sumser, Matt Wade
Project Manager: Richard Dal Porto
Copy Edit Manager: Nicole Flores
Copy Editor: Candace English
Assistant Production Director: Kari Brooks-Copony
Production Editor: Kelly Winquist
Compositor: Diana Van Winkle, Van Winkle Design
Proofreader: Liz Welch
Indexer: Julie Grady
Cover Designer: Kurt Krames
Manufacturing Director: Tom Debolski

Distributed to the book trade worldwide by Springer-Verlag New York, Inc., 233 Spring Street, 6th Floor, New York, NY 10013. Phone 1-800-SPRINGER, fax 201-348-4505, e-mail orders-ny@springer-sbm.com, or visit http://www.springeronline.com.

For information on translations, please contact Apress directly at 2560 Ninth Street, Suite 219, Berkeley, CA 94710. Phone 510-549-5930, fax 510-549-5939, e-mail info@apress.com, or visit http://www.apress.com.

The source code for this book is available to readers at http://www.apress.com in the Source Code/ Download section.

Dedicated to my parents

Contents at a Glance

PART 1 ■ ■ ■ Using RubyGems

PART 2 ■ ■ ■ Using Particular Gems

PART 3 ■ ■ ■ Creating Gems

Contents

PART 1 ■■■ Using RubyGems

PART 2 ■■■ Using Particular Gems

PART 3 ■ ■ ■ Creating Gems

About the Author

DAVID BERUBE is a Ruby developer, trainer, author, and speaker. He's used both Ruby and Ruby on Rails since 2003, when he became a Ruby advocate after he wrote about the language for *Dr Dobb's Journal*. Prior to that he worked professionally with PHP, Perl, C++, and Visual Basic.

David's professional accomplishments include creating the Ruby on Rails engine for Cool-Ruby.com (http://coolruby.com), a site that tracks the latest Ruby developments, and working with thoughtbot (www.thoughtbot.com) on the Rails engine that powers Sermo's America's Top Doc contest. He also worked with the Casting Frontier on the Ruby on Rails backend that is powering their digital casting services for Los Angeles. He has worked on several other Ruby projects, including the engine powering CyberKnowHow's BirdFluBreakingNews search engine.

David's writing has been in print in over 65 countries, in magazines such as *Linux Magazine, Dr Dobb's Journal*, and *International PHP Magazine*. He's also taught college courses and spoken publicly on topics such as "MySQL and You" and "Making Money with Open Source Software."

Feel free to contact the author via his website at http://berubeconsulting.com or via his email address at djberube@berubeconsulting.com.

Acknowledgments

I'd like to thank my parents and my sisters; I can't imagine writing this book without them. I'd also like to thank the many friends that have supported me; in particular, I'd like to thank Wayne Hammar and Matthew Gifford.

I'd also like to thank the vast array of professional associates I've worked with and learned from, and in particular I'd like to thank Terry Simkin, Ted Roche, Bill Sconce, Bruce Dawson, K.C. Singh, and Joey Rubenstein. Thanks to Peter Cooper for introducing me to the possibility of writing this book.

Finally, I'd like to thank my editors, originally Keir Thomas and later Jason Gilmore, as well as my technical reviewer Yan Pritzker, my project manager Richard Dal Porto, and my copy editor Candace English.

PART 1

■■■

Using RubyGems

This section of the book introduces RubyGems and explains how you can start using them in your code.

CHAPTER 1

■ ■ ■

What Is RubyGems?

In short, RubyGems lets you distribute and install Ruby code wherever you can install Ruby.

Specifically, RubyGems is a package-management system for Ruby applications and libraries. It lets you install Ruby code—called *gems*—to any computer running Ruby. It can resolve dependences for you, so if you want to install a given piece of software, RubyGems can handle that for you. It can even resolve version dependencies—so that if a certain gem or your code requires a certain version of another gem, it can take care of that. It also wraps all of this functionality in a very easy-to-use package.

The gems come in a variety of types. For example, if you had a Web application to which your users uploaded pictures from a digital camera, you'd likely need to resize the pictures, which come in a variety of sizes. You could write the resizing code by hand, but it'd be considerably faster to use the rmagick gem to resize the pictures—and you could add additional features like cropping, rotation, sharpening, and so on with just a few extra lines of code, since rmagick includes all of those features. (See Chapter 25 for more details.)

Alternatively, if you want to develop a Web application using Ruby on Rails—which is a full-featured, very powerful Model View Controller (MVC) Web framework—you could install that using RubyGems as well. Rails consists of a number of libraries and utilities—all of which can be installed by RubyGems with just one command. (See Chapter 23 for more information.)

This chapter covers the features of RubyGems and how it differs from other package-management systems.

Why Use RubyGems?

First of all, RubyGems makes it easy use to install Ruby software. For example, Instiki (http://instiki.org/) is a wiki—a kind of content-management system—and if we wanted to install the instiki gem, we could do so with the following command in the Linux/Mac OS X shell or the Windows command prompt:

```
gem install instiki
```

Of course, to do that you'd need RubyGems installed, and we'll cover that in the next two chapters. For now, though, you can see how easy it is to install gems—just one command and RubyGems takes care of the rest.

This can be extremely important; for example, if you had a Web application written in Ruby and your server failed, you'd need to be able to quickly and easily install all of the software that your application needs on a new server.

It Provides a Standard Way to Describe Ruby Software and Requirements.

RubyGems lets you define *gemspecs*. A gemspec describes software—it includes the name, version, description, and so forth. This gemspec can be built into a .gem file, which is a compressed archive containing the gemspec and all of the files that the software requires.

This .gem file can be uploaded to RubyForge, which lets you install it from any Internet-connected RubyGems installation, or it can be distributed via traditional means, like HTTP or FTP. Because the .gem file contains a description of the program, you can also use the gem list command to see the details of the gem or to search for similar gems. (You can find more details on the gem list command in Chapter 3 and you can find out more about building gems in Chapters 34 and 35.)

For example, if you upgrade a version of a gem and the new version has additional requirements, you won't need to scour the documentation for the changes—RubyGems will automatically read the requirements from the gemspec since the format of the gemspecs is standard.

It Provides a Central Repository of Software.

One of the aspects of RubyGems that makes it so appealing is it gives you access to RubyForge —a central repository of Ruby software. You can find out more about RubyForge at, http://rubyforge.org. Without RubyForge, you'd have to locate, download, and then install a gem and its dependencies. With RubyForge, though, RubyGems can automatically locate the software and its dependencies for you.

Although most Rubyists (Ruby programmers and enthusiasts) install gems only from the central repository, you aren't required you to use it—you can install gems from any location you choose. (You can also set up your own gem server, which you'll learn about next.) For example, if you had to move your software from one operating system to another, your operating system's packaging system and repository would be different, but RubyGems would stay the same—you can use RubyForge wherever RubyGems is installed.

It Lets You Redistribute Gems Using a Gem Server.

The technology used to serve gems comes with RubyGems. You can set up your own RubyGems server on a local network or on the Internet without much trouble; if, for example, you'd like to cache all of the gems your development team uses on a local server to speed up downloads, you can do that.

If you'd prefer not to use RubyForge and rather distribute gems via your own website or gem server, you can do that too. You can find more details in Chapter 35.

It Handles Software Dependencies for You.

RubyGems can take care of dependencies automatically. That means that when you install a gem, it can automatically determine what other gems are required and ask you if you'd like to install them.

This can make your life much easier, since a significant amount of Ruby software is built using other Ruby software—and that other Ruby software might require still more software. Without RubyGems, you might have to spend hours installing and researching dozens of packages to get complex software working. With RubyGems, you can just install the gem and let it resolve dependencies for you.

It Handles Multiple Software Versions Intelligently.

RubyGems can store multiple gem versions, and software that uses RubyGems can request particular gem software versions—so, for example, an application that requests the ActiveRecord gem (http://rubyforge.org/projects/activerecord/) could request a gem that's newer or older than a given version. This is very helpful if, for example, a later version of a gem breaks your program, or if your program requires a feature from the latest version of a gem. (You can find more details on how to do this in Chapter 4.)

It Can Be Used Transparently in Place of Regular Ruby Libraries.

RubyGems has a facility that makes it transparent to use gem software. For example, suppose you wanted to use the Camping (http://rubyforge.org/projects/camping/) Web microframework. If you installed Camping the traditional way, you would use the Camping library in your code like this:

```
require 'camping'
```

If you installed it via RubyGems, you use the exact same code. As you can see, using code via RubyGems is transparent, so you can switch back and forth easily; if you distribute your software, the user does not need to have RubyGems installed—only the required library.

Note, however, that if you want to require that a certain version of the software is installed, you'll need to use a special RubyGems statement in your code. (See Chapter 4 for further details.)

It Lets You Use the Same Technology on Any Operating System.

RubyGems targets all platforms that run Ruby. If it runs Ruby, it runs RubyGems. A number of other systems exist to make software installation easier; there's everything from those that simply install software—like Window's MSI installation system—to full package-management systems, like Debian Linux's apt (Advanced Package Tool), Red Hat's yum, or OS X's DarwinPorts. Such systems are generally operating system–dependent, though, as we'll discuss next.

How Does RubyGems Compare to Other Packaging Systems?

Operating system–specific packaging systems, such as apt or yum, can carry Ruby software as well. Since Ruby software can be used by non-Rubyists, this is important. It's also convenient if you need just a few pieces of software. For Rubyists, though, it's usually better to install gems using RubyGems, since RubyGems has the best selection of Ruby software and the latest versions. Additionally, unlike RubyGems, OS-native packagers don't handle multiple gem versions installed simultaneously.

However, it is possible to install a limited selection of Ruby software using other packaging systems. For example, you could install the MySQL Ruby bindings via gem like this:

```
gem install mysql
```

Alternatively, you could install the same library via apt-get under Ubuntu Linux like this:

```
apt-get install libmysql-ruby1.8
```

Finally, you could install it via DarwinPorts under OS X like this:

```
port install rb-mysql
```

Note that those three commands require you to be logged in as root—if you prefer, you can prefix each command with sudo, which will execute that single command with the root-user privileges.

In some cases you can install software via apt or another packaging system. Such systems usually have a very limited selection of Ruby packages, but if they happen to include all of the software you need, you may be able to use them. Consult the documentation that comes with your Linux distribution or other packaging system.

Note, though, that installing gems from your OS distribution is not recommended. It means you have to use the version of the software in your OS's repository, and often this lags significantly behind the RubyGems versions. Using the gem installer, as we do throughout this book, will automatically give you access to the most recent gem versions.

Of course, you can always skip package-management systems entirely—you can install Ruby software by running an install script manually or by copying files into the lib directory of your Ruby installation. If you want to do so, download the software you want from its homepage and consult the included README or INSTALL file.

CHAPTER 2

■■■

Installing RubyGems

You'll need the RubyGems system to follow the examples from this book. The RubyGems system lets you use a vast array of Ruby software packages—including all of the gems we cover in this book. In general, it's fairly easy to install RubyGems. Of course, before you can install RubyGems, you need to install Ruby—we'll cover both in this chapter. Finally, we'll explain how you can update a RubyGems system you've already installed.

■**Note** If you already have RubyGems installed, you can skip this chapter.

Installing Ruby

To follow the examples in this book, and before you install RubyGems, you must have the Ruby programming language interpreter and libraries installed on your machine.

Mac OS X comes with Ruby preinstalled; if you have Mac OS X installed, you can skip straight to the section, "Installing RubyGems under Linux and Mac OS X." Many Linux distributions include Ruby, so we'll cover how you can check if your computer has Ruby installed. Windows does not install Ruby by default, so if you are running Windows, skip straight to "Installing Ruby on Windows Using the One-Click Installer." (If you're using Windows, the One-Click Installer will install both Ruby and RubyGems at once.)

Is Ruby Already Installed on Your Computer?

If you're not sure if you need to install Ruby, run the following command at the OS X/Linux shell or the Windows command prompt:

```
ruby -v
```

If you receive a "command not found" error, you don't have Ruby installed. You should get a message like the following:

```
ruby 1.8.4 (2006-04-14) [i386-mswin32]
```

The version number is the number immediately after the "ruby"—in this case, 1.8.4. Note that to use the RubyGems system (as well as to use a lot of other software that uses Ruby), you'll need version 1.8.4 or later. If you have a lower version, you should upgrade—look for appropriate instructions for your operating system to upgrade your installation.

Installing Ruby on a Linux System

We'll briefly cover three methods of installing Ruby on Linux. The first, apt, is a package manager for Debian-based distributions, such as Ubuntu. The second, yum, is a package manager for Red Hat–based distributions. These both offer an easy way to install Ruby. If your system does not support either apt or yum, you can install Ruby by compiling the source code yourself, which is slightly more complicated. We'll cover that method last.

Installing Ruby on Debian Linux Distributions with apt

apt is a popular package-management system for Debian Linux and Debian-based distributions, such as Ubuntu Linux, Lindows, Xandros, and others. It bears some similarities to RubyGems; for instance, it can download, install, and remove software from the command line. (apt can also be used on non-Debian distributions, but it does not come installed by default.)

If you'd like to use apt to install Ruby, you can do so as follows:

```
sudo apt-get install ruby*
```

This will automatically download and install Ruby, and you can proceed to the "Testing Your Ruby Installation" section of this chapter.

■Note The last two `apt-get` commands install required libraries for installing RubyGems; if you don't plan on installing RubyGems, those aren't absolutely necessary to run Ruby.

Installing Ruby on Red Hat Linux Distributions with yum

yum is another package-management system—it's very similar to apt. It's available on all versions of Fedora Core. If you'd like to use yum to install Ruby, you can do so as follows:

```
yum install ruby
```

This will download and install Ruby and the required libraries for you, and you can proceed to the "Testing Your Ruby Installation" section of this chapter.

Installing Ruby on Linux from the Ruby Source

You'll need to have `gcc` and `make` installed to compile Ruby; if you don't have them installed, consult your distribution's documentation for the installation instructions. First download and uncompress the latest Ruby source tarball from `ftp://ftp.ruby-lang.org/pub/ruby/`, then compile and install Ruby with the following shell commands:

```
./configure
make
make test
make install
```

Once you've done so, your Ruby installation should be ready and you can proceed to the "Testing Your Ruby Installation" section of this chapter.

Installing Ruby on Windows Using the One-Click Installer

The Ruby One-Click installer is very easy to use. It is a precompiled, self-contained Windows installer. It's developed by Ruby Central (`http://rubycentral.org/`), and provides Ruby in the only real way to distribute software for Windows, which is as a binary—after all, Windows does not have any method to compile software by default. (This is true under some Linux distributions as well.)

The installer is very simple, as you can imagine from the name—you won't have to launch multiple programs or type commands into the Windows prompt, so it fits in well with the Windows way of doing things.

You can download the One-Click Installer from `http://rubyinstaller.rubyforge.org/`. Once you've done so, run the program by double-clicking on the icon. You'll be asked a few questions, but if you select the default options you should be all set. Proceed to the "Testing Your Ruby Installation" section of this chapter.

DOWNLOADING FILES WITH WGET

While the most familiar way to download files under Windows is to use a Web browser, there are other options. A popular Linux utility, wget, comes in Win32 form—you can get it at `http://users.ugent.be/~bpuype/wget/`.

wget lets you download files from the command line in just one command. Not all Windows users are comfortable using the command prompt, but once you become comfortable, many people find it easier to use.

Once you've downloaded and installed wget, you can use it to download Ruby from the command prompt like this:

```
wget http://rubyforge.org/frs/download.php/11926/ruby184-20.exe
```

This would save you a number of clicks and the hassle of launching a Web browser.

Testing Your Ruby Installation

How can you be sure that Ruby works? Let's try a very simple test. You can rerun the version command discussed earlier by typing the following command in the Windows command prompt or the Linux/OS X shell:

```
ruby -v
```

You should get a display similar to the following:

```
ruby 1.8.4 (2006-04-14) [i386-mswin32]
```

If you'd like to test an actual line of code, you can do so as follows:

```
ruby -e "puts 'hello world!'"
```

You should get the following output:

```
hello world!
```

Once you've verified that you have Ruby installed, you can install RubyGems; we'll cover that next. If you used the Windows One-Click Installer, it already installed RubyGems for you, so you can skip straight to "Testing Your RubyGems Installation."

Installing RubyGems Under Linux and Mac OS X

It's fairly easy to install RubyGems on Linux, and you can use the same procedure to install RubyGems on Mac OS X. On those systems, use the following shell commands to download and install RubyGems:

```
curl -O http://rubyforge.org/frs/download.php/11289/rubygems-0.9.0.tgz
tar -xvzf  rubygems-0.9.0.tgz
cd rubygems-0.9.0.tgz
ruby setup.rb
```

Once you've done so, set an environment variable, RUBYOPT, using a line in your .profile:

```
export RUBYOPT=rubygems
```

This environment variable causes RubyGems to be run whenever Ruby is run. You can get an similar effect by including the line require "rubygems" in all of your Ruby scripts, but since most Ruby scripts using RubyGems are written assuming that you have RUBYOPT set, that'll require you to modify all of the programs you download—no small task. You can also run your Ruby script with the -rubygems option, but that's a lot of extra typing.

■Note You shouldn't have any negative effects from setting the RUBYOPT variable—even if some of your scripts don't use RubyGems. (Keep in mind that the Windows installer sets the RUBYOPT variable for you unless you explicitly tell it not to.)

At this point, you should have a working RubyGems system, so you can install and use gems. You can now check your installation by following the directions in the next section of this chapter.

Testing Your RubyGems Installation

First let's pull up a list of installed gems. You can use the following command at the Linux/OS X shell or the Windows command prompt:

```
gem --version
```

You should get the following response:

```
x.y.z
```

Note that x.y.z will be replaced by the appropriate directions for your operating system. If you get a "command not found" error, you've done something wrong and you'll want to follow the appropriate instructions again for your operating system; you'll also want to make sure you installed Ruby before you installed RubyGems. Also check that if you already had Ruby installed, it's a version later than 1.8.4. If not, you'll want to install a more recent version.

At this point, you have a working RubyGems install—you can now try all of the examples in this book.

Updating Your RubyGems System After You've Installed It

Once you've installed RubyGems, you can update it easily. You can use the same command on any operating system. Typing the following command at the Linux/OS X shell or the Windows command prompt will update RubyGems:

```
gem update --system
```

This will automatically download and install the latest update of the RubyGems system; you can then use whatever updates have been made available. To check for RubyGems updates, visit http://rubygems.org/.

CHAPTER 3

■ ■ ■

Using RubyGems in Your Code

In this chapter you'll learn how you can use RubyGems in your code. You'll learn about installing individual gems; see a practical example of using them; get debugging tips; and consider a few miscellaneous issues, like unpacking gems so they can be edited, freezing gems so they don't change, and using plugins and engines under Rails.

Getting Started with a Ruby Gem

Before we use a gem, we must install it. The instructions in this chapter assume you have the RubyGems system already installed; if you don't, refer to the previous chapter.

Gems are usually downloaded automatically, since the gem program can fetch gems from the Internet. In fact, you can install most gems with a single command:

```
gem install gemname
```

Replace *gemname* with the name of the gem you want to install. Of course, to do that, you need to know what the gem is called. To demonstrate this and other aspects of gem use, we're going to follow a small demo project.

Suppose you are developing an ecommerce application, and you want a quick way to find out if a credit card number is valid without actually charging the card; that way, you can have immediate feedback in your user interface if a customer mistypes the number.

To find a gem that fits our criteria, we could do a Web search to determine if there are any gems with the functionality we need. However, we can first search the gem repository directly using the gem list command. We can guess that a gem dealing with credit will start with the word *credit*; let's search the repository and see what we get. We can do that with the following shell or Windows Prompt command:

```
gem list -r credit

*** REMOTE GEMS ***

creditcard (1.0)
 These functions tell you whether a credit card number is
 self-consistent using known algorithms for credit card numbers.
```

A few things to note: the -r switch tells the gem command not to search the local repositories, since we'd probably know if we installed a gem that fits our needs. If you omit the -r switch, it'll search both local and remote gems. If you replace -r with the -l switch, you'll search local gems only.

The `credit` part of that command tells the `gem` command to search for gems whose name starts with `credit`. Note that this is part of a regular expression, so if you say `gem list -r .*credit`, you'll search for any gem whose name contains `credit` anywhere in the string.

Also note that you do not need to specify a search criteria; `gem list -r` will give you a complete list of remote gems, and `gem list -l` will tell you all of the gems you've installed locally. (You can save a copy of the remote gem list using your operating system's redirection support: `gem list -r > remote_gem_list.txt` will save a list of all remote gems available into `remote_gem_list.txt`.)

Now that we know the name of the gem, we can install it. Here's the command that will install the `creditcard` gem:

```
>gem install creditcard
Successfully installed creditcard-1.0.0
```

You'll likely need to run this command as root under Linux/OS X. Once you've installed the gem, you can create an application to use it.

Using the creditcard Gem

The `creditcard` gem verifies that credit card numbers are valid. At first glance, it might seem like the gem actually runs cards through a credit card processor; it doesn't. It also does not verify that the account exists, that the expiration date is correct, or that there is sufficient available balance in the account to make a charge; all of those require actually charging the card via a payment gateway or merchant account, which takes time and isn't done until an order is complete.

■**Note** Keep in mind that any given gem won't always solve your problem—you might need to look around a bit to find one that fits, and even when you find it you'll likely need to do some work to get it to solve your particular problem. At times, it may be more work fitting the gem into place than it would be to solve the problem from scratch, particularly if the gem were badly designed—in that case, you'd be better off using custom code.

However, it does verify that a number isn't invalid; it checks the internal checksum of the card number, and that can be done immediately as a user is entering card information. As a result, the `creditcard` gem can help ensure that users entered cards correctly and do not make any typos. Let's write a simple app to use the `creditcard` gem to test credit card numbers.

```
require 'creditcard'

if ARGV[0]
  credit_card_number=ARGV[0]
  if credit_card_number.creditcard?
    puts "Credit card number is valid " <<
    "with type #{credit_card_number.creditcard_type}."
  else
```

```
    puts "Credit card number is not valid."
  end
else
  puts "Please enter a valid credit card number."
end
```

That's pretty simple code for some fairly complex functionality; the statement "require creditcard" gives us the ability to use the full functionality of that gem quite easily on any string.

■**Note** You can download all of the code from this book from the Source Code/Download section of http://www.apress.com/ instead of typing it in.

The ARGV array is a Ruby global variable that contains the command-line arguments to the program. Our program expects you to pass a credit card on the command line, so if there aren't any, the program will print "Please enter a valid credit card number." It'll then call the creditcard? method. This returns true if the string is a valid credit card, and false otherwise. This method takes an optional parameter—if we called it credit_card_number.creditcard? visa, it would return true only if the number were a valid Visa credit card number, and false if it were an invalid credit card number or a non-Visa credit card number. The other method we use is the creditcard_type method; it's also an extension to the String class. That method returns the credit card type, and the preceding listing uses it to print out the credit card type.

Note that no special creditcard objects are created; the creditcard gem extends the String class directly. This is not possible in most languages; however, in Ruby this is called *monkeypatching*, and is common. Also note that both methods end in a question mark. This is a Ruby convention indicating that the method returns a true or false value. The question mark has no special syntactic value—it's just an indication to the programmer. (The other symbol commonly used at the end of method names is the exclamation mark, which means that a method modifies the receiver in place.)

Let's test the program. We'll start by checking that a completely bogus input doesn't work:

```
ruby creditcard_check.rb not-a-number
```

```
Credit card number is not valid.
```

It's good so far. Now let's try with a correctly formatted number that isn't a valid card:

```
ruby creditcard_check.rb 0000-0000-0000-0000
```

```
Credit card number is valid with type unknown.
```

The numbers in Table 3-1 are test card numbers used to debug payment gateways, terminals, and merchant accounts. They are numerically correct, but aren't attached to any charge account. We can use them to test our script.

Table 3-1. *Test Credit Card Numbers*

Card Type	Test Number
Visa	4111-1111-1111-1111
MasterCard	5431-1111-1111-1111
American Express	341-1111-1111-1111
Discover	6011-6011-6011-6611
Diners Club	3530-1113-3330-0000

Let's grab the test numbers from the table and see how well they work:

```
ruby creditcard_check.rb 4111-1111-1111-1111
```

```
Credit card number is valid with type visa.
```

```
ruby creditcard_check.rb 5431-1111-1111-1111
```

```
Credit card number is valid with type mastercard.
```

```
ruby creditcard_check.rb 341-1111-1111-1111
```

```
Credit card number is valid with type american_express.
```

```
ruby creditcard_check.rb 6011-6011-6011-6611
```

```
Credit card number is valid with type discover.
```

```
>ruby creditcard_check.rb 35301113333300000
```

```
Credit card number is invalid.
```

You can see that the gem detects valid test cards without a problem. In a production environment it may be wise to test with a few real cards as well. You can also see that it supports both card numbers formatted with dashes and those without, and a fair number of card types.

So, you can see that the gem works. You can also conclude that it's very simple to use gems in your program: you need only to have the gem installed and use the `require` statement to utilize it. We can't tell from the source how the `creditcard` gem was installed; the script does not care how the `creditcard` library is installed, and the only requirement is that it can be accessed by the `require` statement. This means that if an alternative Ruby library packaging system were developed, our code would work without changes; additionally, if a script is installed manually, it will work out modifications.

Playing Nice with cmdparse Command-Line Parsing

The preceding example was fairly simple—what if we want to use some more-complex functionality in our application? Fortunately, gems remain easy to use even when the gems involved are complex. Our previous example was a command-line application; however, it had a very simple interface. Let's try to make our application more general-purpose: specifically, let's add a gem that gives us the ability to parse complex command-line arguments and, based on the user's input, either give documentation on what the program does or perform an action. Instead of our giving the user all available information, the user can ask for what he wants and receive only that; that's considered a superior approach, since the user can reuse the information in other programs without having to parse our output for the desired answer.

First let's install a gem to help us parse command-line arguments:

```
gem install cmdparse
```

```
Successfully installed cmdparse-2.0.2
Installing ri documentation for cmdparse-2.0.2...
Installing RDoc documentation for cmdparse-2.0.2...
```

■**Note** The `gem install cmdparse` command installed RDocs for us, which are documentation for the gem; the RDocs are stored in the `/path/to/your/ruby/install/lib/ruby/gems/1.8/doc` directory. They include a full class documentation and a browser in HTML format, which you can see with any Web browser. The other gems are there as well, so feel free to browse that directory to see the documentation for any gems you have installed.

Next let's update our example script:

```
require 'creditcard'
require 'cmdparse'

cmd = CmdParse::CommandParser.new( true, true )
cmd.program_name = "creditcard_check"
cmd.program_version = [0, 2, 0]
cmd.add_command( CmdParse::HelpCommand.new,true )
cmd.add_command( CmdParse::VersionCommand.new,true )
```

```
verify = CmdParse::Command.new('verify', false )
verify.short_desc = "Verifies a credit card"
verify.set_execution_block do |args|
  args.each do |arg|
    if arg.creditcard?
      puts "Valid"
    else
      puts "Invalid"
    end
  end
end

type = CmdParse::Command.new( 'type', false )
type.short_desc = "Returns the type of credit card"
type.set_execution_block do |args|
  args.each do |arg|
    if arg.creditcard?
      puts arg.creditcard_type
    else
      puts "Invalid"
    end

  end
end

cmd.add_command( verify, false )
cmd.add_command( type, false)
cmd.parse
```

That was a bit more complicated than our previous example, but still fairly simple. The require cmdparse line lets us automatically include all of the functionality of the cmdparse library—it'll parse our command lines for us.

Specifically, cmdparse lets you parse command lines of the following form:

```
script command1 [options..] command2 [options…]
```

The Linux ifcfg command works like this; so does the Windows NET command. Since our demo credit card program can fit into this mold fairly reasonably, cmdparse is a good option. It won't fit every program—in some cases switches would fit your program better—but it works well here, particularly since you can pass multiple credit card numbers to check or verify at once.

Cmdparse provides us with several predefined commands, which we simply instantiate and add to our cmdparse object: a help command that lists the commands we've added to our cmdparse object, and a version command that lists the current version we've set via cmd.program_version. Cmdparse also gives us a framework to add our own commands: type and verify. These commands will print the type and check the validity of a card number, respectively.

To actually make it possible to use these commands, we create a new CmdParse::Command object for each. We set its *short desc*, which controls its description in the help command, and use set_execution_block to control what actually happens when the command is called.

While our example is fairly simple, it would be trivial to extend this to a great number of options—and what's even better is that cmdparse keeps it simple and clean, so that even at a large number of possible commands our program stays easy to maintain.

Let's take our new program for a test drive:

```
ruby creditcard_check.rb help
```

```
Usage: creditcard_check [options] COMMAND [options] [COMMAND [options] ...] [ar
gs]

Available commands:
 help Provide help for individual commands (=default command)
 type Returns the type of credit card
 verify Verifies a credit card
```

```
>ruby creditcard_check.rb version
```

```
0.2.0
```

```
>ruby creditcard_check.rb verify not_a_number
```

```
Invalid
```

```
>ruby creditcard_check.rb verify 5431-1111-1111-1111
```

```
Valid
```

```
>ruby creditcard_check.rb type 5431-1111-1111-1111
```

```
mastercard
```

```
>ruby creditcard_check.rb type 5431-1111-1111-1111 verify 4111-1111-1111-1111
```

```
mastercard
Valid
```

In this version, we've not only added automatic help and option parsing, but we've made the output cleaner and the interface more powerful; therefore, an outside script could call this script and verify or check the type of card numbers, even if the outside script were written in a different programming language and did not have access to the creditcard gem. Also notice the last example: you can pass multiple commands on the same command line.

Even a very simple program, such as a shell script, can have access to the functionality using this method. Since we used a command-line parsing gem, we can be sure that we didn't leave subtle errors in our parsing routine, and we also saved significant development time and effort.

WHAT IS REQUIRE_GEM?

You may have seen the require_gem statement in a Ruby script, which might seem like the logical way of requiring a gem. However, in the preceding examples, only the require statement was used. This is because under normal conditions, you don't need to use the require_gem statement. Both are necessary only to access special gem-specific functionality.

In particular, require_gem allows you to specify what version of a gem you want to use. In other words, you need use require_gem statements if you need to specify a particular gem version; otherwise you can simply use require.

However, as mentioned previously, you may need more control at times. You might need a gem that's earlier than a given version, since later versions might change the API and break your code. Or you might need a gem that's later than a given version, since earlier versions might not include the functionality you need. Here are three examples of require_gem statements you might use inside Rails:

```
require_gem 'activesupport', '<= 1.0.4'
require_gem 'activesupport', '= 1.0.4'
require_gem 'activesupport', '>= 1.0.4'
```

The first asks for any version of the activesupport gem 1.0.4 or earlier. The second asks for 1.0.4 exactly, and the third asks for 1.0.4 or later. This functionality is very powerful, and quite useful, since much of the Ruby world is changing very rapidly. As a result, specifying your gem versions can keep your application from crashing ignominiously when a new version of a gem is released. It can also provide more understandable error messages; by specifying version requirements, you can get helpful error messages when you deploy on a host that doesn't meet the gem version requirements. That can make a gem-incompatibility issue much easier to fix, since you can quickly and easily determine exactly what's wrong.

Refer to Chapter 4 for more detailed information on how require_gem versioning works; but for now, realize that you can use require for any script in which you don't need a specific gem version, and that you need require_gem only when you have to carefully control the gem versions in use.

Working with Source Gems

Most gems will work under both Linux and Windows since Ruby is an interpreted language and most gems are written in Ruby. However, not all gems are pure Ruby source; some include C extensions or libraries. Those gems must be compiled before they are used. This is normally not an issue; however, many computers—Windows computers in particular—do not have a C/C++ compiler, and not all machines have the proper libraries to install any given gem. As a result, such gems typically come in multiple varieties: a special binary distribution for Windows machines, and a source variety that is portable and will typically work on most Unix-like systems, such as Linux or Mac OS X.

In some cases you'll get a choice of what precompiled versions to install. Here's a quick look at what happens when you try to install Mongrel (see Chapter 17 for more details) on Win32:

```
C:\projects\my_proj>gem install mongrel
```

```
Need to update 10 gems from http://gems.rubyforge.org
..........
complete
Select which gem to install for your platform (i386-mswin32)
 1. mongrel 0.3.13.3 (mswin32)
 2. mongrel 0.3.13.3 (ruby)
 3. mongrel 0.3.13.2 (mswin32)
 4. mongrel 0.3.13.2 (ruby)
… snipped earlier versions…
 42. Cancel installation
> 1
Successfully installed mongrel-0.3.13.3-mswin32
Installing ri documentation for mongrel-0.3.13.3-mswin32...
Installing RDoc documentation for mongrel-0.3.13.3-mswin32...
```

As you can see, the gem command presents you with a list of options. The (ruby) versions work anywhere that has a C compiler; the (mswin32) versions work only under Windows.

However, not all binary gems for Win32 can be downloaded by the gem command; some must be manually downloaded via a Web browser from the gem's Web page. The reason for this is that binary gems often require an extra step, such as running a postinstall.rb file, and so can't be distributed via the gem command. When binary gems are available via the gem install command, you will be presented with a list of platforms and versions for that gem, choose the gem version you'd like for the platform you'd like. Since only Windows typically has difficulty compiling binary gems, the options are usually a Ruby version—which would contain the compilable source—and a Win32 version.

Under Win32 you would download the binary gem, uncompress it, and then use a command like this Rmagick install command (see Chapter 25 for more details) to install the gem from the file:

```
gem install RMagick-win32-x.x.x-mswin32.gem
```

Since it's a local filename, the gem command knows that it should use the local copy instead of downloading the gem. After this, most binary gems include a postinstall process, which will take whatever steps can't be completed by the gem command. You would then run a postinstall command, like this:

```
>ruby postinstall.rb
```

Depending on the gem, of course, the installation process may vary. Binary gems may have other issues, since they are compiled for a certain version of Ruby. Using source gems and compiling them yourself avoids such issues, and you should always compile from source if possible.

When you are installing a source gem on a Linux or Mac OS X system, you won't typically have a problem, assuming you have the dependencies installed properly. The mysql gem, for example, comes in two flavors: one for Win32 and one for everyone else. If you have the MySQL client installed properly, the install should go smoothly.

Here's an Ubuntu Linux example of installing the mysql gem. You'll need to enter the following commands while logged in as root:

```
gem install mongrel
```

```
Attempting local installation of 'mongrel'
Local gem file not found: mongrel*.gem
Attempting remote installation of 'mongrel'
Updating Gem source index for: http://gems.rubyforge.org
Select which gem to install for your platform (i686-linux)
 1. mongrel 0.3.13.3 (mswin32)
 2. mongrel 0.3.13.3 (ruby)
 3. mongrel 0.3.13.2 (mswin32)
 4. mongrel 0.3.13.2 (ruby)
 … snipped earlier versions…
42. Cancel installation
```

2

```
Building native extensions.  This could take a while...
ruby extconf.rb install mongrel
checking for main() in -lc... yes
creating Makefile

make
gcc -fPIC -g -O2  -I. -I/usr/local/lib/ruby/1.8/i686-linux -
I/usr/local/lib/ruby/1.8/i686-linux -I.   -c http11.c
gcc -fPIC -g -O2  -I. -I/usr/local/lib/ruby/1.8/i686-linux -
I/usr/local/lib/ruby/1.8/i686-linux -I.   -c http11_parser.c
gcc -fPIC -g -O2  -I. -I/usr/local/lib/ruby/1.8/i686-linux -
I/usr/local/lib/ruby/1.8/i686-linux -I.   -c tst_cleanup.c
gcc -fPIC -g -O2  -I. -I/usr/local/lib/ruby/1.8/i686-linux -
I/usr/local/lib/ruby/1.8/i686-linux -I.   -c tst_delete.c
gcc -fPIC -g -O2  -I. -I/usr/local/lib/ruby/1.8/i686-linux -
I/usr/local/lib/ruby/1.8/i686-linux -I.   -c tst_grow_node_free_list.c
gcc -fPIC -g -O2  -I. -I/usr/local/lib/ruby/1.8/i686-linux -
I/usr/local/lib/ruby/1.8/i686-linux -I.   -c tst_init.c
gcc -fPIC -g -O2  -I. -I/usr/local/lib/ruby/1.8/i686-linux -
I/usr/local/lib/ruby/1.8/i686-linux -I.   -c tst_insert.c
gcc -fPIC -g -O2  -I. -I/usr/local/lib/ruby/1.8/i686-linux -
I/usr/local/lib/ruby/1.8/i686-linux -I.   -c tst_search.c
gcc -shared  -L'/usr/local/lib' -Wl,-R'/usr/local/lib' -o
http11.so http11.o http11_parser.o tst_
```

```
cleanup.o tst_delete.o tst_grow_node_free_
list.o tst_init.o tst_insert.o tst_search.o
-lc  -ldl -lcrypt -lm   -lc

make install
/usr/bin/install -c -m 0755 http11.so
/usr/local/lib/ruby/gems/1.8/gems/mongrel-0.3.13.3/lib
Successfully installed mongrel-0.3.13.3
Installing RDoc documentation for mongrel-0.3.13.3...
```

As you can see, the extension compiles without much difficulty. There are quite a few lines of output and a number of commands run automatically, but the only command we typed in was 2—selecting the pure Ruby source version.

Debugging Source-Gem Problems

Source gems can sometimes pose difficulties on any operating system. RubyGems can handle dependencies when they are other gems; however, if your source gem requires a system dependency (such as a library) to compile, you'll have to install it manually. Typically, a missing system dependency will result in an error message being displayed; a quick Google search will often reveal the source of the difficulties.

There may also be a system compatibility issue; most source gems will not compile on every platform and environment. Windows tends to be particularly tricky, even if a development environment is installed. If your platform supports it, you may be able to use a binary gem. In other cases, you can use the development environment suggested by the gem maintainers; some gems recommend using MinGW on Windows, and others recommend Cygwin or a particular native compiler, such as MSVC or DJGPP. If you aren't sure what the recommendation of the gem maintainers are, check http://rubyforge.org—it has a page for most gems, and you can typically find the information there. It's likely you'll have the best success when you're using the platform/gem combination that has been tested.

In some cases, you may want to directly edit the gem source to work on your platform. This will result in a forked version of the gem, which means you can't use any future updates of that gem. If a future update contains a bug fix that you need, you'll have to manually re-create the bug fix for your forked version, and this can become time-consuming very quickly. It may be wise to forward your patched version to the maintainers of the gem for possible future inclusion; if they choose to include it you'll have an officially maintained, unforked version of the gem for your platform, which is preferable to maintaining it yourself.

Debugging RubyGems

Sometimes a gem that was working with your code stops working. Often this is a versioning issue: Did you update the gem involved? If not, did you update another gem that updated the first gem? If so, you can roll back to the previous version. Alternatively, because RubyGems does not, by default, remove old versions of gems, you can instruct RubyGems to use an older version instead; see Chapter 1 for details.

If you are using binary gems, your problem may be with your particular installation; binary versions must be run on the Ruby version they were compiled for, or else very erratic behavior results. Even if this is not the case, the gem involved may depend on another gem version; the latest version of Rails, for example, may have broken a plugin that your Rails application uses.

You may also have an issue with locally patched or corrupted gems. RubyGems includes checksums on all gems, so you can see if something has changed. You can use this option as follows:

```
>gem check --alien
Performing the 'alien' operation

win32-file-stat-1.2.2-mswin32 is error-free

win32-process-0.4.2-mswin32 is error-free

RedCloth-3.0.4 is error-free

win32-sapi-0.1.3-mswin32 is error-free

win32-sound-0.4.0 is error-free

win32-dir-0.3.0-mswin32 is error-free

sources-0.0.1 is error-free

win32-file-0.5.2-mswin32 is error-free

windows-pr-0.5.1-mswin32 is error-free

fxruby-1.6.0-mswin32 is error-free

rake-0.7.1 is error-free

cmdparse-2.0.2 is error-free

creditcard-1.0 is error-free

fxruby-1.2.6-mswin32 is error-free

log4r-1.0.5 is error-free

win32-clipboard-0.4.0 is error-free

win32-eventlog-0.4.1-mswin32 is error-free
```

Of course, your output will vary depending on what gems you have installed. This display shows all gems are error-free, but if a gem source file had been edited or if a file had been corrupted, the alien check would have displayed an error, which you could correct by installing the gem again using the gem install command, which should rewrite all of the files with new versions.

## CHAPTER 4

Managing Installed Gem Versions

In this chapter you'll learn how use multiple gem versions in your code. We'll cover installing new gem versions, getting rid of old ones, and making sure your code uses the correct ones.

Gem versioning is very useful—particularly because of the ever-changing nature of the Ruby community. Many gems are changing very fast, and sometimes interfaces change as well. In some ways, this is good—it means that software is improving. On the other hand, it breaks older software. If you have to rely on a certain version of a gem—for example, because a later version disables or changes functionality you currently use—then gem versioning can make your old code run with just a one- or two-line change.

What Is Gem Versioning?

RubyGems has an intelligent versioning-management system. This means that RubyGems can take care of different versions of all installed gems for you; it can store as many versions of as many different gems as you'd like. You can request a specific version of a gem, or you can request any version of a gem that's older or newer than a certain version, and RubyGems will accommodate you.

By default, RubyGems assumes you want to work on the most recent version of a gem. For example, if you use the gem install command to install a gem, RubyGems will install the most recent version of a gem, but you can override this—we'll cover that in the following section.

Normally you'd use the require statement to use a RubyGem in your code—just as in Chapter 3. However, RubyGems lets you use version specifiers so that your code will use a specific gem version—or, alternatively, any version of a gem older or newer than a given version. As you can imagine, this makes the gem-versioning system quite important—you might have a 2.0 version of a gem installed for some programs and a 1.0 version installed for others. RubyGems makes this possible—and easy. (We'll cover this in detail under the heading "Specifying Gem Versions.")

> **Tip** If you're not sure what versions of a gem you have installed locally, you can find out using the `gem list` command. For example, if you've installed the `cmdparse` gem, you could find out which versions you had installed by using the following command at the Linux/OS X shell or Windows command prompt:

```
gem list cmdparse
```

```
*** LOCAL GEMS ***
```

```
cmdparse (2.0.2, 2.0.0)
    Advanced command line parser supporting commands
```

The numbers in parentheses represent the different versions you have installed—in this case, 2.0.2 and 2.0.0.

Installing an Older Gem Version

When installing gems using the `gem install` command, RubyGems will automatically download and install the latest version of the requested gem for you. If you already have an older version installed, RubyGems won't replace the older gem—it will install the newest gem but retain the older one. RubyGems will then automatically use the latest version of that gem; in your code, however, you could use the `require_gem` statement to select which version you'd like to use—see the section "Specifying Gem Versions" for details. If you don't want the older version of the gem installed, see the directions under "Uninstalling Gems" later in this chapter.

However, you may not want the newest version; you may want a particular version of a gem. For example, a newer version may introduce a bug, so you'd like to use an older version that does not contain that bug. Or the newer version might make a change to a method name or class structure that breaks your code.

RubyGems can handle dependencies automatically. If a gem requires a particular version of another gem, when you use the `gem install` command on the first gem, it will automatically install the needed version of the second gem—even if you have a different version of the second gem installed. As a result, you won't need to install old versions manually. However, if you are writing a program that isn't packaged in a gem and you need a particular version for it, you may need to install an older gem version.

If you'd like to install an older gem version manually, you can use the `gem install` command with the `-v` option to manually tell RubyGems which version you'd like to install. For example, if you'd like to install the 1.0.5 version of the `cmdparse` gem, you could do so with the following command in the OS X/Linux shell or the Windows command prompt:

```
gem install -v 1.0.5 cmdparse
```

```
Successfully installed cmdparse-1.0.5
Installing ri documentation for cmdparse-1.0.5...
Installing RDoc documentation for cmdparse-1.0.5...
```

You can also use a gem version constraint to do more-advanced specifications—you could, for example, install any version later than 2.0.0 using this command:

```
gem install -v ">2.0.0" cmdparse'
```

Technically the double quotes aren't necessary with the gem command, but without them your shell or command prompt will think it's an I/O redirection.

■Tip If you'd like to find out what gem versions are available, you can use gem list command with the --remote option. For example, to see what versions of the cmdparse gem are available, we could use the following command at the Linux/OS X shell or Windows command prompt:

```
gem list --remote cmdparse

*** REMOTE GEMS ***

cmdparse (2.0.2, 2.0.1, 2.0.0, 1.0.5, 1.0.4, 1.0.3, 1.0.2, 1.0.1, 1.0.0)
    Advanced command line parser supporting commands
```

The numbers in parentheses represent all of the different versions of the gem available remotely. You can omit the --remote option if you'd like to see what versions you have installed locally.

Updating Gems

You've learned how to install a gem using the gem install command and how to install an older version of a gem. However, installing a gem once isn't enough you might need to update the gem once it is installed.

For example, if we wanted to update the creditcard gem from the last chapter, we could use the following command at the OS X/Linux shell or the Windows command prompt:

```
gem update creditcard
```

```
Need to update 5 gems from http://gems.rubyforge.org
.....
complete
Attempting remote update of creditcard
Successfully installed creditcard-1.0
Installing ri documentation for creditcard-1.0...
Installing RDoc documentation for creditcard-1.0...
Gems: [creditcard] updated
```

This automatically downloads the latest version of a gem and updates your installation appropriately.

Additionally, you can update all of your installed gems at once by entering the same gem update command, but without giving it any arguments. Entering the following command in the OS X/Linux shell or the Windows command prompt will do it:

```
gem update
```

```
Need to update 2 gems from http://gems.rubyforge.org
Updating installed gems...
Attempting remote update of cmdparse
Successfully installed cmdparse-2.0.2
Installing ri documentation for cmdparse-2.0.2...
Installing RDoc documentation for cmdparse-2.0.2...
Attempting remote update of fxruby
Select which gem to install for your platform (i386-mswin32)
 1. fxruby 1.6.1 (ruby)
 2. fxruby 1.6.1 (mswin32)
 3. fxruby 1.6.0 (mswin32)
<snip>
Gems: [cmdparse fxruby] updated
```

In this case, the only gems that needed to be updated were cmdparse and fxruby, and so the gem update command updated them automatically. If there's a choice of different gem platforms, as was the case with fxruby, you can choose which platform you'd like to use.

Uninstalling Gems

At times you'll want to get rid of a certain version of a gem—perhaps an old gem you no longer use or a new version of a gem that contains serious bugs. You might even want to delete all traces of a gem if you are sure you will not need it.

If you'd like to uninstall a particular version of a gem—or if you'd like to remove a gem completely—you can use the gem uninstall command at the OS X/Linux shell or the Windows command prompt as follows:

```
gem uninstall cmdparse
```

```
Select RubyGem to uninstall:
 1. cmdparse-2.0.0
 2. cmdparse-2.0.2
 3. All versions
> 2
Successfully uninstalled cmdparse version 2.0.2
```

If you have just one version of a gem installed, the gem uninstall command will simply delete that version. If you have multiple versions, though, it will ask you which versions you'd like to delete; the final option will delete all versions.

You can also specify a version to delete like this:

```
gem uninstall cmdparse -v 2.0.2
```

That command will uninstall the version 2.0.2 of the cmdparse gem—unlike the gem uninstall cmdparse command, it won't prompt you to select a version, since you specified it on the command line. You can also use a gem version constraint, as detailed in the next section.

Tip Sometimes versioning isn't enough; sometimes you need to start from scratch. You can remove the entire RubyGems system from a Ruby install by deleting both the rubygems.rb file and the rubygems directory—both are in your ruby directory under site/ruby/1.8.

Specifying Gem Versions

At this point we've discussed the various ways you can manipulate gem versions on your local machine—install old versions, upgrade to new versions, and delete unneeded versions. However, you also need to be able to use gems in code. If you use the require statement, as in Chapter 3, RubyGems will always provide you with the latest installed version of a gem. If that's all you need, you'll be set using the require statement.

At times, however, you might need more control over the version of the gem you want to use. In that case, you can use the require_gem statement. Despite having require in its name, require_gem is completely different from the require statement. require_gem activates a particular gem version. That means it tells RubyGems, "Of all the different versions of a gem, I want this one."

AUTOREQUIRE

Confusingly, RubyGems has a feature called autorequire— It's an option you can set when you create a gem. This means that if you use the require_gem statement on a gem with autorequire set, it will automatically require a certain file from the gem. This saves a line of code, but it's confusing because it blurs the line between the require statement and the require_gem statement. It also creates two types of gems— those with autorequire and those without—that are used differently. This makes life much harder for the developer, since you need to know the correct syntax for each gem you use.

autorequire is now deprecated, so future gems should use require_gem only to specify a gem version, and require to actually use the gem.

However, the require_gem statement has the ability to accept a second argument—a version constraint. A version constraint lets you explicitly tell RubyGems which version or versions you'd like to use. There are seven constraints, which are detailed in Table 4-1.

Table 4-1. *RubyGems Version Constraints*

Operator	Description	Example
= *version*	Equal to *version*	require_gem 'cmdparse', '=1.0.0'
!= *version*	Not equal to *version*	require_gem 'cmdparse', '!=1.0.0'
> *version*	Greater than *version*	require_gem 'cmdparse', '>1.0.0'
< *version*	Less than *version*	require_gem 'cmdparse', '<1.0.0'
>= *version*	Greater than or equal to *version*	require_gem 'cmdparse', '>=1.0.0'
<= *version*	Less than or equal to *version*	require_gem 'cmdparse', '<=1.0.0'
~> *version*	Approximately greater than *version*. This works by dropping the final digit from the version and comparing; for our example of '~>1.0.0', it will match any version that starts with 1.0, such as 1.0.1, 1.0.2, or 1.0.9.	require_gem 'cmdparse', '~>1.0.0'

As you can see in Table 4-1, the operators are fairly straightforward. Note that the examples given are for using a gem in your Ruby code via the require_gem statement.

■Tip You can use the same operators on the gem install and gem uninstall commands—so, for example, if you wanted to delete any version of cmdparse earlier than 2.0.0, you could use the following command:

```
gem delete "<2.0.0" cmdparse
```

Let's test several of the version-constraint operators using the irb interactive Ruby shell. First we can launch the shell using the following command at the Linux/OS X shell or the Windows command prompt:

```
irb
```

Next use the following commands to test the require_gem statement:

```
require_gem 'creditcard', '>99.0.0'
```

```
Gem::LoadError: RubyGem version error: creditcard(1.0 not > 99.0.0)

        from c:/ruby/lib/ruby/site_ruby/1.8/rubygems.rb:251:in `report_activate_
error'
        from c:/ruby/lib/ruby/site_ruby/1.8/rubygems.rb:188:in `activate'
        from c:/ruby/lib/ruby/site_ruby/1.8/rubygems.rb:66:in `active_gem_with_o
ptions'
        from c:/ruby/lib/ruby/site_ruby/1.8/rubygems.rb:59:in `require_gem'
        from (irb):1
```

```
require_gem 'creditcard', '=1.0.0'
```

```
=> true
```

```
'not-a-valid-card'.creditcard?
```

```
=> false
```

```
'4111-1111-1111-1111'.creditcard?
```

```
=> true
```

The first line, require_gem 'creditcard', '>99.0.0', requests a version of the creditcard gem greater than 99. Since the only version of the creditcard gem available is 1.0, this fails, giving a RubyGems version error. You'd then need to use the gem install command to install the desired version of the gem—you could even copy the >99.0.0 part right into your gem install command using the following on the Linux/OS X shell or the Windows command prompt:

```
gem install creditcard -v ">99.0.0"
```

Note, of course, that this won't work for our example, since there isn't any version of the creditcard gem greater than 99.

The second statement, require_gem 'creditcard', '=1.0.0', requests a version of the creditcard gem equal to 1.0.0. The next statements test the gem. Since the creditcard gem tests credit card numbers for validity (see Chapter 3), those two statements test an obviously invalid card number and a Visa test-card number—both of which return correct values, so we know that the creditcard gem—and the require_gem statement—works.

Normally you'd have a require statement actually use the gem. But because this particular gem, creditcard, uses the autorequire statement, you can skip the require statement and just start using the gem. (See the sidebar "Autorequire" earlier in this chapter.)

As time goes on, gems will stop using autorequire because it's been deprecated. This doesn't change things much—it just means that you need a require statement for every require_gem statement. For example, if the author of creditcard hadn't used autorequire, the require_gem 'creditcard', '=1.0.0' line from the example would have been written as follows:

```
require_gem 'creditcard', '=1.0.0'
require 'creditcard'
```

As you can see, there isn't much difference between using require_gem and autorequire and using require_gem and the require statement. You can also see that the require_gem statement is fairly straightforward and lets you employ the full power of the RubyGems versioning system in your Ruby applications and scripts.

PART 2

■ ■ ■

Using Particular Gems

RubyGems are powerful extensions to Ruby. In Part 2, I'll provide detailed recipes for exactly how to use a number of gems.

CHAPTER 5

■■■

Data Access with the ActiveRecord Gem

ActiveRecord is an object relationship modeling system—it lets you access databases using a simple object-oriented interface.

ActiveRecord manages database operations for you. It provides an entire set of operations —adding new records, deleting old records, updating records, and searching via a variety of criteria. It provides all of these services without extensive schema configuration. This means that ActiveRecord can read the names and types of your fields from the database directly, so you don't have to specify them manually via a configuration file. You also don't have to mix the schema definition with your code as you do when writing raw SQL—your data and logic layers can be separate. This is a huge boon, since it means that you can quickly change your schema, and that your code becomes lighter and easier to use. It also means that bugs resulting from a mismatch between your program schema and your database schema aren't very likely.

ActiveRecord also makes it easier to manage connections to databases of different kinds; normally when you write database code for a particular database system, it isn't portable to another database system. However, ActiveRecord provides database adapters that manage the connections to the various databases—no matter which database adapter you use, you can employ the same ActiveRecord code. There are a number of ActiveRecord database adapters available, including those for MySQL, PostgreSQL, SQLite, DB2, and more.

■Note A few operations can't be done from ActiveRecord, and you'll need to write raw SQL for that; for example, you can't create triggers or stored procedures from ActiveRecord. However, most operations don't have that problem, and can be used across database systems without incident.

An additional way that ActiveRecord can make your life easier is through "configuration by convention." For example, ActiveRecord has a convention that all tables have an artificial primary key called id, and that foreign keys for the table are the table's name followed by id. You can override this, of course, but following these conventions means that your code is lighter and easier to use; it also means that you need to explicitly mention only the deviations from the norm.

How Does It Work?

ActiveRecord works by letting you define a number of models, which are classes that inherit from the ActiveRecord::Base class, and as such they gain a huge amount of functionality automatically. Special information, such as a table name that ActiveRecord can't infer from the class name or a nonstandard primary key, is specified in the class definition; so are relationships to other models. However, because of configuration by convention, you may not need to place anything in the class definition at all. Once you've created the model class, you can use it to manipulate your data—you can add rows, update rows, delete rows, find rows by primary key or by an arbitrary criterion, and more. The details on both these parts of ActiveRecord—creating your models and using the models—are coming up next.

You can install ActiveRecord with the following command:

```
gem install activerecord
```

■**Note** You can find the ActiveRecord API documentation at http://api.rubyonrails.com/classes/ActiveRecord/Base.html.

Rails depends on ActiveRecord, so if you have Rails installed you'll already have ActiveRecord installed.

ActiveRecord Models

ActiveRecord models are classes that describe your database. Each model is attached to one table from your database; the name of the table is based on the name of your class. Some developers view this as a weakness; it isn't. You can override the name if you'd like, but you should have as few distinct names in your application as possible. For example, if you have a model named images and a table named pictures, it will be easy to transpose them mentally and then use the wrong one in a given context, which slows down development. This could be viewed as restricting your freedom, but it's more accurate to say it increases your freedom to create software with fewer bugs faster. (There are similar aspects to many elements of ActiveRecord; for example, some developers balk that ActiveRecord insists on artificial primary keys named id by default. This choice, however, is often a good one, and the common ground lets you create complex software quickly.)

■**Tip** If you don't like the default ActiveRecord name for your table, and you'd like to set a custom table name for a model, just include a set_table_name statement in your model: set_table_name "my_custom_table_name" tells ActiveRecord that you want a table named my_custom_table_name, for example. You can also use the set_primary_key method in much the same way to set the name of the primary key.

Your ActiveRecord model will also read the structure of a table for you automatically; this means that when you change the schema of your database, you don't need to update anything. It also means you never have to write accessor methods for database fields.

One aspect of your database design that typically can't be read from your database automatically is relationships; however, you can express these attributes in your ActiveRecord model! There are several different kinds of relationships; we'll cover them briefly here but you can get more information at http://api.rubyonrails.com/classes/ActiveRecord/Associations/ClassMethods.html.

For example, suppose you had a MySQL database schema like this:

```
CREATE TABLE clients (
  id int(11) NOT NULL AUTO_INCREMENT,
  name text,
  … other fields required by the application…
  PRIMARY KE Y (id)
);
CREATE TABLE orders (
  id int(11) NOT NULL AUTO_INCREMENT,
  client_id INT(11),
  amount DECIMAL(9,2),
  … other fields required by the application…
  PRIMARY KE Y (id)
)
```

Tip In general, it's a good idea to define your table names in your schema as lowercase—some databases don't handle mixed-case table names well. In your code, you can still use mixed-case table names —Ruby classes must start with an uppercase letter, and ActiveRecord will find the lowercase table names just fine. However, you might have problems, particularly under PostgreSQL. Mixed-case tables are supported in PostgreSQL—the table ORDERS is different from orders. Unfortunately, PostgreSQL automatically lowercases all identifiers that are not surrounded by double quotes, so the following SQL statement will fail on a PostgreSQL table named ORDERS:

```
SELECT * FROM ORDERS;
```

Despite the fact that there is an ORDERS table, it won't work because the table name ORDERS is being lowercased automatically to the table name orders. You'd need to do this:

```
SELECT * FROM "ORDERS";
```

That's confusing, and having lowercase table names neatly avoids the confusion and possible porting issues.

In this case, your model would include a Clients table and an Orders table, and use a has_many relationship to indicate that each customer has many orders. This would automatically create an orders method for you in the customer class, so you could, for example, do the following:

```
class Client << ActiveRecord::Base
  has_many :orders
end
class Order << ActiveRecord::Base
  belongs_to :client
end

myclient = Client.find(3)
myclient.orders.each do |order|
  puts order.amount
end
```

The example code will find a Client with the id 3, and loop through each of the client's orders and print the order amount. The Client table has a has_many relationship with the Order table, and the Order table has a belongs_to relationship with the Client table.

The first model, client, has a has_many relationship with the orders model; this relationship provides a number of things for you: it adds a collection to the Client table, which is accessible via the orders method. This collection has a number of methods: it has an each method, just like a Ruby array, and an add method, which can be used to associate an order with a client. (You can find the full details of what belongs_to does in the Rails documentation at http://api. rubyonrails.com/classes/ActiveRecord/Associations/ClassMethods.html#M000530.)

The complement to this is that the second relationship, Order, belongs to Client, which adds a .client method to the Order class. The Order class can be used to return the Client object, which represents the Client associated with the Order.

There are two other relationships in ActiveRecord: has_one and has_and_belongs_to_many. has_one represents a one-to-one relationship; in such a relationship, the foreign key is in a second table. In a has_one relationship, the second table would have a belongs_to relationship with the first table, so if a Client has a has_one ClientType, then ClientType belongs_to Client. The second type of relationship, a has_and_belongs_to_many relationship (typically called HABTM), represents a many-to-many relationship using a join table. The join table's name comes from the two table names in alphabetical order, separated by an underscore (so a HABTM relationship between the Employees and Clients tables would have a join table named clients_employees).

■**Tip** HABTM is not the only way to represent a many-to-many relationship in ActiveRecord—there's also a relationship called has_many :through, which is similar to HABTM except that the join table is a full model with a primary key—with HABTM, it's just a table with two columns: the primary keys of each table.

Note that some views of database design hold that if a join table has anything besides the two foreign keys, it's indicative of a missing domain model. In any case, you can find a breakdown of the difference between HABTM and has_many :through at http://blog.hasmanythrough.com/2006/04/20/many-to-many-dance-off.

You can find more details on all of the ActiveRecord associations at http://api. rubyonrails.com/classes/ActiveRecord/Associations/ClassMethods.html.

Tip Confused about which class belongs to which? The table in which the foreign key resides in is considered the child table, so in our example the Order table would have a client_id column, and as a result, it would have a belongs_to relationship with the Client table.

Manipulating Data

ActiveRecord provides us with a rich set of tools to manipulate data. For example, we could use the following to add a number of new clients to our earlier example (from the section "ActiveRecord Models"):

```
1.upto(100) do |number|

  newclient =Client.new
  newclient.name = "Client number #{number}"

  neworder = Order.new
  neworder.amount= 33.50
  neworder.save

  newclient.orders << neworder
  newclient.save

end
```

This will create 100 clients with names like Client number 1, Client number 2, and so on. It will also create a single order for each of them, and add the order to the orders association of the client object—which automatically sets the client_id column for us. (We can also do this on a client object that hasn't been saved yet.)

As you can see, it's reasonably natural to use ActiveRecord objects—fields get mapped to methods, the new and save methods work much like you'd expect, and the code is very lean. Let's jump into a more detailed example of using ActiveRecord.

Archiving RSS News with ActiveRecord

To demonstrate ActiveRecord, we're going to create a standalone ActiveRecord application to archive RSS news into a MySQL database. You can find additional examples of ActiveRecord usage in Chapters 7 and 23—both of which use ActiveRecord as part of a Web framework, which is very common.

This example requires the mysql gem to be installed, so if you haven't already installed it, do so via the Linux/OS X shell or Windows command-prompt command gem install mysql.

Listing 5-1 contains the code for our RSS archiver.

Listing 5-1. *rss2mysql.rb*

```
require 'active_record'
require 'feed_tools'

feed_url = ARGV[0]

# This call creates a connection to our database.

ActiveRecord::Base.establish_connection(
  :adapter  => "mysql",
  :host     => "127.0.0.1",
  :username => "root", # Note that while this is the default setting for MySQL,
  :password => "",  # a properly secured system will have a different MySQL
        # username and password, and if so, you'll need to
        # change these settings.
  :database => "rss2mysql")

class Items <  ActiveRecord::Base
end

# If the table doesn't exist, we'll create it.

unless Items.table_exists?
  ActiveRecord::Schema.define do
    create_table :items do |t|
        t.column :title, :string
        t.column :content, :string
        t.column :source, :string
        t.column :url, :string
        t.column :timestamp, :timestamp
        t.column :keyword_id, :integer
        t.column :guid, :string
      end
  end
end


feed=FeedTools::Feed.open(feed_url)

feed.items.each do |feed_item|
  if not (Items.find_by_title(feed_item.title)
        or Items.find_by_url(feed_item.link)
        or Items.find_by_guid(feed_item.guid))
  puts "processing item '#{feed_item.title}' - new"
```

```
    Items.new do |newitem|

      newitem.title=feed_item.title.gsub(/<[^>]*>/, '')
      newitem.guid=feed_item.guid
      if feed_item.publisher.name
          newitem.source=feed_item.publisher.name
      end

      newitem.url=feed_item.link
      newitem.content=feed_item.description
      newitem.timestamp=feed_item.published

      newitem.save
    end
  else
    puts "processing item '#{feed_item.title}' - old"

  end
end
```

A few quick notes on this example. First, it has the connection parameters hard-coded in the `ActiveRecord::Base.establish_connection` call near the top of the script; you might want to change those if your MySQL install has a different username and password. Second, it expects a database named rss2mysql; you can create the database using MySQL's mysqladmin command. (The script will automatically create the required table for you if it does not already exist, so you won't need to populate the table by hand.)

Once you've installed the mysql gem and created the rss2mysql database, you can test the script using the following command:

```
ruby rss2mysql.rb http://coolruby.com/rss
```

```
processing item 'MySQL, some concrete suggestions!' - new
processing item 'Matz, the Khaki Pugilist' - new
processing item 'Senior Web Engineer - Helio' - new
processing item 'Software Development Engineer - Web UI - BINC' - new
processing item 'University of Notre Dame on Rails' - new
…snip..
```

As you can see, the rss2mysql.rb script pulls data from the site you provide and places it in the rss2mysql database. It can then be served by a Web application, viewed with phpMyAdmin or the MySQL command-line client, or processed further.

■**Tip** The rss2mysql.rb script is a simplification of production code used on http://coolruby.com/, which aggregates news about Ruby from a number of sources.

Dissecting the Example

Let's examine a few lines from Listing 5-1.

```
ActiveRecord::Base.establish_connection(
  :adapter  => "mysql",
  :host     => "127.0.0.1",
  :username => "root",# Note that while this is the default setting for MySQL,
  :password => "",   # a properly secured system will have a different MySQL
                     # username and password, and if so, you'll need to
                     # change these settings.

  :database => "rss2mysql")
```

The preceding snippet specifies the details for the connection to the database, such as the database adapter, host, username, and so forth. Several adapters are available for ActiveRecord, including for PostgreSQL, SQLite, DB2, and more—and as you can see from the line :adapter => "mysql", our example uses MySQL. Chapter 7 contains an example of using the SQLite adapter.

Next we'll create a model that represents the news items stored in the database.

```
class Items < ActiveRecord::Base
end
```

It's very simple, but those two lines create a model for our one table, Items. Because it's named Items, it's automatically attached to the items table, which we will create next.

```
unless Items.table_exists?
  ActiveRecord::Schema.define do
    create_table :items do |t|
        t.column :title, :string
        t.column :content, :string
        t.column :source, :string
        t.column :url, :string
        t.column :timestamp, :timestamp
        t.column :keyword_id, :integer
        t.column :guid, :string
      end
  end
end
```

The first line checks if the table for our model exists—if not, it will use ActiveRecord::Schema.define to create it.

Tip The `create_table` and `column` methods used in the preceding snippet are database-independent; this code should work on almost any `ActiveRecord` adapter (as of this writing, all of the `ActiveRecord` adapters except DB2 are supported), so you could switch to, say, PostgreSQL or SQLite without a problem. You could also use an external method to create your database—read the commands in from a .SQL file, for example—but by using `ActiveRecord` our schema becomes database-independent. (Incidentally, you can execute SQL directly using the `execute` command. It takes a single SQL query string as a parameter and executes it. If you need to do a database operation that isn't supported natively by `ActiveRecord`—creating a stored procedure, for example—this could be very useful.)

In fact, the database schema code is a very simple, one-way use of `ActiveRecord` migrations—they can also be used to automatically version schemas and to automatically upgrade or downgrade to any given schema version. You can see the full details at `http://rubyonrails.org/api/classes/ActiveRecord/Migration.html`.

Our last chunk of code uses the `FeedTools` gem to open the URL given on the command line and parse through each of its news items. You can find more details on how FeedTools can be used to parse RSS or Atom feeds in Chapter 10. The following is the `ActiveRecord`-specific code:

```
Items.new do |newitem|

    newitem.title=feed_item.title.gsub(/<[^>]*?>/, '')
    newitem.guid=feed_item.guid
    if feed_item.publisher.name
        newitem.source=feed_item.publisher.name
    end

    newitem.url=feed_item.link
    newitem.content=feed_item.description
    newitem.timestamp=feed_item.published

    newitem.save
end
```

As you can see, it's very easy to use `ActiveRecord` to add new rows, and the process is very similar for updating or deleting rows. There are a few small wrinkles—for example, not all feeds have publisher data, so the `publisher` field is set only if the `publisher.name` value is set—but all in all, it's reasonably easy to follow the code.

Conclusion

ActiveRecord makes database code easy to implement and understand—you don't have to spend time wrestling with the database. At times you may need to override ActiveRecord's defaults; fortunately that's easy to do, so you'll definitely gain time even if you need to tweak the defaults to fit your naming convention. In short, ActiveRecord can make even complex databases easier to use.

■ ■ ■

## CHAPTER 6

Easy Text Markup with the BlueCloth Gem

BlueCloth is an implementation of Markdown (http://daringfireball.net/projects/markdown/), a text-to-HTML converter. It features a simple syntax, and is easy to understand visually. It allows you to write documents and posts in an easy, standard format; additionally, since it's easy to learn, even nontechnical users become comfortable very quickly.

BlueCloth is a very simplified markup language, so not all features of HTML are available; it's very similar to a message-board markup language such as BBCode. BlueCloth isn't designed to replace HTML, but rather to make writing and editing text documents much easier—blog posts, message-board posts, articles, and so forth. As a result, BlueCloth documents can be easily read and written—and even if you aren't familiar with BlueCloth, it's reasonably easy to understand what's going on.

How Does It Work?

BlueCloth's syntax is reasonably simple. It's a plain text format, and additional formatting, like headers, lists, and so forth, all have a simple markup. A few symbols, like number signs, dashes, and so forth, can control your output—as a bonus, they also look very understandable when the document is in text form, in contrast to HTML. Let's examine a few types of BlueCloth syntax.

A header is started with one or more hash marks—the more hash marks the higher the header level, so a single hash mark means an <h1> tag, two means an <h2>, and so forth. For example, the following BlueCloth will produce an <h1> and an <h2>:

```
# I Always Wanted to Learn Lisp

## I Never Wanted to Learn Cobol
```

```
<h1>I Always Wanted to Learn Lisp</h1>

<h2>I Never Wanted to Learn Cobol</h2>
```

Paragraphs are separated by a blank line. Some HTML-to-text converters turn all new lines into line breaks; this means that if a paragraph is wrapped manually, the browser can't rewrap it automatically. BlueCloth is flexible—it will handle paragraphs that are one long line or paragraphs that have multiple hand-wrapped lines.

You can do a number of other things in BlueCloth, of course; for example, code blocks are produced by indenting every line with spacing—at least four spaces or a tab. (This means you can't have a paragraph of noncode text starting with a tab or four spaces, of course.) Consider an example:

```
Some code:

    9.times do
      puts "test"
    end
```

```
<p>Some code:</p>

<pre><code>9.times do
  puts "test"
end
</code></pre>
```

You can get more details at the Markdown homepage, http://daringfireball.net/projects/markdown/.

BlueCloth has a number of other options, for block quotes, tables, and more. You can get more details on BlueCloth syntax at the BlueCloth homepage, http://www.deveiate.org/projects/BlueCloth.

To install BlueCloth, use the gem install command:

```
gem install bluecloth
```

BlueCloth-to-HTML Converter

To demonstrate BlueCloth, let's put together a tiny utility that will convert from Markdown to HTML (see Listing 6-1).

Listing 6-1. *bluecloth2html.rb*

```
require 'bluecloth'

puts BlueCloth.new( ARGF.read ).to_html
```

ARGF is a special variable Ruby provides for our use. It give stream methods, like read, to any files passed on the command line. If no files are passed, then it will read from standard input. A new BlueCloth object is created from the input, and then its to_html method is called —which, of course, converts it to HTML. The HTML is then printed to the screen using puts.

Consider Listing 6-2; the text is placed n a file named `test.txt`.

Listing 6-2. *test.txt*

```
#Why you should use Ruby.

Ruby is an open source, powerful programming language. It's a scripting language,
much like Perl or Python. However, it's surprisingly elegant; complex techniques
can be implemented in just a few lines of code. It's also harmonious, in that
things—even complex things—work the way you might expect them to, even when
used in surprising ways.

For example, Ruby handles iterators in an interesting way. It defines a simple yet
powerful way to deal with arbitrary blocks of code.
The following code prints out 1 through 10:

    1.upto(10){ |x|
      print x
    }
```

We could convert it like this:

```
ruby bluecloth2html.rb test.txt
```

The output would be this:

```
<h1>Why you should use Ruby.</h1>

<p>Ruby is an open source, powerful programming language. It's a scripting
language, much like Perl or Python. However, it's surprisingly elegant; complex
techniques can be implemented in just a few lines of code. It's also
harmonious, in that things—even complex things—work the way you might expect them
to, even when used in surprising ways.</p>

<p>For example, Ruby handles iterators in an interesting way. It defines a simple
yet powerful way to deal with arbitrary blocks of code.
The following code prints out 1 through 10:</p>

<pre><code>1.upto(10){ |x|
  print x
}
</code></pre>
```

As you can see, the converter produces standard HTML. Headers become `<h1>` and `<h2>` tags, ordered lists `<ol>` and `<li>` tags, and so forth. Code blocks use both `<pre>` and `<code>` tags—many Web programmers would use only the `<pre>` tags, but the `<code>` tag is an additional indicator to the browser that it's not just any preformatted text, but specifically preformatted code. (Incidentally, BlueCloth comes with a utility to convert BlueCloth to HTML; it works similar to the example in Listing 6-1.)

bluecloth2pdf BlueCloth-to-PDF Converter

In this section you'll learn how to convert a file marked up with BlueCloth syntax to PDF. This example script is called with two arguments—the input BlueCloth file and the output PDF. If you pass a dash as the input file, it will read from STDIN instead. Figure 6-1 has an example of what our converter looks like when run on the text in Listing 6-2.

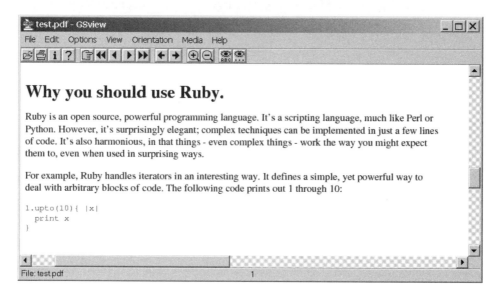

Figure 6-1. *The BlueCloth-to-PDF converter*

To run this example, you will need html2ps and ghostscript installed. Many Linux distributions come with both; for other platforms you can download them from the following URLs, respectively:

```
http://user.it.uu.se/~jan/html2ps.html
http://www.cs.wisc.edu/~ghost/
```

Regardless of platform, you'll need to fill in your full path to each utility in the script, as shown in Listing 6-3.

Listing 6-3. *bluecloth2pdf.rb*

```
require 'tempfile'  # Ruby builtin library - no need to install.
require 'bluecloth'

html2ps_command='/path/to/html2ps'
#on win32, you'll need to prefix this with 'perl '
#    - win32 won't know to run the perl interpreter on it.

ps2pdf_command='/path/to/ghostscript/lib/ps2pdf'
#ps2pdf comes with ghostscript - it'll be in your ghostscript/lib directory.
```

```
if ARGV[0]=='-'
  input_string = $stdin.read
else
  input_string = File.read(ARGV[0])
end
output_pdf_filename =ARGV[1]

# Convert our BlueCloth input into HTML output

bc = BlueCloth::new( input_string )
html_string = bc.to_html

tmp_html_filename ="#{Dir::tmpdir}/#{$$}.html"
tmp_ps_filename = "#{Dir::tmpdir}/#{$$}.ps"

# Next, we take our BlueCloth input and turn it
# into a full HTML document, not just a fragment.

File.open(tmp_html_filename, 'w') do |f|
  f << "<html><head><title>bluecloth2pdf</title></head>"
  f << "<body>"
  f << html_string
  f << "</body>"
  f << "</html>"
end

# First, we convert the HTML and convert it into postscript using
# html2ps, and then convert it into a PDF document using ps2pdf.

`#{html2ps_command} < "#{tmp_html_filename}" > "#{tmp_ps_filename}"`
`#{ps2pdf_command} "#{tmp_ps_filename}" "#{output_pdf_filename}"`
```

Assuming you still have the test.txt file from Listing 6-2, you can test your creation with the following command:

```
ruby bluecloth2pdf.rb test.txt test.pdf
```

This will take the test.txt file and convert it into a PDF. If all goes well, you can verify it by opening the test.pdf file in Ghostview or Adobe Acrobat. If not, check that you've installed both html2ps and ghostscript. Check your paths; it's easy to make a mistake.

Let's briefly recap this relatively complicated script: we took a markdown input, turned it into HTML using the BlueCloth gem, converted that into PostScript using html2ps, and then finally converted the PostScript into PDF using ps2pdf. It's a fairly convoluted process, but the result is transparent to the user and the final PDF is very slick.

There are other options for each step, of course; you could modify the BlueCloth gem to use the pdfwriter gem as output, although that would be fairly complicated. Depending on your circumstance, you might wish to use an alternate HTML conversion tool, such as HTMLDOC. You can get more information on HTMLDOC at http://www.htmldoc.org/.

Tip You also could use Ghostscript to output to formats other than PDF: you could output to PNG or JPEG snapshots. For example, we could replace the last line of the script with this:

```
`gs -sDEVICE=jpeg -sOutputFile="#{output_pdf_filename}" "#{tmp_ps_filename}"`
```

That will print to a JPEG filename—just like the first version printed to a PDF. (You should probably refactor the output_pdf_filename variable to a different name, of course, since you won't be outputting to PDF files.)

Additionally, you could use Ghostscript's printer drivers to create a hard copy; you can get the full details on Ghostscript printer drivers—as well as other Ghostscript output devices—at http://www.cs.wisc.edu/ ~ghost/doc/cvs/Devices.htm.

Dissecting the Example

Let's take a look at a few important lines from Listing 6-3. The first few lines set up the paths to the two programs we'll use in this script: html2ps and ps2pdf. The next few lines parse the input—if the input argument is a dash, then parse from the standard in or STDIN—typically the keyboard. Otherwise, read from the file provided. Next we hard-code the paths to the various programs we will use later:

```
html2ps_command='/path/to/html2ps'
```

```
ps2pdf_command='/path/to/ghostscript/lib/ps2pdf'
```

Next we create a new BlueCloth object from the input and turn it into HTML using the to_html method:

```
bc = BlueCloth::new( input_string )
html_string = bc.to_html
```

Next we create two temporary filenames: one for the HTML input to html2ps, and one for the intermediate PostScript file. It uses the Dir::tmpdir variable to locate the temporary directory for your operating system; to access this variable, we must have the require tempfile statement, even though we aren't using the tempfile class.

```
tmp_html_filename ="#{Dir::tmpdir}/#{$$}.html"
tmp_ps_filename = "#{Dir::tmpdir}/#{$$}.ps"
```

The HTML temporary file is filled with the output from BlueCloth surrounded by the the skeleton of an HTML document, as follows:

```
File.open(tmp_html_filename, 'w') do |f|
  f << "<html><head><title>bluecloth2pdf</title></head>"
  f << "<body>"
  f << html_string
  f << "</body>"
  f << "</html>"
end
```

html2ps needs the `<body>` and `<html>` tags, but since `BlueCloth` produces only HTML fragments and not complete documents, we need to add them ourselves. Note that this is a good thing: it means you can use `BlueCloth` to represent blog posts, for example, and put the output HTML inside a larger document.

Finally, we have two backtick commands:

```
`#{html2ps_command} < "#{tmp_html_filename}" > "#{tmp_ps_filename}"`
`#{ps2pdf_command} "#{tmp_ps_filename}" "#{output_pdf_filename}"`
```

These run system commands; specifically, the first runs `html2ps`, connecting its input to the temporary HTML file and its output to the temporary PostScript flie. The second command calls `ps2pdf`, but unlike `html2ps` it takes input and output files as arguments, so we don't need the redirection. Its input is the temporary PostScript file that `html2ps` produced; its output is our output PDF file. Once the second command is run, our program is finished.

Conclusion

BlueCloth is a powerful, easy-to-use way to write and edit documents, and it'd fit in well in a variety of environments, including online content-management systems, blogs, forums, software changelogs, and much more.

CHAPTER 7

■■■

Creating Web Applications with Camping

Camping is a microframework for developing Web applications.

Whereas a typical Web framework is designed to make large Web applications easier to write, a microframework is designed to make short scripts easier to write. Camping is very lightweight, but still elegant. Further, because it uses ActiveRecord (discussed in Chapter 5) and is similar to Rails in a number of ways, you can transition smoothly to Rails if necessary.

The small size of Camping apps is quite useful; you can create an entire application, with separate views, models, controllers, and it will all fit in a single file. Rails apps have quite a few files and directories before you even start writing custom code; it's awkward for small applications, since a relatively small amount of code will end up spread out over quite a few files. Rails gives you a distinct advantage in a large project, but in a small project—with just a few views and controllers   the single file approach of Camping is superior.

Note, though, that Camping has a great deal of power despite being short—you can use routing, generate fully compliant XHTML/HTML with Markaby (short for "markup as Ruby"), use both layouts and views, and access databases with ActiveRecord models. For example, Camping is great for writing guest books, blogs, and virtually any other short application.

How Does It Work?

Much like Rails, Camping is a Model View Controller (MVC) framework. MVC refers to the three principal parts of the framework. The model is the code that controls the data stored in the database—this includes the code that validates the data and all other data-level manipulations. The view is the code that actually displays information to the user—in a Web application, this is typically HTML, but it may be formats like RSS, other XML, HTML, PDF, or plain text. Finally, the controller is responsible for responding to user actions, like saving, deleting, and searching.

At first the distinction between models, views, and controllers may seem artificial; all programming paradigms are artificial distinctions. However, this is a particularly useful one. It's an integral part of Ruby on Rails, and Rails has been reported to have nearly mythically fast development speed compared to other solutions. Rails, though, is designed for larger applications; Camping, on the other hand, is designed to "fit in a backpack"—Camping apps are small, they're easily understood, and they fit in one file.

One of the big differences between Rails and Camping is that a Camping application is a single Ruby script. Rails applications have an entire directory structure with a great number of files and an entire array of generators to create often-used code; Rails' competitors

CakePHP and `Nitro` are similar. `Camping` applications are much smaller; in fact, the distribution version of the entire `Camping` framework is under 4KB.

The `Camping` framework comes in two varieties: the first, `Camping.rb`, is for distribution, and is stripped of whitespace and comments. This is slightly faster to load, and matches `Camping`'s lightweight philosophy. The other version is `Camping-unabridged.rb`, which includes comments and documentation. The two versions are functionally identical; the second just has more comments, so unless you are reading the source code directly, you won't notice the difference.

`Camping` provides three modules: `Camping::Models`, `Camping::Controllers`, and `Camping::Views`. Your script is responsible for placing classes in each module; models go in `Camping::Models`, controllers in `Camping::Controllers`, and views in `Camping::Views`. You can get the full details on `Camping` at the `Camping` homepage, `http://code.whytheluckystiff.net/camping`. You can install `Camping` using the `gem install` command:

```
gem install camping
```

The Camping::Models Module

`Camping::Models` uses `ActiveRecord`. Here's a short example:

```
module Blog::Models
  class Actor; has_and_belongs_to_many :movies; end
  class Movie; has_and_belongs_to_many :actor; end
end
```

That example creates two classes: `Actor` and `Movie`. Each represents a table in the database. No specific fields are referenced; it automatically adds methods for each field based on the table that each represents. Each model is automatically connected to the table of the same name. The only thing that should be specified is the relationships between the tables; in this case, we specify two `has and belongs to many` relationships. Other types of relationships include `belongs to`, `has one`, and `has many`.

In this particular case, the `has_and_belongs_to_many` relationship is appropriate because each actor belongs to many movies, but also each movie has many actors. The `belongs_to` relationship would work if each actor had just one movie, or vice versa. The `has_one` relationship is quite similar; the difference is that in a `belongs_to` relationship, the foreign key is in the source table. In a `has_one` relationship, it's the opposite: in a `model_a has_one :model_b`, the key is in `model_b`. Typically, `model_b` would have a `belongs_to` relationship with `:model_a`.

A `has_many` relationship works much like a `has_one`, except that it can have more than one row in the destination table. This also adds iterator methods, like `each` and `reverse_each`. These methods let you loop over all over the items in a collection. You can access other functionalities that `ActiveRecord` provides, like using the `<<` operator to automatically add to a collection. (See Chapter 5 for more details about features provided by `ActiveRecord`.)

The Camping::Controllers Module

The second module, `Camping::Controllers`, is different from `Rails` controllers. `Rails` controllers and routes are separate; further, `Rails` controllers have many actions, each of which can be given a `POST`, `GET`, or other HTTP request. Camping controllers can be given different

HTTP requests, but they don't get separate actions. In other words, to delete a blog post in a Rails application, your URL might be /blog/delete/3. In Camping, it might be /delete_blog/3, or perhaps you'd use an HTTP DELETE action on /blog/3. (Since Camping applications are small, you might even just do /delete/3—if your application includes multiple types of resources to delete, you may want to consider splitting it up or moving to Rails or Nitro. You can find out more about Nitro at http://nitroproject.org/.)

The Camping::Views Module

Unlike Rails, Camping controllers don't have an associated view; you use render to specify which view you'd like to use. Camping controllers can set class variables that views can see, so you can pass controller-specific data to your view.

Views are fairly simple in Camping. They can be called by any number of controllers. There is a special view, named layout, which is called to display each view. Layout is usually used to add content to every page—like page titles, copyright notices, navigation menus, and so forth. Typically, views are written using Markaby (http://redhanded.hobix.com/inspect/markabyForRails.html). (You can get more details on Markaby in Chapter 14.) Markaby consists of Ruby functions that produce HTML. Consider the following script, which outputs a few lines of HTML:

```
require 'markaby'

builder = Markaby::Builder.new

builder.html do
  head do
    title "test tile"
  end
  body do
    h1 "tests"
    p "test paragraph"
    ul do
        li "item 1"
        li "item 2"
        li "item 3"
    end
  end
end

puts builder.to_s
```

Executing this script produces the following:

```
<?xml version="1.0" encoding="UTF-8"?>
<!DOCTYPE html PUBLIC "-//W3C//DTD XHTML 1.0 Transitional//EN" "DTD/xhtml1-trans
itional.dtd">
<html xmlns="http://www.w3.org/1999/xhtml" lang="en" xml:lang="en">
<head>
<meta content="text/html; charset=utf-8" http-equiv="Content-Type"/>
```

```
<title>test tile</title>
</head>
<body>
<h1>tests</h1>
<p>test paragraph</p>
<ul>
<li>item 1</li>
<li>item 2</li>
<li>item 3</li>
</ul>
</body>
</html>
```

You'll notice that Markaby automatically produces the <?xml..?> and <!DOCTYPE..> tags. It also handles closing tags automatically. In fact, if Ruby Markaby code will run, it will produce valid XHTML 1.0.

Tracking Time with Camping

To demonstrate Camping, we'll develop an application to track time. Specifically, we'll track billable hours, by client, using stopwatch-style start and stop features. The application will use a simple Web interface developed in Camping.

Since this is a fairly long listing, it's split into three parts; each will be preceded by a brief description, and I'll cover them in detail under the heading "Dissecting the Examples."

Listing 7.1 contains the model and schema for our application; that's the part of the program relating to the database. It also contains the code that detects if the table has been created yet; if it hasn't, the code will create the database.

Note that the listing is split into three parts for readability.

Listing 7-1. *tracktime.rb, Part One*

```ruby
#!/usr/bin/ruby

%w(rubygems camping ).each { |lib| require lib }

# Populate our namespace with Camping functionality.
Camping.goes :TrackTime

#
# Contains the application's single model, ClientTime.
#
module TrackTime::Models
  #Sets or retrieves the schema.
  def self.schema(&block)
    @@schema = block if block_given?
    @@schema
  end
```

```
  #
  # The single model for this application.
  # It inherits from ActiveRecord,
  # so you can use it like any Rails
  # model.
  #
  class ClientTime < Base

    # Returns the difference between the starting
    # and stopping times - if the entry hasn't been
    # stopped yet, it will return the time elapsed
    # since it was started.
    def elapsed
      diff=((stop || Time.now) - start)
      format("%0.2f",(diff/3600))
    end
  end
end


#
# Sets the schema, defining our single table.
#
TrackTime::Models.schema do
  create_table :tracktime_client_times, :force => true do |t|
    t.column :client, :string, :limit => 255
    t.column :start, :datetime
    t.column :stop, :datetime
    t.column :created_at, :datetime
  end
end


#
# Get ready to run by creating the database
# if it doesn't already exist.
#
def TrackTime.create
 unless TrackTime::Models::ClientTime.table_exists?
   ActiveRecord::Schema.define(&TrackTime::Models.schema)
   TrackTime::Models::ClientTime.reset_column_information
 end
end
```

Listing 7-2 contains our controllers, which contains the program logic.

Listing 7-2. *tracktime.rb, Part Two*

```
#
# Contains all of the controllers for the application.
```

```ruby
#
module TrackTime::Controllers

  #
  # Homepage for the application.
  #
  class Index < R '/'
    def get

      @times=ClientTime.find_all
      render :homepage
    end
  end


  #
  # Controller which creates a new timer.
  #
  class Start < R('/start/')
    def get
      @text='Started!'
      new_time=ClientTime.create :client=>@input[:client], :start=>Time.now
      render :statictext
    end
  end


  #
  # Controller for stopping a timer.
  #
  class Stop < R('/stop/(\w+)')
    def get(id)
      @text='Stopped!'
      old_time=ClientTime.find id

      if !old_time
        @text="failed on stopping time # #{id}"
      else
        old_time.update_attributes :stop=>Time.now
      end

      render :statictext
    end
  end


  #
  # Deletes a timer.
  #
  class Kill < R('/kill/(\w+)')
    def get(id)
```

```
      @text='Killed!'

      deleted_successfully=ClientTime.delete id

      @text="failed on killing time # #{id}" unless deleted_successfully

      render :statictext
    end
  end

end
```

Our next chunk of code (Listing 7-3) contains our views (the part of our application that interacts directly with the user). It produces the HTML that is sent to the Web browser.

Listing 7-3. *tracktime.rb, Part Three*

```
#
# Contains all of the views for the application.
#
module TrackTime::Views
  TIME_FORMAT="%H:%M:%S"

  #
  # View which statically shows a message with a
  # redirect back to the homepage.
  #
  def statictext
    h1 { a @text, :href=>R(Index), :style=>'text-align:center'}
  end

  #
  # View which shows the homepage.
  #
  def homepage
    div do

      table :cellpadding=>5, :cellspacing=>0  do
        tr do
          th :colspan=>6 do
            form :action=> R(Start) do
              p  do
                strong 'start timer: '
                br
                label 'client name'
                input :name=>'client', :type=>'text', :size=>'5'
                input :type=>'submit', :value=>'start'
              end
            end
```

```ruby
            end
          end
          tr do
            th 'Client'
            th 'Start'
            th 'Stop'
            th 'Elapsed'
          end
          (@times || []).each do |time|
            tr :style =>"background-color: #{(time.stop ? 'white' : '#FFEEEE')}" do
              td time.client
              td time.start.strftime(TIME_FORMAT)

              if time.stop
                td time.stop.strftime(TIME_FORMAT)
              else
                td {a 'Stop now', :href=>R(Stop,time.id) }
              end
              unless !time.start

                td "#{time.elapsed} hrs"
              end

              td {a 'kill', :href=>R(Kill, time.id)}
            end
          end

        end
      end
    end

    #
    # Layout which controls the appearance
    # of all other views.
    #
    def layout
      html do
        head do
          title 'TrackTime'
        end
        body do
          h1 "welcome to tracktime"
          div.content do
            self << yield
          end
        end
      end
    end

  end
```

You can run the combined example as follows:

```
camping tracktime.rb
```

You can now see the example by pointing your Web browser to http://localhost:3301/.

■**Tip** You can use the camping command to run on different ports and addresses. For example, you can use the -h option to specify an IP address to bind to—the default is all available addresses. You can also use the -p option to specify which port you want to use—the default port is 3301. The following command would run Camping on the localhost (127.0.0.1) address only and on port 3030:

```
camping tracktime.rb -p 3030 -h 127.0.0.1
```

You should see a Welcome to Tracktime greeting and a Start Timer option. You'll also see a blank table with no entries in it—it will hold our saved times. Enter a name in the client's name box (any name will do), then click Start.

You'll see a Starting! screen. Click on the link, and you'll be sent to the main screen again, but you'll see an entry—it'll be highlighted in red, which indicates that the timer is running. You can add another entry if you'd like, although your customers might not appreciate double billing.

Click Stop to stop the timer. Click past the Stopped! message, and you'll see that your entry is no longer white—this indicates that the timer has stopped.

On the left, there's a link marked Kill. This link will delete an entry.

At this moment, we're using Camping to run the application, but there are other ways. As I mentioned, you can run the app through a Web server in a variety of ways. You can also use *postambles* to let Ruby apps run stand-alone, with a command like ./tracktime.rb on OSX or Linux and ruby tracktime.rb on Win32. Postambles are added to the end of the program; if the program is run stand-alone, the postamble kicks in and starts a mini Web browser. The documentation for Camping has a number of postambles; you can use either WEBrick, which is pure Ruby but fairly slow, or Mongrel, which is fast but is written in a mixture of C and Ruby.

For example, if you use the mongrel postamble, you can run it easily without a stand-alone launcher; it allows you to use the command ruby tracktime.rb to launch the server. The mongrel postamble is as follows:

```
if __FILE__ == $0
  TrackTime::Models::Base.establish_connection :adapter => 'sqlite3',
          :database => 'tracktime.db'
  TrackTime::Models::Base.logger = Logger.new('tracktime.log')
  TrackTime::Models::Base.threaded_connections=false
  TrackTime.create
  require 'mongrel'
  server = Mongrel::Camping::start("0.0.0.0",3301,"/",TrackTime)
  puts "**TrackTime is running on Mongrel - check it out at http://localhost:3301/"
  server.run.join
end
```

You'll need Mongrel installed—you can install it via the command gem install mongrel. Once it's installed, you can launch the app as follows:

```
ruby tracktime.rb
```

```
**TrackTime is running on Mongrel—check it out at http://localhost:3301/
```

You can get other postambles for serving Camping apps in different ways at http://code. whytheluckystiff.net/camping/wiki/PostAmbles.

Dissecting the Examples

Let's examine a few lines from Listings 7-1 through 7-3.

The first statement requires two libraries:

```
%w(rubygems camping ).each { |lib| require lib }
```

The %w(…) is Ruby syntax for arrays; it returns an array of the words inside the parentheses, separated by spaces. The .each iterates over each one, and the require lib statement requires each library. Although slightly more compact, functionally it's identical to require rubygems followed by require Camping.

This line uses Camping's method to fill the :TrackTime module with the Camping framework:

```
Camping.goes :TrackTime
```

You could modify the Camping module directly, but that'd prevent you from mounting multiple applications in the same process, and so it's always preferable to use Camping.goes.

This module was populated by the Camping.goes line:

```
module TrackTime::Models
  def self.schema(&block)
    @@schema = block if block_given?
    @@schema
  end

  class ClientTime < Base
    def elapsed
      diff=((stop || Time.now) - start)
      format("%0.2f",(diff/3600))
    end
  end
end
```

It has our single model, ClientTime. Camping uses ActiveRecord, and so the table name for the ClientTime model is tracktime_client_times. You can find out more about ActiveRecord's pluralization and table-naming rules by turning to Chapter 5, which discusses ActiveRecord. (Camping changes the typical ActiveRecord convention slightly: Camping apps have table names that start with the current application name.)

The self.schema method lets us set the class variable @@schema to a block, which can then be run if our tables don't exist. (Incidentally, the database connection is created by the Web server, not by our script. By default, it uses a sqlite3 database, but you can use any database adapter ActiveRecord supports, including MySQL, PostgreSQL, and more.)

The next block of code sets the schema for our application:

```
TrackTime::Models.schema do
  create_table :tracktime_client_times, :force => true do |t|
    t.column :client, :string, :limit => 255
    t.column :start, :datetime
    t.column :stop, :datetime
    t.column :created_at, :datetime
  end
end
```

While most functions that take a block execute the code immediately, this isn't required and this example doesn't do it. The block then sets the @@schema variable to this block of code, and if the database is blank, this block of code (which creates our single table) will run.

This ActiveRecord schema is database-agnostic—you can run it on almost any database supported by ActiveRecord, including MySQL, PostgreSQL, or, as we are doing here, SQLite 3 or later. In some cases, you might need to use database-specific functionality; ActiveRecord includes an execute command to execute arbitrary SQL.

You'll notice that the table name is tracktime_client_times; this is different from Rails table names, which would usually be client_times. Camping has the application name prepended to the table name, which lets you have multiple applications in the same database without a risk of table-name collisions.

The following code defines a method, TrackTime.create, which is called by the Camping framework when the application is first launched:

```
def TrackTime.create
  unless TrackTime::Models::ClientTime.table_exists?
    ActiveRecord::Schema.define(&TrackTime::Models.schema)
    TrackTime::Models::ClientTime.reset_column_information
  end
end
```

If the ClientTime table doesn't exist, then the code will create it by using ActiveRecord::Schema.define and the schema that we set earlier. It will then call reset_column_information—which will cause ActiveRecord to load the column names and types that we just created.

Our next block of code is for controllers, which specify the logic for the pages that will be displayed:

```
module TrackTime::Controllers
  class Index < R '/'
    def get
      @times=ClientTime.find_all
      render :homepage
    end
  ... snip ...
```

The first controller is Index; it's represented by a class inside of TrackTime::Controllers. This controller is attached to the route '/'—this means that the root of our application will call the Index controller, in this case http://localhost:3301/. You might find the < R '/' confusing—it looks like inheritance, but the end looks like a function call. Both are correct—the function returns a class. It takes a regular expression that indicates what kind of URL will respond to this controller.

If you'd like, you can specify multiple routes like this: R '/', '/index', '/home'. That would specify http://localhost:3301/, http://localhost:3301/index, and http://localhost:3301/home all to correspond to the same action.

Inside of that class, a single method is defined—get. This corresponds to the GET HTTP method—you can also definite POST, DELETE, and PUT methods. This is different from Rails—in Rails, you have controller names followed by action names. In Camping, a single route is mapped to a single controller.

Inside of the get method, @times is assigned to ClientTime.find_all. The find_all call returns all of the records in the ClientTime array. It's assigned to @times, which is an instance variable, since it is prefixed with @. Since it's an instance variable, the view can access it.

The view is then called by the render :homepage statement. In Rails, unless you specify otherwise, the view with the same action and controller name as the current request is automatically called; in Camping, you create your views and decide when to call which—no automatic mapping.

The following controller, Start, creates a new ClientTime record, setting the client name to whatever the user enters and setting the start time to the current time.

```
  ... snip ...
  class Start < R '/start/'
    def get
      new_time=ClientTime.create :client=>@input[:client], :start=>Time.now
      if new_time
@text='Started!'
      else
        @text='Failed!'
      end
      render :statictext
    end
  end
  ... snip ...
```

If the save succeeded then the @text variable is set to Started!, and if it failed it's set to Failed!. The statictext view is then shown—as we'll see in the listing after next, the statictext view shows the text present in the @text class variable.

Our next controller will stop a running timer:

```
... snip ...
class Stop < R('/stop/(\w+)')
  def get(id)
    @text='Stopped!'
    old_time=ClientTime.find id

    if !old_time
      @text="failed on stopping time # #{id}"
    else
      old_time.update_attributes :stop=>Time.now
    end

    render :statictext
  end
end
... snip ...
```

The Stop controller uses slightly different routing—it includes capturing parentheses, (\w+). The get function takes a single parameter. The \w+ means *any number of nonwhitespace characters*, and the contents of the capturing parentheses are passed to the id function. This means that if you request http://localhost:3301/TrackTime/Stop/5, it passes 5 to the Stop controller.

It uses the find method of the ClientTime model to find the record. Since the find method looks for records by primary key, we just pass ID to the method and it returns the matching record. If there isn't a matching record, we set @text to a failure message. If there is, we use the update_attributes method to set the stop time to the current time. We then render the statictext view, as we did in the previous controller. Incidentally, if we didn't want to find by primary key, we could use a :conditions parameter, which would let us use any arbitrary condition.

This is our first view, statictext:

```
module TrackTime::Views

  def statictext
    h1 { a @text, :href=>R(Index), :style=>"text-align:center;" }
  end
  ... snip ...
```

It's pretty simple, and it's also not much like an eRuby or other type of Ruby HTML view you might find in Rails or Nitro. It's Markaby. (Chapter 14 has more details on Markaby.) It's Ruby syntax converted into HTML; the h1 takes a block and wraps the result in appropriate <h1> and </h1> tags. Inside the h1 block is an a tag—an anchor tag that we can hyperlink back to the index page. The :href parameter to that anchor specifies the URL for the link. The URL is generated by the R function—that's the same function that produces the classes for the controllers, but when you pass it an existing class, it produces the URL for that class instead. Finally, it's also passed an :style=>"text-align:center;" parameter. This is a cosmetic change to let us center the link.

The last view is the homepage view:

```
... snip ...
TIME_FORMAT="%H:%M:%S"

def homepage
  div do

    table :cellpadding=>5, :cellspacing=>0  do
      tr do
        th :colspan=>6 do
          form :action=> R(Start) do
            p  do
              strong 'start timer: '
              br
              label 'client name'
              input :name=>'client', :type=>'text', :size=>'5'
              input :type=>'submit', :value=>'start'
            end
          end
        end
      end
    end
... snip ...
```

The homepage view displays the home, or index, page for our app. It uses Markaby to produce the HTML, as we did before. It creates a table with cell padding of 5 and no cell spacing, and then creates a form in a table header that spans the entire table width. There are other ways to do the formatting, of course.

At the top of the function is a constant, TIME_FORMAT, which controls the output of the times. You can modify this if you'd like—you might want to change it to display a date, although that will clutter the output.

The following code outputs the headers for the table, and then loops through each timer and displays a new row for it:

```
... snip ...
  tr do
    th 'Client'
    th 'Start'
    th 'Stop'
    th 'Elapsed'
  end
  @times.each do |time|
    tr :style =>"background-color: #{(time.stop ? 'white' : '#FFEEEE')}" do
      td time.client
      td time.start.strftime(TIME_FORMAT)
```

```
              if time.stop
                td time.stop.strftime(TIME_FORMAT)
              else
                td {a 'Stop now', :href=>R(Stop,time.id) }
              end

              td "#{time.elapsed} hrs"


              td {a 'kill', :href=>R(Kill, time.id)}
            end
          end

      end
    end
  end
```

If the timer has been stopped, it'll be displayed in white; running timers will be displayed in red. Stopped timers will also have a display of the stop time; running timers get a Stop Now link. All rows also get an Elapsed Time display and a Kill link.

The Kill and Stop links use the R function to generate the URL—but this time, it also passes the time.id link to it. The R function can handle this, fortunately, and produce valid URLs. This is very convenient for you—if the routing changes or if the format of the URLs changes somehow, the R function will work seamlessly.

The layout function, demonstrated in the following snippet, produces the layout for the application—this is HTML code above and below every view in the application.

```
def layout
  html do
    head do
      title 'TrackTime'
    end
    body do
      h1 "welcome to tracktime"
      div.content do
        self << yield
      end
    end
  end
end
```

In this case, it produces the header, which has the title tag setting the title of the page, and then produces a welcome to tracktime <h1> tag. Camping doesn't call view methods directly—instead it passes the views to the layout function. Since these views are blocks, the layout function uses yield to append the output of the block to the current object, self.

Conclusion

Camping apps are tiny, easy to write, and easy to comprehend—perfect for writing small Web applications very quickly.

CHAPTER 8

■ ■ ■

Creating Command-Line Utilities with cmdparse

The cmdparse gem provides support for writing command toolkits. Specifically, you can create command-based command-line programs—programs that take a number of commands, with each command able to have a varying number of arguments. This style of program is what the gem command uses, and it is a bit more flexible than parsing based on switches, which is what many other Linux, OS X, and Windows commands use. In any event, cmdparse lets you create such programs quickly and efficiently—letting you worry about your program and not about how it receives input from the user. cmdparse also gives you free functionality, such as a help command which will go through all of your available commands and display them, their descriptions, and their options to the user.

How Does It Work?

Command-line programs use a variety of different methods to specify arguments. The most familiar method comes in the format of switches or options, which is how most Linux and Windows programs specify arguments for most of their commands. For instance, traditional shell commands use switches, like the familiar Linux/OS X ls command—in ls -al for example, the -al specifies two options, -a and -l. Those two options tell the ls command to behave differently—the first tells it not to hide files whose names start with a period, and the second tells to use the long list format, which contains more information.

The Windows command dir works similarly, so if you specify dir /ad /P, it will specify the /ad and the /P options. These types of commands often take filenames—for example, in the command tail -f /var/log/somefile it runs tail, which uses the -f option on the file /var/log/somefile. If you'd like to use this style of arguments, you can use Ruby's built-in library optparse. (See Chapter 18 for an optparse example.)

The second method involves using a command-based syntax, such as that supported by cmdparse. This method is more verbose and is often used for commands that don't manipulate files—such as the Windows NET command. RubyGems also works like this; the gem command, for example, takes cmdparse-style arguments. Your program has multiple "commands" that you allow the user to run, and each command has multiple possible arguments—as well as options and switches. Let's see a quick example at the Windows command prompt:

```
net send my_machine Hello!
```

That will send the message Hello to the computer named my_machine—assuming it's running the Windows Messenger service, of course. send is the command, and my_machine and Hello! are the arguments.

For example, we could create a simple Hello World application using cmdparse as follows:

```
require 'cmdparse'

cmd = CmdParse::CommandParser.new( true, true )

cmd.program_name = "helloworld"

cmd.add_command( CmdParse::HelpCommand.new, true )

new_command= CmdParse::Command.new('hello', false )
new_command.short_desc = 'Say hello.'
new_command.set_execution_block do
  puts 'Hello World'
end

cmd.add_command( new_command)
cmd.parse
```

This creates a simple application using cmdparse: it has two commands, help and hello. The first lists the available commands along with a short description; the second simply prints the phrase "Hello World!" Note that the help command is built into cmdparse—we didn't need to write it by hand. Also note that the help command uses the short_desc property of the hello command; that's how the help command gets descriptions of the functionality.

Let's take a look at how the application works:

```
ruby hello_world.rb help
```

```
Usage: helloworld [options] COMMAND [options] [COMMAND [options] ...] [args]

Available commands:
  hello         Say hello.
  help          Provide help for individual commands (=default command)
```

```
ruby hello_world.rb hello
```

```
Hello World
```

As you can see, it's reasonably easy to put together a simple application with cmdparse. You can use the following command to install cmdparse:

```
gem install cmdparse
```

A Job-Search Tool Built with cmdparse

To demonstrate cmdparse, we're going to build a short program that will assist in performing Web-based job searches. It will have three different commands, each of which can take options to modify the way they behave. The first will be a search of Indeed.com, the Internet search engine; it will take a search phrase and return all of the jobs found at that location. Next will be a Ruby job lister; it will take jobs from jobs.coolruby.com and display them. Finally, our last command will be a Craigslist searcher—it will generate a Google URL you can visit, which will display all of the Craigslist entries updated in the last 30 days and that match your search.

Listing 8-1. *Searching Jobs with cmdparse (jobsearch.rb)*

```
require 'feed_tools'
require 'cmdparse'
require 'date'
require 'uri'

# Create a new CmdParse object -
# we're going to use this to parse
# our command line arguments.

cmd = CmdParse::CommandParser.new( true, true )
cmd.program_name = "jobsearch "
cmd.program_version = [0, 1, 0]

# These are two commands that come with CmdParse -
# the first displays a list of commands, and the
# second displays the current program version.

cmd.add_command( CmdParse::HelpCommand.new, true )
cmd.add_command( CmdParse::VersionCommand.new )

# This object will represent our first command -
# - the indeed command, which searches Indeed.com

indeed = CmdParse::Command.new('indeed', false )
indeed.short_desc = "Searches for jobs via Indeed.com "
indeed.short_desc  << " and prints the top ten results."

indeed.description = 'This command searches Indeed.com for jobs matching [ARGS].'
indeed.description << 'You can specify a location to search via '
indeed.description << 'the -l and -r switches.'

# This block of code sets the optional switches for our command.
indeed.options = CmdParse::OptionParserWrapper.new do |opt|
  opt.on( '-l', '--location LOCATION',
   'Show jobs from LOCATION only' ) { |location| $location=location }
  opt.on( '-r', '--radius RADIUS',
```

```ruby
        'Sets a distance in miles from LOCATION to search from. ' <<
        'This option has no effect ' <<
        'without the -l option.' ) { |radius| $radius=radius }

end

# This block sets the code which will be executed when the
# command is run.

indeed.set_execution_block do |args|
  search_string= args.join(' ')
  feed_url = 'http://rss.indeed.com/rss?'
  feed_url << 'q=#{URI.escape(search_string)}'
  feed_url << '&l=#{$location}&sort=date&radius=#{$radius}'
  puts "Jobs matching \"#{search_string}\" from indeed.com"
  puts "for more detail, see the following URL:\n\t#{feed_url}\n\n"

  feed= FeedTools::Feed.open(feed_url)
  feed.items.each do |item|
    puts "#{item.title}"
  end
end

# This is similar to the previous command, but
# searches jobs.coolruby.com.

coolruby = CmdParse::Command.new( 'coolruby', false )
coolruby.short_desc = "Shows Ruby jobs from jobs.coolruby.com"
coolruby.description = "This command takes no arguments."
coolruby.set_execution_block do |args|
  feed_url = "http://jobs.coolruby.com/rss"
  puts "Jobs from coolruby.com"
  puts "for more detail, see jobs.coolruby.com.\n"

  feed= FeedTools::Feed.open(feed_url)
  feed.items.each do |item|
    puts "#{item.title}"
  end
end

# This final command searches Craigslist sites.

craigslist = CmdParse::Command.new( 'craigslist', false )
craigslist.short_desc = "Searches all Craigslist sites for jobs"
craigslist.description = "Displays results from all craigslist sites which "
craigslist.description  << " match [ARGS]. Only displays recent results - "
craigslist.description  << " by default, results from the last "
```

```ruby
craigslist.description << " thirty days, but this can be overridden "
craigslist.description << " with the -d option."

craigslist.options = CmdParse::OptionParserWrapper.new do |opt|
  opt.on( '-d', '--days DAYS',
  'Show jobs from last DAYS days only' ) { |days| $days=days }
  opt.on( '-s', '--section SECTION',
    'Show jobs from SECTION section of craigslist only. ' <<
    'cpg searches computer gigs, for example, ' <<
    'and sof searches software jobs.' ) { |section| $section=section }

end
craigslist.set_execution_block do |args|
  search_string= args.join(' ')
  $days||=30

  query_string = "#{search_string}"
  query_string << " site:craigslist.org"
   query_string << " inurl:/#{$section}/" unless $section.nil?

   query_string << " daterange:#{(Date.today-$days.to_i).jd}-#{Date.today.jd}"

    google_url="http://www.google.com/search?q=#{URI.encode(query_string)}"

  puts "Jobs matching \"#{search_string}\" in the last "
  puts #{$days} days from all craigslist via google.com"
  puts "You can use the following Google search string:"
  puts "\t#{query_string}"
  puts "You can also use the following URL:"
  puts "\t#{google_url}"

end


# We've created the command objects, but we haven't added
# them to our parser, so we'll do that next:

cmd.add_command( indeed )
cmd.add_command( coolruby )
cmd.add_command( craigslist )

# Finally, we need to actually parse the command.
# This runs the commands indicated
# on the command line

cmd.parse
```

Save this example as `jobsearch.rb`. You can run our example using the following command:

```
ruby jobsearch.rb help
```

```
Usage: jobsearch  [options] COMMAND [options] [COMMAND [options] ...] [args]

Available commands:
    coolruby        Shows Ruby jobs from jobs.coolruby.com
    craigslist      Searches all Craigslist sites for jobs
    help            Provides help for individual commands
    indeed          Searches for jobs via Indeed.com and prints the top ten results
    version         Show the version of the program (=default command)
```

As you can see, `cmdparse` provides us with a `help` command that will summarize our commands. When called without any arguments, it lists all of the commands that our script supports. When called with a specific argument, it provides us with detailed help on any particular command:

```
ruby jobsearch.rb help indeed
```

```
indeed: Searches for jobs via Indeed.com and prints the top ten results.
This command searches Indeed.com for jobs matching [ARGS]. You can specify a
location to search via the -l and -r switches.

Usage: jobsearch indeed [options] [ARGS]

    -l, --location LOCATION         Show jobs from LOCATION only
    -r, --radius RADIUS             Sets a distance in miles from LOCATION to
search from. This option has no effect without the -l option.
```

Note that this is built from our program itself; if we add an option to the `indeed` command, it will automatically appear here, so our documentation needs less maintenance.

Let's try out the `coolruby` command—it will display Ruby jobs from `jobs.coolruby.com`. We can use it by entering the following command:

```
ruby jobsearch.rb coolruby
```

```
Jobs from coolruby.com
for more detail, see jobs.coolruby.com.
Web Application Database Developer - AIDT
Web Developer - Indianapolis Star
Web Designer/Flash Developer - Indianapolis Star
Software Engineer - Intern - Snapvine
...snip...
```

As you can see, the command successfully connected to jobs.coolruby.com, downloaded the RSS feed, and displayed it for us. In most cases, of course, it's easier to simply visit jobs. coolruby.com via a Web browser, but this way, you could put it into a cron job or a Windows Scheduler task and have the output emailed to you automatically.

Next let's try the Craigslist search functionality. This won't display any results, but it will let us produce a very useful Google URL.

```
ruby jobsearch.rb craigslist java developer
```

```
Jobs matching "java developer" in the last 30 days from all craigslist via
google.com
see the following URL:

http://www.google.com/search?q=java%20developer%20site:craigslist.org%20daterange:24
53981-2454011
```

The daterange: and site: operators are the keys: the first shows us recent results only, and the second restricts the results to craigslist.com and its subdomains.

We can also search for listings updated within the last five days, and we can even pin it down to a certain section of Craigslist. For example, let's say we wanted to search all of the Craigslist sites for Rails developer jobs, but we didn't want to visit them all by hand. First we'd visit just one of the Craigslist sites and note that the software jobs all had sof in the URL— that's the category shorthand for *software job*. We can then use our script to construct a Google query to search all of the Craigslist sites for software-developer jobs that match our criteria. We can do so using the following command:

```
ruby jobsearch.rb craigslist rails developer -s cpg -d 5
```

```
Jobs matching "rails developer" in the last 5 days from all craigslist via
google.com
You can use the following Google search string:
        rails developer site:craigslist.org inurl:/cpg/ daterange:2454006-245401
1
You can also use the following URL:

http://www.google.com/search?q=rails%20developer%20site:craigslist.org%20inurl:/cpg/
%20daterange:2454006-2454011
```

Finally, we can also search Indeed.com using the indeed command. The indeed command even lets us specify a location and a maximum distance from that location, so we can pin our jobs down by preferred city or state. Let's try it out using the following command:

```
ruby jobsearch.rb indeed rails developer
```

```
Jobs matching "rails developer" from indeed.com
for more detail, see the following URL:
        http://rss.indeed.com/rss?q=rails%20developer&l=&sort=date&radius=

SDE MT502024 - Comsys -  Seattle, WA
Web Developer (PHP, MySQL, AJAX) - A Prime Solution -  Charleston, SC
Server Developer - Ruby on Rails -  Portland, OR
Sr. Software Developer -  East Bay, CA
Something so much better than Social Ntwkg looking for Lead Developer -  Manhatt
an, NY
Web Designer Developer - DIRECT MAIL EXPRESS -  Daytona Beach, FL
Sr. Software Developer to $110k+ DOE - Act 1 Technical -  San Francisco, CA
...snip...
```

As you can see, we've gained quite a bit of power using the cmdparse interface. Let's take a look at exactly how our code works.

Dissecting Our Example

After we've used the require statement on the various libraries used by our code, our code creates a new command parser object and describes our program as follows:

```
cmd = CmdParse::CommandParser.new( true, true )
cmd.program_name = "jobsearch "
cmd.program_version = [0, 1, 0]
```

The first line creates a new CommandParser object for us—the first argument tells our program to handle exceptions gracefully by showing an error message and then the help screen, and the second argument tells CommandParser that we would like to use partial command matching—this means that if someone types ruby jobsearch.rb cool instead of ruby jobsearch.rb coolruby it will still work. Next, the program_name and program_version properties are set, which describe the name and version of the program. Those are used by cmdparse's built-in commands, which will we use next:

```
cmd.add_command( CmdParse::HelpCommand.new, true )
cmd.add_command( CmdParse::VersionCommand.new, false )
```

These two lines each add a command to our parser; the first adds the built-in command help, and the second the built-in version command. The second argument specifies whether the command should be a default command—since the second argument is true for the command help, the help command will be the default command. Both commands work via the data we've already entered: help works by listing all of the available commands and their descriptions and arguments, and version works by printing out the version we entered earlier in our code.

Next let's look at how the indeed command works:

```
indeed = CmdParse::Command.new('indeed', false )
indeed.short_desc = "Searches for jobs via Indeed.com "
```

```
indeed.short_desc << "and prints the top ten results."
indeed.description = 'This command searches Indeed.com for jobs matching [ARGS].'
indeed.description << 'You can specify a location to search '
indeed.description << 'via the -l and -r switches.'
```

The first line creates a new generic command named indeed, and the next two lines set up a short and a long description. The short description is shown on the help page summarizing available commands; both the short and the long descriptions are shown on the specific help page for the indeed command. Next we'll specify which options the indeed command can accept.

```
indeed.options = CmdParse::OptionParserWrapper.new do |opt|
  opt.on( '-l', '--location LOCATION',
  'Show jobs from LOCATION only' ) { |location| $location=location }
  opt.on( '-r', '--radius RADIUS',
  'Sets a distance in miles from LOCATION to search from. ' <<
  'This option has no effect without the -l option.' ) { |radius| $radius=radius }

end
```

This code creates a new OptionParserWrapper class, which parses optional arguments for us. The opt.on calls each specify a short and a long version of a given argument, as well as what to do when that argument is called. Each argument sets a variable that we can retrieve when the indeed command is called.

■Note Internally it uses the optparse library to parse options; the library is used in Chapter 18, among others.

```
indeed.set_execution_block do |args|
  search_string= args.join(' ')
  feed_url = 'http://rss.indeed.com/rss?'
  feed_url << 'q=#{URI.escape(search_string)}'
  feed_url << '&l=#{$location}&sort=date&radius=#{$radius}'
  puts "Jobs matching \"#{search_string}\" from indeed.com"
  puts "for more detail, see the following URL:\n\t#{feed_url}\n\n"

  feed= FeedTools::Feed.open(feed_url)
  feed.items.each do |item|
    puts "#{item.title}"
  end
end
```

This block of code uses the set_execution_block method to set what actually happens when the indeed command is run from the command line. It takes the command-line arguments, joins them into one search string, and produces an rss.indeed.com URL from them. Note that this is only the arguments to the indeed command—options such as -l and -r are stripped out, as is the word indeed itself; only actual arguments and not options or commands are passed to this code. Finally, FeedTools—an RSS parsing and output library for Ruby—is used to open the feed and print out each of its items. You can find out more about FeedTools in Chapter 10. (Note that the generated URL includes the $location and $radius variables even if you don't set them—this is because Indeed.com still works when those fields are blank.)

The coolruby and craigslist commands work similarly—the first takes an RSS feed from jobs.coolruby.com/rss and displays it, and the second simply produces a URL from the provided arguments. Let's look at how this all ties together:

```
cmd.add_command( indeed )
cmd.add_command( coolruby )
cmd.add_command( craigslist )

cmd.parse
```

The first three lines add our newly created commands to our parser, giving us a total of five commands—the custom indeed, coolruby, and craigslist commands, and the two built-in commands help and version. The final line, cmd.parse, hands control off to the parser, which will then call whichever command the user asked for on the command line.

HOW DOES THE GOOGLE SEARCH WORK?

The google command creates a search string that will search all of the Craigslist sites for recent listing. It uses Google's operators to cut down on extra results—specifically, it uses the daterange: operator to ensure that the listings are recent. It also uses the site: operator to make sure that the results are all from craigslist.org, and the inurl: operator to let you display only results from a certain section. This is quite useful, since you can search only one Craigslist site at a time using Craigslist's built-in tools.

For example, the following command will produce a URL to search for Craigslist jobs matching ruby programming in the Computer Gigs section of all the different Craigslist sites:

```
ruby jobsearch craigslist ruby programming -s cpg
```

Note that the Computer Gigs section is slightly different from the Software Jobs section—computer gigs are typically jobs for freelancers or moonlighters. You can search the software jobs section with the argument -s sof. Note that the argument isn't set by our program—it's an artifact of the way Craigslist sets up its sites. All of the Computer Gigs sections are in a cpg directory, so by searching for cpg in the URL, we can find results only from that section. Software jobs, likewise, are in the sof directory; there are other options, such as crg for Creative Gigs, and so on—you can find out more by visiting any Craigslist site and looking for the directory for the section you'd like to search.

Here's the algorithm we use to produce a Google string:

1. Start with the search string—this will be passed directly into the result search string as the q parameter.

2. Use Google's site: operator to add a term that will require the results to be from craigslist.org.

3. If the user wants to search only part of Craigslist, add an inurl: term which restricts the results to URLs containing that string.

4. Finish the query string by using the `datetime:` operator to restrict the results to those posted within the last `$days` days. Note that the `daterange:` operator requires the dates to be in Julian date format, and so we use the `jd` method to retrieve the Julian date. (Julian dates are the number of days that have elapsed since Monday, January 1, 4713 BC—like most date systems, it's fairly arbitrary, but fortunately it's easy to convert the dates appropriately.)

5. Finally, print the search string for cutting and pasting into Google. We'll also interpolate our query string into a Google search URL and then print the result, so you can just cut and paste the URL into your browser.

Conclusion

As you can see, `cmdparse` is a powerful and lightweight solution to providing a command-based interface. You could easily customize the example shown in this chapter for your own ends, and fortunately `cmdparse` is easy enough to use that most of the code in your program will be dealing with its unique issues and not with parsing commands.

## CHAPTER 9

HTML Templating with erubis

erubis is an implementation of the eRuby markup language, which allows you to weave Ruby code into HTML pages. In fact, eRuby lets you use the entire power of Ruby to output HTML. Of course, you could achieve similar functionality with puts statements embedded in Ruby code, but it'd be awkward and very difficult to maintain. As a bonus, some editors, such as gvim and radrails, support editing eRuby templates directly. Embedding code manually is painful and difficult—you have to constantly weave your HTML inside of your double quotes, your HTML isn't syntax-highlighted, and it's easy to miss a double quote, breaking your code.

There are three notable eRuby implementations. Specifically, there is erb, which ships with Ruby, and there's also a confusingly named implementation of eRuby called eRuby, which is faster than erb but slower than erubis. (Incidentally, erb is the implementation of eRuby used by Ruby on Rails.) Additionally, erubis is very extensible. For example, it ships with a number of extensions that change the way it parses eRuby, and you can easily create your extensions. It's also a pure Ruby library, so it can run wherever Ruby can run.

How Does It Work?

First let's look at how eRuby works in general, and then we'll discuss erubis in particular.

As mentioned, eRuby is a mix of Ruby and HTML. HTML code is passed to the browser as is but embedded Ruby code is executed. In particular, there are several kinds of delimiter tags that mark text as being embedded Ruby code, the most common being <%=..%> and <%..%>. The first executes code and inserts it into the output; the second simply executes code, which is useful for loops, conditional statements, and so forth. Here's a brief example:

```
<p>5 + 1 = <%=5+1%></p>
```

When executed by an eRuby parser, that line of eRuby will output the following:

```
<p>5 +1 = 6</p>
```

However, HTML can also be placed inside blocks of Ruby code —you can have a loop that outputs HTML on each iteration. Here's eRuby code that does just that:

```
<ul>
<% 1.upto(3) do |item_number| %>
  <li>List item #<%=item_number%>!</li>
<% end %>
</ul>
```

The output is as follows:

```
<ul>
  <li>List item #1!</li>
  <li>List item #2!</li>
  <li>List item #3!</li>
</ul>
```

As you can see, eRuby is reasonably easy to work with; it lets you use both Ruby code and HTML easily, and neither makes the other hard to read—which is quite unlike using hard-coded strings and puts statements.

erubis is an implementation of eruby. It's purported to be faster than any other available implementation, which is a bonus. It's also easily customized via subclasses, and it has a few features other libraries don't have. For example, it has a <%==..%> tag, which automatically sanitizes HTML—that is, it encodes the data as HTML so that HTML tags in your data become literal text instead of being misinterpreted. Text misinterpreted as HTML could cause your display to be really messed up—suppose, for example, you were viewing data that had the value </table> in it. This would cause your table to end prematurely, leaving all of the subsequent data to be displayed wrongly. In fact, if this was a publicly accessible system, this could even be used to insert malicious JavaScript code, which could be a very big security problem indeed.

Of course, you don't always want to sanitize HTML, since at times you may insert HTML into your output. Often, though, when you are reading data from a database that may contain HTML, you'll want to sanitize the output since you want to display the data as text and not HTML. The same is likely true of user-submitted input.

Let's look at an erubis example.

```
require 'erubis'

template = "<html><head>This is a test document!</head>
<body>
<h1>Hi!</h1>
<%1.upto(10) do |number|%>
  <p>This is paragraph number <%=number%>!</p>
<%end%>
</body>
"
eruby_object= Erubis::Eruby.new(template)

puts eruby_object.evaluate()
```

The output of the snippet is as follows:

```
<html><head>This is a test document!</head>
<body>
<h1>Hi!</h1>
        <p>This is paragraph number 1!</p>
        <p>This is paragraph number 2!</p>
```

```
        <p>This is paragraph number 3!</p>
        <p>This is paragraph number 4!</p>
        <p>This is paragraph number 5!</p>
</body>
```

As you can see, it's reasonably easy to evaluate an eRuby template using erubis; you simply call `Erubis::ERuby.new` and pass it the template as a string; you then use the object's `evaluate` method to get the output.

Incidentally, `Ruby on Rails` uses eRuby templates, although it uses the erb library instead of the erubis gem. If you'd like to use erubis instead of erb in a `Rails` application, see the instructions on the erubis home page. You can get those instructions as well as the erubis documentation at the erubis home page:

```
http://www.kuwata-lab.com/erubis/
```

■**Tip** There's an optional parameter to the `evaluate` method. It specifies the binding for which the eRuby code is evaluated, so you can specify what scope all of the local variables will come from. This is the same kind of facility used by `Ruby on Rails` to pass values from controllers to views.

To install erubis, enter the following OS X/Linux shell or Windows command-prompt command:

```
gem install erubis
```

HTML MySQL Table Viewer with erubis

The following script will demonstrate erubis by creating a MySQL table viewer. It will open a MySQL connection using `ActiveRecord` and then dump the table using an erubis template. (See Chapter 5 for more details.) The erubis template will be in a separate file; this separates the presentation of the data from the flow control of the program so you can edit the template easily without disrupting the program's main logic. The script handles things like reading command-line arguments, setting up the connection to the database, loading the data, and so forth, and the template has to handle only the actual display of the data.

You'll need `ActiveRecord` installed; if you don't have it installed, you can install it via the Windows command prompt or OS X/Linux shell command `gem install activerecord`.

```
require 'erubis'
require 'active_record'
require 'optparse'

$options = {}

opt=OptionParser.new do |opts|
  opts.banner = "Usage: #{$0} [options] hostname.com file1 file2 file3..."
```

```ruby
    opts.on("-H", "--host HOST", "host") { |h|    $options[:hostname] = h }
    opts.on("-u", "--username USERNAME",
            "username") { |u|    $options[:username] = u }
    opts.on("-p", "--password PASSWORD",
            "password") { |p|    $options[:password] = p }
    opts.on("-o", "--port PORT", "port") { |p|    $options[:port] = p }
    opts.on("-d", "--database DATABASE", "DATABASE") { |d|
            $options[:database] = d }
    opts.on("-t", "--table TABLE", "TABLE") { |t|    $options[:table] = t }
    opts.on_tail("-h", "--help", "Show this message") { puts opts.help; exit }

end
opt.parse!

(puts "Please specify a table name to print.\n" << opt.help;
  exit) unless $options[:table]
(puts "Please specify a database to print.\n" << opt.help;
  exit) unless $options[:database]

$options[:hostname] ||= 'localhost'
$options[:username] ||= 'root'
$options[:password] ||= ''
$options[:port] ||= 3306

ActiveRecord::Base.establish_connection(
  :adapter  => "mysql",
  :host     => $options[:hostname],
  :username => $options[:username],
  :password => $options[:password],
  :database => $options[:database])

class OutputTable <  ActiveRecord::Base
  set_table_name $options[:table]
end

context={:table=> OutputTable, :print_data=>OutputTable.find_all}

eruby_object= Erubis::Eruby.new(File.read('template.rhtml'))

puts eruby_object.evaluate(context)
```

Save this as mysql2html.rb, and the save the following erubis code as template.rhtml:

```html
<html>
  <head>
    <title>MySQL Dump of <%=@table.table_name.titlecase%></title>
  </head>
  <body>
```

```
    <h1><%=@table.table_name.titlecase%><h1>
    <table>

      <tr>
        <%@table. column_names.each do |col|%>
            <th><%=col %></th>
        <%end%>
      </tr>

      <%@print_data.each do |row|%>
        <tr>
        <%@table.column_names.each do |col|%>
            <td><%==row[col]%></td>
        <%end%>
        </tr>
      <%end%>

    </table>
  </body>
</html>
```

To test the example, let's create a simple MySQL database using the following Windows command prompt or Mac OS X/Linux shell commands:

```
mysql
```

```
Welcome to the MySQL monitor.  Commands end with ; or \g.
Your MySQL connection id is 40 to server version: 4.1.9-nt

Type 'help;' or '\h' for help. Type '\c' to clear the buffer.
```

```
mysql> create database mysql2html_test;
```

```
Query OK, 1 row affected (0.00 sec)
```

```
mysql> use mysql2html_test;
```

```
Database changed
```

```
mysql> create table users (logon text, password text, joined timestamp);
```

```
Query OK, 1 row affected (0.08 sec)
```

```
mysql> insert into test (logon, password) values ('Mister X','eagle/beagle//3');
```

```
Query OK, 1 row affected (0.00 sec)
```

```
mysql> insert into test (logon, password) values ('Star Captain Y','tender++camel');
```

```
Query OK, 1 row affected (0.00 sec)
```

```
mysql> insert into test (logon, password) values ('Doctor Z','beable+proge-3');
```

```
Query OK, 1 row affected (0.00 sec)
```

Note that if the default username and password aren't correct for your system, you can use the -u and -p options to change them—if you had username fred and password john, you could do the following as the initial command: mysql -u fred -p john. The remainder of the commands would be the same.

At this point, you should have a working MySQL database with a few tables in it. You can then test the script using the following command:

```
ruby mysql2html.rb -d mysql2html_test -t test
```

```
<html>
  <head>
    <title>MySQL Dump of Users</title>
  </head>
  <body>
    <h1>Users<h1>
    <table>

      <tr>
        <th>Logon</th>
        <th>Password/th>
        <th>Joined</th>
```

```
      </tr>

      <tr>
        <td>Mister X</td>
        <td>eagle//beagle/3</td>
        <td>Mon Oct 09 14:56:58 Eastern Daylight Time 2006</td>
      </tr>

      <tr>
        <td>Star Captain Y</td>
        <td>tender++camel</td>
        <td>Mon Oct 09 14:57:01 Eastern Daylight Time 2006</td>
      </tr>

      <tr>
        <td>Doctor Z</td>
        <td>beable+proge-3</td>
        <td>Mon Oct 09 14:57:04 Eastern Daylight Time 2006</td>
      </tr>
    </table>
  </body>
</html>
```

As you can see, our script and template will produce nicely formatted HTML output from a MySQL database; let's take a look at how it works behind the scenes.

Dissecting the Example

Let's examine our program. First we retrieve the various connection settings from the command line and then we create an ActiveRecord object. The program will die if the command is not called with both a database name and a table name, since both are required to locate the table. The parsing of the various switches is done using optparse. If you are curious as to how the optparse library works, you can get the full details at the following URL:

http://www.ruby-doc.org/stdlib/libdoc/optparse/rdoc/classes/OptionParser.html

After creating a connection to the database, the bulk of the work is accomplished by the following lines. First we create an ActiveRecord model to represent our table. By default, ActiveRecord models have a table name based on their class name. In this case, though, we'll be accessing a user-specified table, so we override the default with the $options[:table] variable—which corresponds to the table set by the user on the command line.

```
class OutputTable < ActiveRecord::Base
  set_table_name $options[:table]
end
```

Next we create a context variable—this is a hash of all of the variables that will be accessible to our Ruby template. The first is the variable OutputTable, which will be accessible through the variable @table; the second is all of the data from that table, retrieved using the find_all method, which will be accessible through the variable print_data. Note that the names used by the template correspond to the keys in the hash, and not to the original variable names.

```
context={:table=> OutputTable, :print_data=>OutputTable.find_all}
```

The next line creates an erubis object by calling Erubis::ERuby.new() with the contents of our template file as an argument. All that's left is to print the results of evaluating—that is, running—the code using the variables we created on the context=… line. At this point, the control is handed off to the template, and then the result is printed.

```
eruby_object= Erubis::Eruby.new(File.read('template.rhtml'))

puts eruby_object.evaluate(context)
```

As you can see, the control code is very simple and clean—it's easy to extend this to having multiple templates or storing the templates in the database, or to scale it up to more templates and more data.

Next let's look at the template internals:

```
<table>

  <tr>
    <%@table. column_names.each do |col|%>
        <th><%=col %></th>
    <%end%>
  </tr>

  <%@print_data.each do |row|%>
    <tr>
    <%@table.column_names.each do |col|%>
        <td><%==row[col]%></td>
    <%end%>
    </tr>
  <%end%>

</table>
```

This is the heart of our template—it contains three loops, the first of which prints out all of the column names from the @table variable passed from our controller. The second loops through each row of data, and the third loops through each column of each row, printing the data. As you can see, it's fairly simple—and you can easily modify the presentation of the code without changing the logic behind the controller.

Conclusion

erubis is a great way to use eRuby templates. It's fast, it's customizable, and it's easy to use; any time you need eRuby, you should think about using erubis.

CHAPTER 10

■ ■ ■

Parsing Feeds with feedtools

The feedtools gem helps you parse feeds in either the RSS or Atom format. RSS and Atom are formats used to publish frequently updating digital content, such as blogs, news, wikis, or podcasts. Both formats allow programs to programmatically retrieve the information from such sites; often, programs will aggregate multiple feeds together and display the results of several sites at once.

feedtools is an excellent choice for writing those sorts of aggregators. It can be useful in a variety of contexts; for example, you could use it to add a sidebar displaying news from CNN or BBC to your rails application. You could also use it to display search-engine results, such as a job search on Indeed.com or a blog search on Google Blog Search. You can even use it to display videos from Yahoo! News or YouTube.

How Does It Work?

The feedtools gem helps you parse newsfeeds. Newsfeeds—typically in the Atom or RSS format—let you track changes to your favorite websites. Since there is a huge number of sites on the Internet and since many of them change incredibly fast, such feeds can make your life much easier. RSS and Atom both provide a standard XML file format for describing news—such as current events, blog posts, or changes to a site. Nearly all blogs offer RSS and Atom feeds, and so do most news sites, like Google News, CNN, BBC, and so forth.

Atom and RSS are both XML formats, so you could parse them using a Ruby library like the standard Ruby library REXML or the xml-simple gem (see Chapter 33 for more details.) However, using feedtools means that you can take advantage of a powerful newsfeed-specific interface, which makes your life much easier. For example, here's how easy it is to print out the titles from a newsfeed:

```ruby
require 'feed_tools'
newsfeed=FeedTools::Feed.open('http://rss.coolruby.com/')
newsfeed.items.each do |item|
  puts item.title
end
```

LAMP developers - S & A Associates
using iText in JRuby to Create PDF
Computer Systems Analysts - BAE SYSTEMS
The Least Surprised #13: Those Are Stars In Our Eyes

```
Server Engineer - Cross Creek Systems
Senior Software Engineer - Harvard Law School
Developer, Internet Software - Tribune Company
Senior Software Engineer - Harvard University
Ajax Web Developer - Global Software Technologies
CSS Web Developer - Global Software Technologies
Software Architect - J2EE/.NET - Riviera Partners
```

The second line creates a new FeedTools:Feed object using the open method. The URL specified is http://rss.coolruby.com/, which is the RSS feed for http://coolruby.com. The next line uses the .items method of the feed and call its .each method to iterate through each feed item, then the .title method of each item is used to print out the item titles. You can access other attributes of each item, of course—the URL of the full view of the item, the date it was updated, and so forth. In some cases—many blogs, for example—the full text of an item is included in the .description attribute.

You can use the following command to install feedtools:

```
gem install feedtools
```

CACHING WITH FEEDTOOLS

feedtools has caching built in; it can store RSS data locally, and download the feeds only when they have changed. This is useful, since it means that your application won't use any more bandwidth than necessary. Unfortunately, it's designed for Rails applications. It can't be used without a database connection, and it expects Rails-style paths, with a YAML markup file specifying the database details. (YAML is the markup language Rails uses to specify the database-configuration information.) This is convenient for use in Rails, but awkward outside of Rails.

Note, though, that feedtools will cache transparently, without any extra code in the script, if you fulfill two requirements. First, you'll need a database.yml file, using the same format that Rails does, and it needs to be placed in a config/ directory—so if your script is in /home/someuser/myscript, the full path to your database.yml file will be /home/someuser/myscript/config/database.yml. You'll need a database specified for the production environment—see Chapter 23 for more details on Rails database.yml files. Second, the database needs to have the feedTools caching table in it—you can find the schema definition for your database in the ruby\lib\ruby\gems\1.8\gems\feedtools-x.y.z\db directory, where x.y.z is the version of the feedtools gem that you have installed. (Note that if you are using feedtools from inside a Rails app, the first requirement will be taken care of—you'll only need to add the feedtools caching table to your app.)

You can find out more about using the feedtools cache at the following URL:

http://dekstop.de/weblog/2005/12/feedtools_cache_in_ruby_scripts/

A News Search Tool Built with feedtools

To demonstrate feedtools, we're going to build a short program (Listing 10-1) that will show the top ten or so Yahoo! News results. It will use feedtools to download and parse the feed, and then use Camping to serve a web page that has the news items on it. We can then use our Web browser to see the feed. (You can see more feedtools examples in Chapters 5 and 8.)

Note you'll need Camping installed—you can use the gem install camping command at the windows command prompt or Linux/OS X shell to install it. You can find out more about Camping in Chapter 7.

Listing 10-1. *Searching News Feeds with feedtools (news.rb)*

```ruby
require 'camping'
require 'feed_tools'
require 'uri'


Camping.goes :News

module News::Controllers
  class Index < R '/'
    def get
      render :frontpage
    end
  end
end

module News::Views
  @@search_term= 'ruby on rails'
  def frontpage
    h1 "News about #{@@search_term.titlecase}"

    ul do
      url="http://news.search.yahoo.com/news/rss?" <<
          "ei=UTF-8&p=#{URI.encode(@@search_term)}&eo=UTF-8"
      feed=FeedTools::Feed.open(url)

      feed.items.each do |feed_item|
        div do
          a :href=>feed_item.link do
            feed_item.title
          end
        end
      end
    end
  end
end
```

Save this example as `news.rb`. You can run the code using the following Windows command prompt or Linux/OS X shell command:

```
camping news.rb
```

```
** Camping running on 0.0.0.0:3301.
```

You can now access the application in your Web browser at the following address:

```
http://127.0.0.1:3301
```

You'll then see a simple Web page with the latest `Ruby on Rails` news on it.

Dissecting the Example

First, our script requires the `Camping` gem, the `feedtools` gem, and the `URI` module that is part of Ruby. The `Camping` gem is a Web framework—it's covered in detail in Chapter 7. The `URI` module is used to dynamically the create the Google search string—its encode method lets us encode our search string into our Google search URL. Next, it uses the `Camping.goes` method to create a new `Camping` application namespace—you can find out more about this in Chapter 7 as well. You can see all of our controller code in this section of the code:

```
module News::Controllers
  class Frontpage < R '/'
    def get
      render :frontpage
    end
  end
end
```

This snippet defines just one controller—`Frontpage`—which renders our one and only page. This corresponds to the root of our Web server—by default, the Web address `http://localhost:3301/`. This controller simply calls our singular view, which is shown here:

```
module News::Views
  @@search_term= 'ruby on rails'
  def frontpage
    h1 "News about #{@@search_term.titlecase}"
    url="http://news.search.yahoo.com/news/rss?" <<
        "ei=UTF-8&p=#{URI.encode(@@search_term)}&eo=UTF-8"
    feed=FeedTools::Feed.open(url)

    feed.items.each do |feed_item|
      div do
        a :href=>feed_item.link do
          feed_item.title
        end
      end
    end
```

```
  end
end
```

This module contains our single `Camping` view. It uses `Markaby` to output HTML—you can find out more about the `Markaby` gem recipe in Chapter 14. The `@@search_term` variable is a class-level variable, which has a permanently hard-coded search term—by default, it's `ruby on rails`, but you can change that if you'd like. The `h1` method outputs a header for the page, and then we create a URL for the page by inserting the search term into our template URL.

Next we use the `FeedTools::Feed.open` method to create a new `feedtools` object. This automatically opens and downloads our newsfeed. Finally, we loop through the `feed.items` array, creating a `div` element with the title of the item and a link to the news item.

Conclusion

As you can see, the `feedtools` interface is very intuitive, and you can quickly create sites and applications that use RSS and Atom feeds using `feedtools`.

CHAPTER 11

■■■

Creating Graphical User Interfaces with fxruby

While Ruby is perhaps best known for the Rails Web-application toolkit (introduced in Chapter 23), it's also possible to create excellent graphical applications using Ruby. The FOX GUI toolkit is a cross-platform (Mac OS X, Linux X11, and Windows) toolkit, and the fxruby gem lets you use Ruby to create FOX applications.

How Does It Work?

Since FOX is designed for multiple platforms, programming FOX is slightly different than programming graphical applications on each individual platform. It's reasonably easy to pick up, however, even if you have no experience writing graphical applications.

FOX applications are composed of one or more windows, and each window can have various widgets: menus, text boxes, check boxes, command buttons, and so forth. Each of these items can have events which are composed of methods in our Ruby code that respond to a given user's action.

For example, in a hypothetical text editor written in Ruby, when the user clicks the File menu and then the Save As menu item, it will create a click event. The Ruby application will respond to the click event, just like a Rails application would respond to a request for a Web page. When no events are happening, your application is essentially in a holding pattern—waiting to receive an event. Fortunately, fxruby takes care of the difficult work, leaving us with a nice object-oriented interface to let us create windows and controls and then attach code to them.

Listing 11-1 contains a brief example.

Listing 11-1. *test_application.rb*

```
require 'fox16'

include Fox

myApp = FXApp.new

# FXMainWindow objects are windows;
# our single control will be inside this
# window.
```

```
mainWindow=FXMainWindow.new(myApp, "Test App")

# FXButton objects are clickable buttons.

my_button= FXButton.new(mainWindow, 'Click Me!')
my_button.connect(SEL_COMMAND) do
  my_button.text="I've been Clicked!"
end

myApp.create

mainWindow.show( PLACEMENT_SCREEN )

myApp.run
```

This example will show a single, small window with the caption *Test App*; it will have a single clickable button labeled Click Me (Figure 11-1), and when you click it, the label changes to I've been Clicked (Figure 11-2).

Figure 11-1. *The example before being clicked*

Figure 11-2. *The example after being clicked*

You can use the following command to install fxruby:

```
gem install fxruby
```

Under Linux or OS X, you'll need to have the FOX toolkit installed before you install fxruby; you can get it here:

```
http://www.fox-toolkit.org/
```

Dynamic MySQL Data Form with fxruby

The script in Listing 11-2 demonstrates fxruby by creating a form to insert data into a MySQL table. It uses ActiveRecord to read the table information, and then create a form based on those table names. (You'll need to install the ActiveRecord gem as well; see Chapter 5 for more information.) It will use ActiveRecord's Inflector.Humanize method to create friendly table labels, and it will work on any MySQL table, since ActiveRecord provides database reflection. You can see the result in Figure 11-3.

You'll also need to be running a graphical interface, of course, such as the default interface on Mac OS X, Windows, and X11 Linux.

■**Note** Chapter 26 has an additional example of using fxruby.

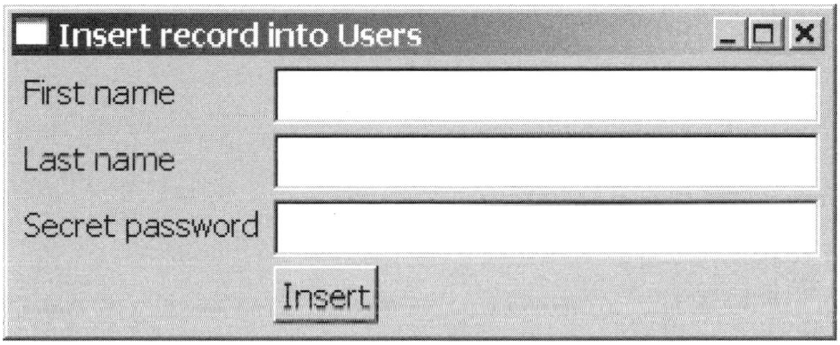

Figure 11-3. *The application in use*

Listing 11-2. *fxruby.rb*

```
require 'fox16'
require 'active_record'
require 'optparse'

$options = {}

opt=OptionParser.new do |opts|
  opts.banner = "Usage: #{$0} [options]"
  opts.on("-H", "--host HOST", "host") { |h|  $options[:hostname] = h }
  opts.on("-u", "--username USERNAME", "username") { |u| $options[:username] = u }
  opts.on("-p", "--password PASSWORD", "password") { |p| $options[:password] = p }
  opts.on("-o", "--port PORT", "port") { |p|  $options[:port] = p }
  opts.on("-d", "--database DATABASE", "DATABASE") { |d| $options[:database] = d }
  opts.on("-t", "--table TABLE", "TABLE") { |t| $options[:table] = t }
  opts.on_tail("-h", "--help", "Show this message") { puts opts.help; exit }

end
opt.parse!

(puts "Please specify a table name.\n" << opt.help; exit) unless $options[:table]
(puts "Please specify a database.\n" << opt.help; exit) unless $options[:database]
```

```ruby
$options[:hostname] ||= 'localhost'
$options[:username] ||= 'root'
$options[:password] ||= ''
$options[:port] ||= 3306

#First, we connect to the database that the user specified...
ActiveRecord::Base.establish_connection(
  :adapter  => "mysql",
  :host     => $options[:hostname],
  :username => $options[:username],
  :password => $options[:password],
  :database => $options[:database])

# and then we create an ActiveRecord model to represent it...

class OutputTable <  ActiveRecord::Base
  set_table_name $options[:table]
end

include Fox

fox_application=FXApp.new

# we're going to create a single window for our application;
# it will be titled according to the name of our table.

main_window=FXMainWindow.new(fox_application, "Insert record into " <<
  #{Inflector.humanize($options[:table])}", nil, nil, DECOR_ALL )

# This matrix is like a table for our controls;
# it's a MATRIX_BY_COLUMNS matrix with two columns,
# which means that our app will have two columns of
# controls, which will line up nicely. The first
# column will be our labels, and the second column
# will be our text boxes.

control_matrix=FXMatrix.new(main_window,2, MATRIX_BY_COLUMNS)

# This array will contain all of our data entry controls -
# we'll need this to insert the data into our model.

field_controls = []

OutputTable.columns.each do |col|
  FXLabel.new(control_matrix, Inflector.humanize(col.name))
  field_controls << [col.name,FXTextField.new(control_matrix, 30)]
end
```

```
# This is a blank frame; it does nothing but take up a space in
# the matrix.
# if this wasn't here, our "Insert button" would line up with
# our labels, but it looks nicer lined up with the text boxes.

FXHorizontalFrame.new(control_matrix, LAYOUT_FILL_X )

# This creates our "Insert button", and attaches some code
# to the SEL_COMMAND event; this event controls what happens
# when we click on it.

FXButton.new(control_matrix, 'Insert').connect(SEL_COMMAND) do
  OutputTable.new do |rec|
    field_controls.each do |field_control|
      name, control = *field_control
      rec.send("#{name}=", control.text)
    end
    rec.save
  end

  FXMessageBox.new(main_window, "Data Inserted",
  "Data inserted into table '#{Inflector.humanize($options[:table])}'.\n\nThanks!",
  nil, MBOX_OK | DECOR_TITLE).execute

end

fox_application.create

main_window.show( PLACEMENT_SCREEN )

fox_application.run
```

Save this as `fxruby_demo.rb`. To test our example, let's create a simple MySQL database using the following commands:

```
mysql
```

```
Welcome to the MySQL monitor.  Commands end with ; or \g.
Your MySQL connection id is 40 to server version: x.y.z

Type 'help;' or '\h' for help. Type '\c' to clear the buffer.
```

```
mysql> create database fxruby_test;
```

```
Query OK, 1 row affected (0.00 sec)
```

```
mysql> use fxruby_test;
```

```
Database changed
```

```
mysql> create table users (first_name text, last_name text, secret_password text);
```

```
Query OK, 1 row affected (0.08 sec)
```

Note that if the default username and password aren't correct for your system, you can use the -u and -p options to change them—if you had username *fred* and password *john*, you could do the following as the initial command: mysql -u fred -p—you can then enter the password when prompted. The remainder of the commands would be the same.

At this point, you should have a working MySQL database with a single table in it. You can then test the script using the following command:

```
ruby fxruby_demo.rb -H localhost -u root -d fxruby_test -t test
```

As you can see, this brings up a new record form. You can enter some test data, and click Insert—you'll then get a dialog confirming the insertion and the data will be added.

Dissecting the Example

Let's examine Listing 11-2—first we retrieve the various connection settings from the command line and then we create an ActiveRecord object. This works the same as the optparse example in Chapter 9; additionally, you can find the API reference at the following URL:

```
http://www.ruby-doc.org/stdlib/libdoc/optparse/rdoc/classes/OptionParser.html
```

We then set up an example table model, just like we did in Chapter 9. This table is called OutputTable, and represents whatever table is specified on the command line. Next we create a new application window based on the data from that table.

```
fox_application=FXApp.new
```

```
main_window=FXMainWindow.new(fox_application, "Insert record into " <<
  "#{Inflector.humanize($options[:table])}", nil, nil, DECOR_ALL )
```

The first line creates an FXApp object that represents the new application. The next line creates a new FXMainWindow object—the first parameter specifies that the parent FXApp object will be the one we just created. The second parameter is the table title—the call to `Inflector.humanize` means that it "humanizes" the table name; for example, it converts underscores into spaces, capitalizes the first character of each word, and so forth.

```
control_matrix=FXMatrix.new(main_window, 2, MATRIX_BY_COLUMNS)

field_controls = []

OutputTable.columns.each do |col|
  FXLabel.new(control_matrix, Inflector.humanize(col.name))
  field_controls << [col.name,FXTextField.new(control_matrix, 30)]
end
```

The first line creates an `FXMatrix`—it's an object that holds controls in a matrix or table format. It will fill up either top to bottom or left to right, depending on the third parameter. Additionally, the second parameter specifies the number of columns or rows. The first parameter specifies the parent object.

We then loop through each column in the table, and create a label and a new `FXTextField` control for each. The label is purely cosmetic—it shows the humanized label for the text field, based on the name of the table. We create a new text field as well, which will be used for the end user to enter their data for each field. We also add the text field control to the `field_controls` array, which means we can access it later when we add the record into the table.

Because we specified two columns for each row in the `FXMatrix` creation line, each label and text-field combination will be on its own row.

Next we need to create a button that actually adds the data to the table. This chunk of code does just that:

```
FXHorizontalFrame.new(control_matrix, LAYOUT_FILL_X )
FXButton.new(control_matrix, 'Insert').connect(SEL_COMMAND) do
  OutputTable.new do |rec|
    field_controls.each do |field_control|
      name, control = *field_control
      rec.send("#{name}=", control.text)
    end
    rec.save
  end

  FXMessageBox.new(main_window, "Data Inserted",
"Data inserted into table '#{Inflector.humanize($options[:table])}'.\n\nThanks!",
 nil, MBOX_OK | DECOR_TITLE).execute

end
```

We create a new `FXHorizontalFrame`—since we ended the loop on a new row, the horizontal frame will take up the first cell. The horizontal frame can also hold controls, but in this example we use it only as a placeholder. The new `FXButton` control is what Windows programmers call a "command button"—in HTML it would be called a "submit control." It's a control with a label you can click on to perform an action. In this case, it's an action to add the new record, and we connect the block of code we specify to the `SEL_COMMAND` message. The

SEL_COMMAND message kicks in when the control is clicked or activated using the keyboard. (Under Windows, for example, you can tab to the control and then press the spacebar.)

When the FXButton control is activated, the OutputTable.new line prepares a new record to be added into the table. We then loop through each control and set the appropriate field for each control to the entered value. Finally, we save the new record using the .save method.

The last three lines create the application object, which loads all of the controls we created already; after that, we just need to show our main window and run the program.

```
fox_application.create

main_window.show( PLACEMENT_SCREEN )

fox_application.run
```

The first of these three lines creates the application's resources; that is, it calls the operating-system-specific APIs to instantiate our main window, our labels and text boxes, and so forth. The second line shows the main window, since it's invisible by default. The sole parameter to that function call is the PLACEMENT_SCREEN constant, which centers the window on the screen. The final call takes over control of the program—turning it into an event-driven program that simply responds to user events. The function call will return when the application is exited.

Conclusion

fxruby provides access to a fast, flexible, cross-platform GUI toolkit, and you can quickly create virtually any kind of graphical application with it.

CHAPTER 12

■■■

Retrieving Stock Quotes with YahooFinance

The YahooFinance gem provides an interface to the Yahoo! Finance API for the retrieval of stock quotes. This service is free, unlike many other services, and it's much easier to use the YahooFinance gem to extract quotes from Yahoo! than it is to extract quotes via screen scraping.

Using the YahooFinance gem, you can easily retrieve current stock quotes on most international stock markets, and get information on some indexes and mutual funds. You could use the gem to create a stock ticker, for example, or a program that automatically downloads the current value of your stock portfolio and emails it to you. Finally, you can also use it to get historical information on stocks (for more information on this, see the sample application in Chapter 22).

How Does It Work?

The YahooFinance gem retrieves stock quotes from http://finance.yahoo.com. Of course, this means that you'll need an Internet connection to use the YahooFinance gem. The gem is fairly easy to use. For example, suppose you wanted to print the most recent quotes for Yahoo! and Microsoft stock. You can use the following code to do that:

```
require 'yahoofinance'

YahooFinance::get_standard_quotes('MSFT,YHOO').each do |symbol, quote|
  puts "#{symbol}: #{quote.lastTrade}"
end
```

The get_standard_quotes function takes a comma-separated list of symbols and returns a hash with symbol and quote information; the quote information is in the form of an object with reasonably straightforward properties: lastTrade represents the last trade price, open represents the opening price, previousClose represents the previous day's closing price, and so forth. In the preceding snippet example, we use the lastTrade property.

Running that Ruby code produces a result similar to this:

```
YHOO: 29.74
MSFT: 28.98
```

Of course, the exact values will vary—both Yahoo! and Microsoft stocks will change values throughout the trading day. In any case, as you can see, it's pretty easy to retrieve quotes on various symbols. Note that Yahoo! Finance delays its quotes by about 20 minutes, so the values you retrieve with YahooFinance won't be up-to-the-minute.

You can find the documentation for the YahooFinance gem here:

```
http://www.transparentech.com/projects/yahoofinance
```

■**Note** The YahooFinance gem is at the heart of the Grism stock-market tool—Grism lets you watch stocks graphically using a GTK interface. You can find out more at the following Web address:

```
http://www.grism.org/
```

The following command installs the YahooFinance gem:

```
gem install yahoofinance
```

Displaying a Stock-Market Ticker with YahooFinance

The example application in Listing 12-1 uses the YahooFinance gem and the fxruby gem (see Chapter 11) to display a graphical stock ticker. The example takes stock symbols on the command line, and for each symbol specified, it will constantly scroll the name and price in a graphical window. The prices are updated once a minute.

Listing 12-1. *A Graphical Stock Ticker with YahooFinance (ticker.rb)*

```ruby
require 'yahoofinance'
require 'fox16'
include Fox

# Exit if the user did not pass any symbols
# on the command line.
(puts "Usage: ruby #{$0} STOCK_SYMBOL STOCK_SYMBOL..."; exit) unless ARGV.length>0

# These values can be changed; they represent
# time in milliseconds.

@scroll_interval = 25
@update_interval = 6000

@fox_application=FXApp.new
```

```ruby
@main_window=FXMainWindow.new(@fox_application, "Stock Ticker ",
                              nil, nil,
                              DECOR_ALL | LAYOUT_EXPLICIT)
@tickerlabel = FXLabel.new(@main_window, '', nil, 0,  LAYOUT_EXPLICIT)

# The following method updates the ticker text.
# It's called by a timer once a minute.

def update_label_text
  label_text = ' '
  # Loop through all of the symbols, retrieve
  # the most recent quotes, and update the
  # label with the most recent information.
  YahooFinance::get_standard_quotes( ARGV.join(',')).each do |symbol, quote|
    label_text << "#{symbol}: #{quote.lastTrade} ... "
  end
  @tickerlabel.text = label_text
end

# The following method scrolls the ticker across
# the screen.
#
# It's called by a timer every 25ms.

def update_label_position

  @left_position = @tickerlabel.x if @left_position.nil?

  # Move the ticker back to the left once
  # it reaches the right edge.

  if(@left_position > @main_window.width)
    @left_position = -@tickerlabel.width
  end

  @left_position = @left_position + 3

  @main_window.padLeft = @left_position
end

update_label_text

@left_position=nil

# These following two functions manage
# the timing of the update and scroll
# functions; FOX doesn't have a permanent
```

```
# timer - just one-shot timeouts - so
# every time one of these functions is called,
# we need to set the timeout again.
#
def scroller(sender, sel, ptr)
  update_label_position
  @fox_application.addTimeout(@scroll_interval, method(:scroller))
end

def updater(sender, sel, ptr)
  update_label_text
  @fox_application.addTimeout(@update_interval, method(:updater))
end

# Initialize the two timer functions...

@fox_application.addTimeout(@scroll_interval, method(:scroller))
@fox_application.addTimeout(@update_interval, method(:updater))


# Create the window, show it,
# and then run the application.

@fox_application.create

@main_window.show( PLACEMENT_SCREEN )

@fox_application.run
```

Save this script as `ticker.rb`. You can then run it using the following command:

```
ruby ticker.rb msft yhoo
```

As you can see in Figure 12-1, this script displays a graphical ticker with the stock symbols specified on the command line; they scroll from left two right. Every minute, the stock prices update.

Figure 12-1. *The stock ticker*

Dissecting the Example

Most of the program in Listing 12-1 uses fxruby to prepare the stock-ticker window; the stock-label ticker, for example, is scrolled across the rest of the screen by the update_label_position function, which simply moves the label toward the right of the window and resets it once it scrolls out of view.

However, the heart of the the program is a single function, update_label_text, which grabs the values and places them in the stock ticker as follows:

```
def update_label_text
  label_text = ' '
  # Loop through all of the symbols, retrieve
  # the most recent quotes, and update the
  # label with the most recent information.
  YahooFinance::get_standard_quotes( ARGV.join(',')).each do |symbol, quote|
    label_text << "#{symbol}: #{quote.lastTrade} ... "
  end
  @tickerlabel.text = label_text
end
```

The get_standard_quotes function returns a hash; each element returns a symbol and a quote object. The quote object has various properties that describe the stock quote that was retrieved; the property used here is lastTrade, which refers to the last price at which the stock traded. Each stock's symbol and last trading price is concatenated into a single string, which is then assigned to the label.

Conclusion

YahooFinance lets you quickly access stock quotes from the Yahoo! Finance service; it's not as quickly updated as various commercial providers are, but it's free and it's easy to use.

CHAPTER 13

■ ■ ■

Parsing HTML with hpricot

The hpricot gem provides a fast Ruby HTML parser; it's partially implemented in C to increase performance. hpricot has two big advantages: it's easy to use and it's fast. It combines an elegant interface with the ability to search by CSS selectors, element IDs, tag types, and so forth. At the same time, it's also high-performance, so you can process even fairly large HTML documents quickly.

For example, you can use hpricot to pull information from virtually any Web page. This process, called *screen scraping*, allows you to take information provided by a Web page and translate it into a different form. You could download information provided by a site and index it into a Web page, for example, or you could write a script that automatically logs on to, say, your bank's website, downloads your latest statement, and then places the result in a MySQL database. You could also use hpricot to automatically parse your website and check for accuracy by comparing the data your site is displaying to a source that is known to be accurate.

Note If you are performing any significant amount of data retrieval—and doubly so if it's commercial—you should obtain written permission from the site in question before starting. Bandwidth costs money, and otherwise you may find your IP banned. In a worst-case scenario, you could face legal action.

How Does It Work?

The hpricot gem helps you do two things: First, it lets you parse HTML, including possibly broken HTML, such as is commonly found on the Web. Second, it lets you update HTML so that you could, for example, add a certain attribute to all tags of a certain CSS class. hpricot lets you use an intuitive interface to parse HTML in a variety of ways.

Let's look at a brief example (Listing 13-1). We'll pull all of the list items out of an HTML list and print them out using hpricot.

Listing 13-1. *Parsing HTML with hpricot (hpricot_parse_by_tag.rb)*

```
require 'hpricot'

document= <<END
<p>This is the first test paragraph.</p>
<ul>
```

```
  <li>This is the first list item.</li>
  <li>This is the second list item.</li>
</ul>
END

parser=Hpricot.parse(document)

(parser/:li).each do |list_item|
  puts list_item.inner_html
end
```

Save this code as hpricot_parse_by_tag.rb. You can run this code with the following command:

```
ruby hpricot_parse_by_tag.rb
```

```
This is the first list item.
This is the second list item.
```

The first line requires the hpricot library, and the next few lines use a "here document" to have the HTML stored directly in the Ruby script. The next line uses the .parse method of hpricot to parse the HTML. The line after that looks like this:

```
(parser/:li).each do |list_item|
```

The use of the divide operator (/) is convenient—it is equivalent to the .search method in this line:

```
parser.search(:li).each do |list_item|
```

Both lines search the HTML for the specified tag. Also note that the divisor—in this case, :li—can be either a string literal or a symbol. That means that the following lines are also the same as the preceding two lines:

```
(parser/'li').each do |list_item|
parser.search('li').each do |list_item|
```

There are other specifiers, as well. For example, you can use the [] operator to pull out just one element, and there are a number of other selectors—such as by the ID of the element or by class. Listing 13-2 shows both of those techniques.

Listing 13-2. *Selecting HTML Elements by ID (hpricot_ select_by_id.rb)*

```
require 'hpricot'
document= <<END
<h1 class="big_header">This is a header.</h1>
<h1 class="big_header">This is the second big header.</h1>
<p>This is the first test paragraph.</p>
<ul>
<li>This is the first list item.</li>
```

```
<li>This is the second list item.</li>
</ul>
<p id="footer_paragraph">Lorem dolor sit amet...</p>
END

parser=Hpricot.parse(document)

puts (parser/'#footer_paragraph').inner_html

(parser/'h1.big_header').each do |list_item|
  puts list_item.inner_html
end
```

Save this code as hpricot_select_by_id.rb. You can run this code with the following command:

```
ruby hpricot_select_by_id.rb
```

```
Lorem dolor sit amet...
This is a header.
This is the second big header.
```

Just like before, we use a here document to load the HTML fragment. In this case, there are two <h1> tags with the CSS class big_header and one paragraph with the id footer_paragraph, and we are going to pull out those three elements using hpricot. As before, we use the divide operator and two types of selectors. The first is the #id selector, which specifies the ID of the element we want—we just have to precede the ID we want with a hash mark (#). The second selector is the .classname selector, as in h1.big_header, which specifies that we want all h1 tags with a classname of big_header.

You can use the following Linux/OS X shell or Windows command-prompt command to install the hpricot gem:

```
gem install hpricot
```

■**Note** There are two versions of this gem: one for Windows and one for every other operating system. If you're on Windows, use the win32 distribution—otherwise use the ruby distribution.

Screen-Scraping a Catalog with hpricot

Our sample application (Listing 13-3) will use hpricot to search an ecommerce site, http://practicalrubygems.com/examplestore. It's a fictional musician's catalog full of products like guitars and saxophones. You can search and view products, but you can't actually order anything. This is somewhat similar to our job-search script in Chapter 8, but unlike that example, this script doesn't require an RSS feed. Of course, this code may break if the site changes significantly.

Listing 13-3. *Screen-Scraping an Online Catalog with hpricot (search_catalog.rb)*

```ruby
require 'uri'
require 'open-uri'
require 'hpricot'

(puts "usage: #{$0} search_term "; exit) unless ARGV.length>0

search_term = ARGV.join(' ')

url = "http://practicalrubygems.com/examplestore/search/#{URI.encode(search_term)}"

doc = Hpricot(open(url))

products=[]
doc.search("table#products").each do |item|
  (item/'tr td').each do |td|
    product=Hash.new

    (td/"a").each do |navigation|
      product[:title]= navigation.inner_html
      product[:link]=  navigation.attributes['href']
    end

    price= (td/"span.price")
    product[:price]= price.inner_html if price.any?

    products << product
  end
end

products.each do |product|
  puts "#{product[:title]}, #{product[:price]}\n#{product[:link]}\n\n"
end
```

Save this script as search_catalog.rb. You can then run it using the following command:

```
ruby search_catalog.rb example manufacturer
```

```
Example Manufacturer Ultra Acoustic Guitar, Price: $599.95
http://practicalrubygems.com/examplestore/product/Example-Manufacturer-Ultra-
Acoustic-Guitar?sku=463131

Example Manufacturer Speaker Cab, Price: $499.98
http://practicalrubygems.com/examplestore/product/Example-Manufacturer--Speaker-
Cab?sku=463131
```

Ultra Light CD player, Price: $199.98
http://practicalrubygems.com/examplestore/product/Ultra-Light-CD-player?sku=463131

Example Manufacturer Super Acoustic Guitar, Price: $399.99
http://practicalrubygems.com/examplestore/product/Example-Manufacturer-Super-
Acoustic-Guitar?sku=463131

Learning Jazz Bass Amp by Example Manufacturer, Price: $299.99
http://practicalrubygems.com/examplestore/product/Learning-Jazz-Bass-Amp-by-Example-
Manufacturer?sku=463131

As you can see, this script will print out the various the results of the search we specified
on the command line. If we wanted to, we could have exported into a CSV file or used
ActiveRecord to export it into a MySQL database. (See Chapter 5 for more detail.)

Dissecting the Example

The program in Listing 13-3 essentially works in two parts: the first loops through the various
TD elements. Note that TD is short for *table data*; each one represents a single cell of data in an
HTML table, and in this case, each TD element represents a result. For each result, we pull out
the link:

```
doc.search("/table#products").each do |item|
  (item/'td.nav_content').each do |td|
    product=Hash.new

    (td/"a").each do |navigation|
      product[:title]= navigation.inner_html
      product[:link]= navigation.attributes['href']}
    end

    price= (td/"span.price")
    product[:price]= price.inner_html if price.any?

    products << product
  end
end
```

We search for the table with the ID product, and then we look for all of the cells inside
that table. Each of those cells represents one result, and for each result we look for an <a> tag
inside it—this represents the name of the result and the URL for the full page. Finally, we grab
the price from the span with the CSS class price. We then add the data we've collected to our
array of products:

```
products.each do |product|
  puts "#{product[:title]}, #{product[:price]}\n#{product[:link]}\n\n"
end
```

Once we've looped through all of the elements, we can then loop through the stored elements and print out the results, as shown in the preceding code.

Conclusion

`hpricot` is a powerful, easy way to parse HTML, and it's fast and flexible enough to be used on projects ranging from the very small to the very large.

## CHAPTER 14

Writing HTML as Ruby with Markaby

Markaby—short for "markup as Ruby"—is a Ruby library that lets you output HTML using Ruby code. Whenever you output HTML from a Ruby application, you have a number of options, ranging from manually outputting the HTML with puts statements to using a templating system like erubis (see Chapter 9). Markaby, though, has a distinct advantage over the other options: it turns HTML tags into Ruby methods so that instead of having a mixture of HTML strings and Ruby code, you only have Ruby code. It's elegant, it's easy to read, and it gives your entire program a harmonious feel because it's all pure Ruby code.

Caution Most graphical HTML editors, such as Dreamweaver or FrontPage, can't edit Markaby files. This can be a problem if you need to work extensively with graphic designers. (On the other hand, Markaby can utilize CSS style sheets provided by graphic designers without a problem.)

How Does It Work?

You can use Markaby to produce HTML using simple, easy-to-write and easy-to-read Ruby code. Unlike eRuby—which we covered in Chapter 9—Markaby code is not mixed Ruby and HTML. It's Ruby code that produces HTML—that is, it's a series of Ruby classes and methods converted into HTML. This is very valuable for a number of reasons—for one, you don't have any long strings interspersed with short bits of Ruby code, which can be visually confusing. Instead, you simply have Ruby code—which the Ruby interpreter can verify is correct.

Note Markaby also guarantees correct HTML output, since the Ruby interpreter checks the validity of your Ruby code—if you missed a closing table tag, for example, your program wouldn't run.

Listing 14-1 displays a brief example of creating HTML with Markaby.

Listing 14-1. *Short Markaby Demo (test_markaby.rb)*

```
require 'markaby'

mab=Markaby::Builder.new
mab.html do
  head do
    title 'Test Title'
  end
  body do
    h1 'Test Header'
    p 'Lorem ipsum dolor sit amet.'
  end
end

puts mab.to_s
```

This example outputs the following HTML:

```
<html><head><meta content="text/html; charset=utf-8" http-equiv="Content-Type"/>
<title>Test Title</title></head><body><h1>Test Header</h1><p>Lorem ipsum dolor s
it amet.</p></body></html>
```

You'll note that HTML start and end tags are automatically created from the Ruby code blocks, and that the various methods called on the `Markaby::Builder` object—`html`, `head`, `body`, `h1`, and `p`—all correspond to tags in the output HTML.

You'll also note that `Markaby` automatically adds a `<meta>` tag with encoding information. `Markaby` also maintains a list of valid attributes for each tag, so you can't set inappropriate attributes for any tags—you can't have a `<P>` tag with an `HREF` attribute, for example. If you attempt to do so, `Markaby` will throw an exception.

`Markaby` helps in other ways, too—it automatically escapes data passed to the helper functions, so that you can be sure that your display output is exactly what you want. As a result, `Markaby` ensures that you output valid HTML.

For full details on the `Markaby` gem, visit this URL:

```
http://markaby.rubyforge.org/
```

You can use the following OS X/Linux shell or Windows command-prompt command to install `Markaby`:

```
gem install markaby
```

Graphical HTML Stock Charts with Markaby

The script in Listing 14-2 will demonstrate `Markaby` by drawing stock charts. We'll retrieve the stock quotes using the code from Chapter 12, and then use `Markaby` to produce an HTML graph.

You'll need YahooFinance installed; if you don't have it installed, install it via the Windows command prompt or OS X/Linux shell command gem install yahoofinance. You can find more information on YahooFinance in Chapter 12.

You'll also need a Web browser to view the resulting HTML, although if you are familiar with HTML, you can get the gist of the example without a Web browser.

Listing 14-2. *Graphical HTML Stock Chart Application (markaby_stock_charts.rb)*

```ruby
require 'markaby'
require 'yahoofinance'

(puts 'Usage: ruby stockgraph_markaby.rb ' <<
      'STOCK_SYMBOL STOCK_SYMBOL...'; exit) unless ARGV.length>0

graph=Hash.new

max=nil
min=nil

ARGV.each do |symbol|
 graph[symbol]=[]
 quotes=YahooFinance::get_HistoricalQuotes_days( symbol, 30 ) do |s|
   open_price=s.open
   date=s.date
   graph[symbol] << [date , open_price]
   max=open_price if max.nil? or (open_price > max)
   min=open_price if min.nil? or (open_price < min)
 end
end

builder=Markaby::Builder.new

builder.html do
  head do
    title "Stock Charts for #{ARGV.join(', ')}"
  end
  body do
    graph.each do |key, value|
      table :style=>"float:left; margin-right:2em;" do
        th "#{key.upcase}"
        value.each do |val|
          tr do
            td
          date, open = *val
          td "#{date} (#{open}) \t"
            td do
              div :style=>"width:  #{((open.to_f - min)/(max - min) * 100) }px;" <<
```

```
                        "background-color:black;" do
                " "
              end
            end
          end
        end
      end
    end
  end
end
```

```
puts builder.to_s
```

Save this as `markaby_stock_charts.rb`. To test our example, use the following command:

```
ruby markaby_stocks.rb msft yhoo amd > output.html
```

The arguments to the script—`msft yhoo amd`—specify the stocks we'd like to graph, and the `> output.html` portion tells the operating system to redirect the output of the script to the file `output.html`. You can open `output.html` in a Web browser; you should see a page similar to the one in Figure 14-1.

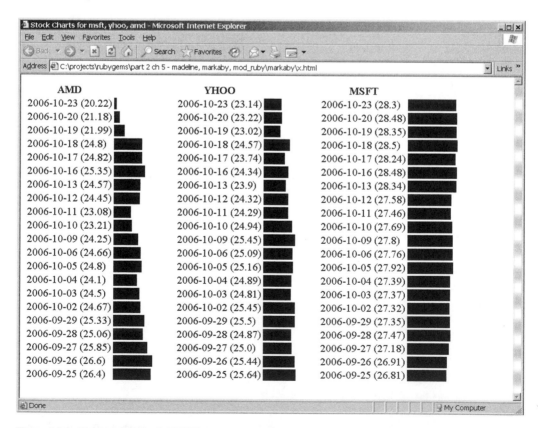

Figure 14-1. *The stock-graph HTML*

Dissecting the Example

Let's examine Listing 14-2—first we use YahooFinance to produce an array of stock values. We start the document using the .html method, as follows:

```
builder.html do
  head do
    title "Stock Charts for #{ARGV.join(', ')}"
  end
```

The head section contains a call to a title method, which produces a `<title>` tag; the text of the `<title>` tag will show up in the title bar of your Web browser. We could also put style sheet or JavaScript links there if so desired. Let's take a quick look at the body of our code:

```
body do
  graph.each do |key, value|
    table :style=>"float:left; margin-right:2em;" do
      th "#{key.upcase}"
      value.each do |val|
        tr do
          td
          date, open = *val
          td "#{date} (#{open}) \t"
          td do
            div  :style->"width:  #{((open.to_f - min)/(max - min) * 100) }px;" <<
                        " background-color:black;" do
              " "
            end
          end
        end
      end
    end
  end
end
```

The body block contains the `<body>` part of our HTML. We then loop through each of the stock symbols and create a table for it. Then we loop through each of the days we retrieved from the Yahoo! Finance service, and for each item we add a new div code element with a width based on the stock value. It's much like our Chapter 12 example, except that we use divs instead of asterisks inside of tables.

USING MARKABY IN RAILS

Markaby can also be used as a `Rails` plugin—this gives you an additional type of view to use in your projects. You can install it as follows:

```
script/plugin install http://code.whytheluckystiff.net/svn/markaby/trunk
```

Once you've installed it, you can then create `.mab` templates—they work identically to `.rhtml` templates, but they have `Markaby` code inside instead of eRuby code. You can get the full details at RedHanded, the blog of `Markaby`'s author:

```
http://redhanded.hobix.com/inspect/markabyForRails.html
```

Conclusion

As you can see, `Markaby` methods can be used to easily produce even complex HTML objects fairly easily. There are other options, of course, but `Markaby` is an elegant, easy way to encode HTML from your application.

■■■

## CHAPTER 15

Parsing CSV with fastercsv

The fastercsv gem is a fast CSV parsing library. CSV—short for comma-separated values—is an unstandardized data-exchange format. Unlike XML—which has a formal standard and programs that can check a data file for validity—CSV has a great many different forms. However, CSV is also extremely easy to output, and quite common; for example, you can easily export and import CSV from desktop applications such as Microsoft Office or OpenOffice.org. Additionally, CSV is often used for business purposes, such as transferring millions of rows of inventory data.

For example, if you wanted to sell inventory from a partner's website on your website, you might get his inventory in CSV form; that way, you'd have access to all of your partner's product descriptions, images, and so forth.

Unfortunately, despite its being very common, the many different forms in which CSV can come makes parsing it very difficult, and parsing it quickly even harder. Fortunately, fastercsv makes CSV parsing both easy and fast so you can concentrate on other aspects of your application.

How Does It Work?

fastercsv is a pure Ruby library for parsing CSV. We'll cover the details in this chapter. (Incidentally, if you'd like to parse XML, you can see how to do that in Chapter 33.)

■**Note** fastercsv isn't the only option (though it is the fastest); if you don't want to install an external gem, you can also parse CSV using Ruby's built-in CSV module—you can get the full details at http://www.ruby-doc.org/stdlib/libdoc/csv/rdoc/index.html.

The simplest scenario is when you have a string consisting of CSV, and you'd like to parse it one row at a time, as in this example:

```
require "fastercsv"
csvdata = "jones,bob,165\n"
csvdata << "smith,tim,100\n"
csvdata << "doe,john,135\n"
```

```
fastercsv.parse(csvdata) do |row|
  lastname, firstname, iq = *row
  puts "#{firstname} #{lastname} has an IQ of #{iq}"
end
```

This example uses the `parse` method of `fastercsv` to loop through each row. As you can imagine, you can also use this exact same technique on data read from a file. This example has the following result:

```
bob jones has an IQ of 165
tim smith has an IQ of 100
john doe has an IQ of 135
```

`fastercsv` can also create CSV from a Ruby array:

```
require "fastercsv"

inventory_array = [['Expensive DVD', '$39.95'],
                   ['Normal DVD', '$19.95'],
                   ['Cheap DVD', '$9.95']]

inventory_array.each do   |line|
  puts line.to_csv
end
```

This example loops through each element of our array, calls the `to_csv` method (provided by `fastercsv`) on it, and prints out the result. (We can't just call `to_csv` on the entire array because `to_csv` expects just one row at a time—if we did that, it would treat our entire array as one long row of data.) This example has the following result:

```
Expensive DVD,$39.95
Normal DVD,$19.95
Cheap DVD,$9.95
```

This CSV data could then be loaded into a CSV-compliant application, like Microsoft Access, Microsoft Excel, or OpenOffice.org. Additionally, many businesses accept CSV input for interbusiness communication—for example, if you want to upload a few hundred vehicle advertisements at once to AutoTrader.com, you can upload your data in CSV format; that will save you a significant amount of time, since otherwise you'd need to enter all of the data by hand.

■Note Unfortunately, unlike XML, CSV is not standardized. There are a great many kinds of CSV. As you can imagine, fields are separated by commas. What happens, though, when your data contains commas? Some CSV implementations surround fields with double quotes, which means you need a way to escape the double quotes when you want to store double quotes. Some people solve this by doubling up the double quotes, and others use backslashes to escape the double quote. Fortunately, fastercsv is fairly flexible, so it can handle the various situations well.

You can use the following Windows command-prompt command or Linux/OS X shell command to install fastercsv:

```
gem install fastercsv
```

Processing Census Data with fastercsv

To demonstrate fastercsv, we're going to build a short program that will download and then display census data for all of the U.S. states (Listing 15-1).

Listing 15-1. *Census Data Viewer (census_data_viewer.rb)*

```
require 'fastercsv'
require 'open-uri'

url='http://www.census.gov/popest/national/files/NST_EST2005_ALLDATA.csv'

data=open(url)

fastercsv.parse(data) do |row|
  area=row[4]
  population=row[5]
  puts "#{area} #{population}"
end
```

Save this example as census_data_viewer.rb. You can run the example using the following command:

```
ruby csv_test.rb
```

```
STNAME CENSUS2000POP
United States 281421906
Alabama 4447100
Alaska 626932
Arizona 5130632
Arkansas 2673400
California 33871648
```

```
Colorado 4301261
Connecticut 3405565
Delaware 783600
District of Columbia 572059
Florida 15982378
Georgia 8186453
Hawaii 1211537
Idaho 1293953
Illinois 12419293
Indiana 6080485
Iowa 2926324
Kansas 2688418
Kentucky 4041769
Louisiana 4468976
Maine 1274923
Maryland 5296486
Massachusetts 6349097
Michigan 9938444
Minnesota 4919479
Mississippi 2844658
Missouri 5595211
Montana 902195
Nebraska 1711263
Nevada 1998257
New Hampshire 1235786
New Jersey 8414350
New Mexico 1819046
...
```

As you can see, our script will print out the 2000 census population figures, which were automatically downloaded from the U.S. Census Bureau website. Note that the first line of our output—STNAME CENSUS200POP—is the column headers, which some CSV files include. (Note that those headers come from the input file—there's quite a few more fields available in the input file.) If you desired, you could strip these out by ignoring the first line of the file, but in this case it's a nice visual aid for the following lines of output.

Dissecting the Example

Let's take a quick look at the core of Listing 15-1:

```
fastercsv.parse(data) do |row|
  area=row[4]
  population=row[5]
  puts "#{area} #{population}"
end
```

The `.parse` method loops through each row of CSV data and grabs two different CSV cells from it. The single argument to our block is the `row` variable, which is an array containing all of the data parsed from the CSV file. In particular, we grab indexes 4 and 5 and print them out. Note that this corresponds to the fifth and sixth field, since the indexes start at zero.

The data file has a number of other fields—you can see the full details on the census data here:

```
http://www.census.gov/popest/datasets.html
```

Conclusion

CSV is far from perfect, but it's common and you'll need to deal with it often. At times you may need to deal with only a few rows of CSV, and at other times you may be working with several million rows—in either case `fastercsv` is an effective and efficient way to deal with CSV.

■ ■ ■

## CHAPTER 16

Multiple Dispatch with multi

multi adds support for multiple dispatch to Ruby. In short, *multiple dispatch* is a powerful functional programming technique that makes it possible to have some or all of the arguments to a function be used in determining which function to call.

Let's look a little deeper into multiple dispatch. Programming languages separate code into blocks—called, depending on the language, functions, methods, subroutines, and so forth. Each one of these blocks—called methods or functions in Ruby—takes one or more arguments, which communicate between the function and its caller. For example, the puts method—which prints text to the screen—takes a single argument, which specifies the text to be printed. There is only one puts function; that same function will be called no matter what arguments are specified. That's fine for the puts function—its behavior will always be the same—but what if a function's behavior varies widely based on the arguments?

Multiple dispatch essentially allows you to have multiple versions of a function that are differentiated based on the type or value of their arguments. For example, suppose you had an ecommerce site, and you had a function that calculated the tax rate of the user's order; the calculations for each state would likely be very different and unrelated to each other. You could use multiple dispatch to separate those behaviors into separate function definitions, but to the caller the function would appear harmonious and still be easy to use.

How Does It Work?

Normally, Ruby has single dispatch. This means that for each function name, you have one definition. Using multiple dispatch, on the other hand, you can have a function that is split up into multiple versions: one version that takes a string, one version that takes an integer, and one version that takes both a string and an integer.

For example, let's briefly implement a Fibonacci number finder using both single dispatch and multiple dispatch. We'll write a program to find the 17th number in the sequence. The following is a simple example with single dispatch:

```
def fib(i)
  if i==0 or i==1
    i
  else
    fib(i-1) +fib(i-2)
  end
end

print fib (16)
```

It could be more complicated, but it's not especially elegant and it only gets worse with more special cases. On the other hand, the following code uses multiple dispatch thanks to the `multi` gem:

```
require 'multi'

multi(:fib, 0) {0}
multi(:fib, 1) {1}
multi(:fib, Integer) { |i| fib(i-1)+fib(i-2)}


print fib(16)
```

As you can see, the multiple dispatch is a bit clearer; it's even more so if you have a great many special cases. It's also nice since the unrelated special cases are grouped in different functions—the edge cases can be completely separated. Of course, with a simple case like a Fibonacci sequence it's quite possible to wrap your mind around the two special cases, but in a more complex algorithm it may be more difficult.

In any case, there's an even more powerful aspect of the `multi` gem we'll discuss next: destructuring.

Destructuring means taking a complex structure and breaking it down. Many languages—Ruby included—can do some kinds of automatic destructuring for you, such as for parallel assignment or for turning an array into a list of parameters. `multi` includes support for a kind of destructuring in which the argument to the function will be partially destructured and two arguments will be passed: the element that was extracted and the remainder of the structure. This lets you parse complex data structures using a few simple functions, which are differentiated based on what part of the structure they expect next; for example, if you were parsing HTML, you might have a version of a function that expects a `<p>` tag and responds accordingly, one that expects an `<h1>` tag, and so forth. Of course, this is possible to do without `multi`; `multi` can simply make the process faster and easier.

`multi` offers two kinds of destructuring: array and string. Array destructuring takes a piece off of the front of the array and passes it to the function. This is offered by `multi`'s `amulti` library. String destructuring works by stripping off a piece of the string—delimited by a regular expression—and passing that to the function. This is offered by the `smulti` library, which is part of `multi`. A powerful benefit is that each implementation of the function can have a different regex, so the various implementations don't need to parse by one fixed delimiter. The other significant benefit is that because the string destructurer handles only one bit of the string at a time, you can pass control onto a completely different parser and then back again at will. Therefore, you can apply totally different rules easily to, say, a certain part of a string.

You can install multi using the following command:

```
gem install multi
```

Formatting SQL for Legibility Using multi

Listing 16-1 will demonstrate parsing text using multiple dispatch and string destructuring via the multi gem. Specifically, it will parse SQL and output HTML-formatted SQL—highlighting keywords, logical operators, and typenames. Since SQL queries can be very long, it can be useful to view a nicely formatted version of the query.

Note that this approach is not exhaustive—for one thing, your particular database will likely have a different set of keywords and types.

Listing 16-1. *Formatting SQL with multi (sql_hilighter.rb)*

```
require 'multi'
require 'smulti'

class SQL
  def keyword_regex
   /^(SELECT|FROM|WHERE|ORDER\s+BY|GROUP\s+BY|INSERT\s+INTO|
    UPDATE|INNER|OUTER|LEFT|RIGHT|JOIN|AS|ON|CREATE|
    TABLE|VIEW|SEQUENCE|FUNCTION|TRIGGER)$/ix
  end
  def logical_regex
    /^AND|OR|NOT$/i
  end
  def types_regex
    /^CHAR|VARCHAR|TINYTEXT|TEXT|BLOB|MEDIUMTEXT|MEDIUMBLOB|
    LONGTEXT|LONGBLOB|BLOB|INTEGER|TINYINT|SMALLINT|MEDIUMINT|
    INT|BIGINT|FLOAT|DOUBLE|DECIMAL|DATE|DATETIME|TIMESTAMP|
    TIME|ENUM|SET$/ix

  end

  LITERAL_COLOR = '#0e6e6e'
  LOGICAL_COLOR = '#8e4e2e'
  TYPE_COLOR    = '#9eaeae'

  def initialize(in_sql)
    @sql=in_sql
    @output=''
    smulti :parse, /[\s,\(\)\n]+/ do |match, remainder|
      @output << match
      parse remainder
    end
    smulti :parse, /;/ do |match, remainder|
      @output << "#{match}<br>"
      parse remainder
    end
```

```
smulti :parse, /$/ do |match, remainder|
  @output
end
smulti :parse, /[^0-9"'\s(),]+/ do
    |match,remainder|
     if keyword_regex.match(match)
      @output << "<b>#{match.upcase}</b>"
    elsif logical_regex.match(match)
      @output << "<font color=\"#{LOGICAL_COLOR}\">#{match.upcase}</font>"
    elsif types_regex.match(match)
      @output << "<font color=\"#{TYPE_COLOR}\">#{match.upcase}</font>"
    else
      @output << "<i>#{match}</i>"
    end
    parse remainder
end
smulti :parse, /["']/ do |match, remainder|
  @string_delimiter=match
  @output << "<font color=\"#{LITERAL_COLOR}\">#{match}"
  string_parse remainder
end
smulti :parse, /[0-9]/ do |match, remainder|
  @output << "<font color=\"#{LITERAL_COLOR}\">"
  number_parse "#{match}#{remainder}"
end

smulti :string_parse, /[^'"]+/ do |match, remainder|
  @output << match
  string_parse remainder
end
smulti :string_parse, /['"]/ do |match, remainder|
  if match==@string_delimiter
    @output << "#{match}</font>"
    parse remainder
  else
    @output << match
    string_parse remainder
  end
end
smulti :string_parse, /$/ do |match, remainder|
  @output
end

smulti :number_parse, /[0-9.]+/ do |match, remainder|
  @output << match
  number_parse remainder
end
```

```ruby
      smulti :number_parse, /[^0-9.]/ do |match, remainder|
        @output << "</font>"
        parse "#{match}#{remainder}"
      end
      smulti :number_parse, /$/ do |match, remainder|
        @output
      end
    end
    def highlight
      parse(@sql)
    end
  end
end

puts '<pre>'

STDIN.read.each_line  do | line |
  puts SQL.new(line).highlight
end
puts '</pre>'
```

Save this file as `sql_hilighter.rb`.

As mentioned, this program will read from the standard input and write to the standard output when the user runs it. As a result, we'll need some SQL in a text file before we can run the code from Listing 16-1, so put the following in a text file called `create_users_table.sql`:

```sql
CREATE TABLE "users" (
  "id" integer auto_increment not null,
  "total_paid" decimal(9,2),
  "customer_id" integer,
  "date" timestamp
);
```

You can then run the program as follows:

```
ruby sql_hilighter.rb < create_users_table.sql
```

```
<b>CREATE</b> <b>TABLE</b> <font color="#0e6e6e">"users"</font> (
  <font color="#0e6e6e">"id"</font> <font color="#9eaeae">INTEGER</font>
 <i>auto_increment</i> <font color="#8e4e2e">NOT</font> <i>null</i>,
  <font color="#0e6e6e">"total_paid"</font> <font color="#9eaeae">DECIMAL</font>
(<font color=#6e0e6e>9</font>,<font color="#6e0e6e">2</font>),
  <font color="#0e6e6e">"customer_id"</font> <font color="#9eaeae">INTEGER</font>,
  <font color="#0e6e6e">"date"</font> <font color="#9eaeae">TIMESTAMP</font>
);<br>
```

If you view the output in a Web browser, you'll see a multicolored output highlighting types, strings, and numbers, as in Figure 16-1.

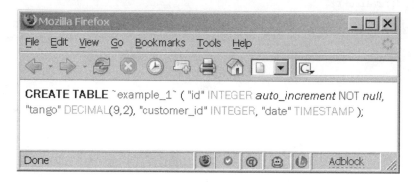

Figure 16-1. *The HTML-highlighted SQL*

Dissecting the Example

Let's examine a few lines from Listing 16-1.

```
def keyword_regex
  /^(SELECT|FROM|WHERE|ORDER\s+BY|GROUP\s+BY|INSERT\s+INTO|
  UPDATE|INNER|OUTER|LEFT|RIGHT|JOIN|AS|ON|CREATE|
  TABLE|VIEW|SEQUENCE|FUNCTION|TRIGGER)$/ix
end
def logical_regex
  /^AND|OR|NOT$/i
end
def types_regex
  /^CHAR|VARCHAR|TINYTEXT|TEXT|BLOB|MEDIUMTEXT|MEDIUMBLOB|
  LONGTEXT|LONGBLOB|BLOB|INTEGER|TINYINT|SMALLINT|MEDIUMINT|
  INT|BIGINT|FLOAT|DOUBLE|DECIMAL|DATE|DATETIME|TIMESTAMP|
  TIME|ENUM|SET$/ix

end
```

The first few methods of our class define three methods that return a regular expression describing one of three classes of words, each of which are highlighted differently: keywords, logical operators (AND, OR, and NOT), and data types. If you so desire, you can fairly easily change the distinctions made—for example, you could have highlighted all operators. Or you could have highlighted operators by class—one color for arithmetic operators, one for Boolean, and one for set operators, for example.

```
smulti :parse, /[\s,\(\)\n]+/ do |match, remainder|
  @output << match
  parse remainder
end
smulti :parse, /;/ do |match, remainder|
  @output << "#{match}<br>"
```

```
    parse remainder
end
smulti :parse, /$/ do |match, remainder|
  @output
end
smulti :parse, /[^0-9"'\s(),]+/ do
    |match,remainder|
    if keyword_regex.match(match)
      @output << "<b>#{match.upcase}</b>"
    elsif logical_regex.match(match)
      @output << "<font color=\"#{LOGICAL_COLOR}\">#{match.upcase}</font>"
    elsif types_regex.match(match)
      @output << "<font color=\"#{TYPE_COLOR}\">#{match.upcase}</font>"
    else
      @output << "<i>#{match}</i>"
    end
    parse remainder
end
```

These lines constitute the core parser of our SQL highlighter. The first definition of the parse function grabs all of the delimiters—specifically whitespace, commas, and parentheses—and simply passes them on to the output buffer. (The output buffer holds the HTML output.) The parse function is called again—passing the remainder of text back to the same parser we are currently running.

The next definition handles a semicolon—note that because we later pass control to a different parser while parsing strings, semicolons inside of a string won't cause this to trigger. When this function definition is called, it will send a line break to the output buffer—that means the next output will be displayed on a different line in our Web browser. The call to parse means that control remains with the current parser.

The next definition handles the end of the string—if we hit the end of the string in this parser, we'll just return the output buffer. Since we have no more string remaining to parse, we won't call the parse function.

Next, the definition /[^0-9"'\s(),]+/ handles almost everything else. It grabs all the characters in a row that aren't digits, string delimiters, whitespace, parentheses, or commas—this includes keywords like CREATE or INSERT as well as barewords like unquoted table names. Inside of this function it checks the match against the regular expressions we defined at the beginning of our class and highlights it appropriately. Keywords are displayed in bold, logical operators and data types are displayed in colored text, and everything else is displayed in italics. parse is then called so that the rest of the string will be processed.

```
smulti :parse, /["'  ]/ do |match, remainder|
  @string_delimiter=match
  @output << "<font color=\"#{LITERAL_COLOR}\"#{match}"
  string_parse remainder
end
smulti :parse, /[0-9]/ do |match, remainder|
  @output << "<font color=\"#{LITERAL_COLOR}\">"
  number_parse "#{match}#{remainder}"
end
```

This is the final part of our main parser—it's responsible for passing off control to our other two parsers. The first function matches a double quote or a single quote. The particular one that caused the function call is saved into the `@string_delimiter` instance variable so that the `string_parse` function can later ensure it exits only on a matching delimiter—a double-quoted string can have single quotes inside of it, for example. The next line outputs a `<font>` tag to the output buffer. The `string_parse` function is called, which passes control of the parsing to our special string parser.

Note All three delimiters are considered string delimiters by this parser, but often one or more will actually delimit identifiers, not strings—you may wish to highlight differently for identifiers, in which case you should be able to modify the highlighting function fairly easily. The exact meaning of each delimiter will depend on your database engine.

The second function matches any digit. It outputs a `<font>` tag, which will color the number in the HTML output. Next, control is passed to our `number_parse` function, which is a specialized parser that handles numbers. Note that we pass both the `match` and the `remainder` variables into the `number_parse` function—this is because the delimiter is part of the number, which we want the `number_parse` function to parse.

```
smulti :string_parse, /[^'  "]+/ do |match, remainder|
  @output << match
  string_parse remainder
end
smulti :string_parse, /['  "]/ do |match, remainder|
  if match==@string_delimiter
    @output << "#{match}</font>"
    parse remainder
  else
    @output << match
    string_parse remainder
  end
end
smulti :string_parse, /$/ do |match, remainder|
  @output
end
```

The aforementioned three function definitions define our special string parser. The first function matches anything that's definitely not a delimiter and sends it to the output buffer. The second function matches anything that might be a delimiter—it checks it against the `@string_delimiter` variable, which contains the opening delimiter for our string. If the two are different, we output the match and continue parsing. If the two are the same, then our string is over and we output the match and pass control back to our main parser. (Note that handling escaped string delimiter is left as an exercise to the reader.)

   The last function definition handles the situation of our query ending inside of a string. This isn't valid SQL, of course, but it might happen in any event, particularly if we had the job of highlighting only a SQL fragment and not an entire query. In this case, we simply return the output buffer.

```
smulti :number_parse, /[0-9.]+/ do |match, remainder|
  @output << match
  number_parse remainder
end
smulti :number_parse, /[^0-9.]/ do |match, remainder|
  @output << "</font>"
  parse "#{match}#{remainder}"
end
smulti :number_parse, /$/ do |match, remainder|
  @output
end
```

   These definitions constitute our number parser. It will accept any combination of 0 through 9 and periods, and once it reaches something that isn't a digit 0 through 9 or a period, it will return control to the main parser. Like our string parser, the last function definition handles the string ending before we exit this parser; if it does end before the parser is finished, it simply returns the output buffer.

Conclusion

You can see that the multiple-dispatch and string-deconstruction techniques that `multi` provides are powerful. Of course, neither is absolutely required—it's definitely possible to write a SQL highlighter using regular expressions alone—but they can definitely help you write code that is both powerful and simple.

CHAPTER 17

■ ■ ■

Serving Web Applications with mongrel

mongrel is an HTTP library and server for Ruby. It's very fast, since critical areas have been optimized with C code. It can be used to run `Rails`, `Camping`, or `Nitro` apps; you can also use it to create custom Web-server applications.

One of the occasional criticisms of Ruby is that it is not fast enough for heavy-duty Web applications. `mongrel` can speed up Ruby Web applications significantly; it is much more stable than using FastCGI or CGI, so your visitors can be sure that they are going to receive the Web page that they requested. Note that `mongrel` is designed specifically for hosting Ruby applications, so you can't host, say, PHP scripts with it; typically, static portions of the site—such as graphics and static HTML—will be served with a different Web server, such as Apache, since servers are faster at serving such content than `mongrel` is.

You can use `mongrel` to host any application written in any popular Ruby Web framework. For example, you could have an Apache Web server that uses several Mongrel processes to serve `Rails` or `Camping` applications. Static content would be served by Apache, and all dynamic requests to the `Rails` application would be sent to Mongrel; in that way, you can have the best of both worlds. This is a powerful setup that can scale very well, and is used by many `Ruby on Rails` deployments, including startups like The Casting Frontier (`http://castingfrontier.com/`), a digital film/television casting firm, and DormItem (`http://www.dormitem.com`), a Web 2.0 college classifieds site.

How Does It Work?

`mongrel` is designed to be simple and fast. It's designed to provide HTTP services to a Web application behind a larger Web server, such as Apache or LightTPD; it can also be used to directly provide simple Web-server needs directly during development. It works well in either usage. `mongrel` is capable of working as a stand-alone file server, but it's slower than Apache or LightTPD at serving static files, so typically a combination of both is used.

It's very fast; it's optimized by using a C extension to do the URI and HTTP parsing. However, traditional Web servers can still be faster for serving large numbers of static files, and can provide a number of other services that `mongrel` doesn't; in those cases, you can use `mongrel` between the `Rails` application and the Web server, as described under the subheading "mongrel Serving a Rails App via Apache 2.2."

You can install `mongrel` using the command `gem install mongrel`, but there's a small caveat: `mongrel` is a source gem with C components, so it comes in two flavors—`win32` and ruby. The first is for Windows environments, and the second is for other environments that have a C compiler, which include Linux and Mac OS X. When you install mongrel, it'll ask which you want. The win32 flavor comes precompiled; it doesn't need any special configuration, unlike some binary gems, so you can pick the win32 option when prompted by the installer if you are on Windows 2000 or later, and it should work seamlessly. The ruby option is for all other environments; it'll compile the C source for you, and should also work seamlessly. Here's the command again:

```
gem install mongrel
```

If you are running on Windows, and you want to run mongrel as a service, you can install service support for mongrel as follows:

```
gem install mongrel_service
```

This will give you a number of additional options to use with mongrel under Windows—you can stop and start mongrel from the Windows Services console, and so on. I'll cover the details later in this chapter in the "mongrel Running Rails as a Service on Win32" section. You won't need mongrel_service to do development with mongrel—just to have long-running background services under Win32.

Using mongrel as a Rails Development Server

One of the great aspects of Rails is that it can be used easily on a development machine; you can test Rails locally on virtually any development system. Note, though, that the default server, WEBrick, is quite slow—mongrel is faster, and the faster your development environment is, the faster you can develop. To use mongrel as a development server, you can employ the mongrel_rails helper script.

For example, using the sample Rails app we developed in Chapter 23, you can start using mongrel_rails like this:

```
# cd /path/to/example/rails/application
# mongrel_rails start
```

```
* Starting Mongrel listening at 0.0.0.0:3000
* Starting Rails with development environment ...
* Rails loaded.
* Loading any Rails specific GemPlugins
* Signals ready.  INT => stop (no restart).
* Mongrel available at 0.0.0.0:3000
* Use CTRL-C to stop.
```

At this point, you can browse to http://localhost:3000 and access the Rails application. It will work much like the default WEBrick server that ships with Rails, but it will be much quicker, and since you are likely to load and reload pages hundreds or thousands of times during a development session, that can add up to a lot of time saved.

■**Note** The server states that it is listening at 0.0.0.0:3000—the 3000 is the port, but 0.0.0.0 is not a valid IP address. It is shorthand for "listening on all adapters," however—in many environments, that means that it's listening on both `localhost` and on your network adapter. This may be undesirable; during development you might want it to listen on `localhost` only, in which case you can do `mongrel_rails start -a 127.0.0.1`, which will accept requests from your local machine only.

There are other command-line options, as well: you can use `-e` to specify the `Rails` environment, such as development or production environments. You can use `-p` to specify a port to listen to, which can be very useful during development. Additionally, `-l` can specify a log-file location. You can get a full listing of the `mongrel_rails` options by running the following command:

```
mongrel_rails start -h
```

mongrel Running Rails as a Service on Win32

If you are running mongrel on Windows, you'll probably want to install mongrel as a service. This allows you to start and stop mongrel services from the Windows Services management console—just like any other long-running Windows process.

If you haven't already installed the mongrel_service gem, do it now:

```
gem install mongrel_service
```

You can create the mongrel service as follows:

```
mongrel_rails_service install -n name_of_your_rails_application
          -r path/to/rails/application -p 3000 -e production
```

Note that the above is split onto two lines, but you'll need to type it on one line. You'll need to substitute the name of your `Rails` application and its full path for `name_of_your_rails_application` and `/path/to/rails/application`, respectively. That example starts a `Rails` server service on port 3000 and using the production environment. It doesn't start the service, though: you can use the Services applet inside of the Microsoft Management console to start it. You can also create multiple services from the same application, as in the following example:

```
mongrel_rails_service install -n app_name -r C:\rails\path -p 3000 -e production
mongrel_rails_service install -n app_name -r C:\rails\path -p 4000 -e development
```

This will start two Windows services: one on port 3000 and running in the production environment, and one on port 4000 and running in development. You could also have them run on the same port and start and stop them as needed.

mongrel Running Camping

mongrel also works well with Camping, which was introduced in Chapter 7. Camping is a Web microframework—much like Rails, but smaller and designed to make small applications easy to write. mongrel is much faster than WEBrick, so using mongrel to serve Camping applications is an easy way to get extra speed in a Camping application.

For example, if we'd like to use mongrel to serve our TrackTime example from Chapter 7, we can do so by adding the following code, called a *postamble*, to the end of the example:

```
if __FILE__ == $0
  TrackTime::Models::Base.establish_connection :adapter => 'sqlite3',
    :database => 'tracktime.db'
  TrackTime::Models::Base.logger = Logger.new('camping.log')
  TrackTime::Models::Base.threaded_connections=false
  TrackTime.create

  server = Mongrel::Camping::start("0.0.0.0",3000,"/tracktime",TrackTime)
  puts "**TrackTime is running on Mongrel - " <<
       "check it out at http://localhost:3000/tracktime"
  server.run.join
end
```

We can then run the app as follows:

```
ruby tracktime.rb
```

This will start mongrel and mount our app at /tracktime, much like the Camping server did in Chapter 7. We can then access it at http://localhost:3000/tracktime/.

This postamble uses sqlite3 to set up our database connection. Camping is generally database agnostic; the database connection is considered part of the application setup and not part of the application itself. If we prefer, we could change the establish_connection line to use MySQL or another database.

Incidentally, the first line of the postamble, if __FILE__ =$0, causes the postamble to kick in only when the script is run directly—you can still run it using the camping command.

The last line, server.run.join, runs the server and joins it to the current thread. Note that this means no code will run after this line. If you simply replace that with server.run, the mongrel thread will exit when the main thread exits, which is a problem. You could loop, waiting for the mongrel thread to exit, but since our application has no work left in any case, it is simplest to replace the current thread with the Mongrel thread.

As you can see from the mongrel::Camping::start line, mongrel has Camping support built in. However, mongrel can do more than run Web frameworks—you can use it as a Web framework directly. The example in the following section does just that.

mongrel as a Small Web Server

mongrel can act as a small Web server. While it's relatively uncommon to write your own Web server, there may be times when you wish to have a very lightweight Web server—if you have a large Ruby application running on a server, for example, you could add a mongrel Web server displaying the current application status, and it'd likely have a much smaller footprint than a larger Web server like Apache. The following is a small example that will display the current time:

```
require 'mongrel'

class TimeHandler < Mongrel::HttpHandler
  def process(request, response)
    response.start(200) do |headers, output_stream|
      headers["Content-Type"] = "text/plain"
      output_stream.write("My current time is #{Time.now}.\n")
    end
  end
end

puts "** Time server on Mongrel started!"

mongrel_server = Mongrel::HttpServer.new("0.0.0.0", "3000")
mongrel_server.register("/", TimeHandler.new)
mongrel_server.run.join
```

If you browse to http://localhost:3000/, you'll get a page showing the current time. This application is fairly simple: it creates a new class, derived from mongrel:HttpHandler, and connects it to /—the root of the Web server. You could, if you so desire, connect additional classes to other mount points underneath.

The HttpHandler class, TimeHandler, has just one custom method—process. This method takes two parameters: request and response. The first is an object describing the request, and the second is an object describing the response. The method always returns an HTTP code of 200, a content-type header of text/plain, and an output containing the current time. It ignores the path and filename of the request, so all requests return the same result—http://localhost:3000/test and http://localhost:3000/ return the same result.

This server is pretty simple, but you can extend the example to suit your needs. In fact, extending it is simple enough that mongrel can be added on to an existing application as, say, a status monitor without much effort. Because it is so trivial, Web interfaces become feasible in situations where they normally aren't, and you can use them to save significant time, effort, and money.

mongrel Serving a Rails App via Apache 2.2

mongrel is slower than a regular Web server for some tasks—serving static files, for example; Additionally, mongrel does not distinguish between different domains; Apache can serve hundreds of domains, each with different content. For both those reasons, Rails apps are often deployed with mongrel running inside of another server. An excellent way to do this is via proxying: set up a Apache 2.2 or higher server to automatically send requests to a different server—in this case, a mongrel server.

In this example, we'll use Apache to serve a `Rails` app via the proxy mechanism—we'll run five `mongrel` servers on different ports, and we'll use `mod_proxy_balancer` to balance between them.

Add the following lines to the end of your `httpd.conf` file:

```
LoadModule proxy_module modules/mod_proxy.so
LoadModule proxy_balancer_module modules/mod_proxy_balancer.so
LoadModule proxy_http_module modules/mod_proxy_http.so
```

```
<Proxy balancer://my_cluster>
    BalancerMember http://127.0.0.1:6001
    BalancerMember http://127.0.0.1:6002
    BalancerMember http://127.0.0.1:6003
    BalancerMember http://127.0.0.1:6004
    BalancerMember http://127.0.0.1:6005
</Proxy>
```

Next, comment out this line in your `railsapp/public/.htaccess` file:

```
RewriteRule ^(.*)$ dispatch.cgi [QSA,L]
```

Insert this line:

```
RewriteRule ^(.*)$ balancer://my_cluster%{REQUEST_URI} [P,QSA,L]
```

At the shell or the Windows prompt, use the following commands to start up the five `mongrel` instances we'll need:

```
cd /path/to/rails/application
mongrel_rails cluster::configure -p 6001 -N 5
mongrel_rails cluster::start
```

The preceding code is equivalent to these shell or prompt commands:

```
cd /path/to/rails/application
mongrel_rails start -d -p 6001
mongrel_rails start -d -p 6002
mongrel_rails start -d -p 6003
mongrel_rails start -d -p 6004
mongrel_rails start -d -p 6005
```

You can access the application at `http://locahost/`—the other ports are only for `mod_proxy`. The number of `mongrel` processes and the specifics can vary, of course—you may find you get the best performance with more or fewer processes.

This example works by having Apache automatically send the requests to the `mongrel` servers. When you request a dynamic page, Apache's `mod_proxy_balancer` will distribute it to one of the `mongrel` processes; if it's a static element, like an image, Apache will serve it directly.

Some people have reported problems with mod_proxy_balancer balancing unevenly; in that case, you may wish to use an external load balancer, such as nginx (http://nginx.net/). You'd still use mod_proxy, but with just a single entry pointing to the nginx server, and nginx would distribute the incoming requests to the remaining nginx processes.

Conclusion

mongrel is a powerful, easy-to-use way to host Ruby Web applications. It scales well, so whether you're catering to one user or one million users, mongrel is an excellent starting point.

■ ■ ■

## CHAPTER 18

Transferring Files Securely with net-sftp

The net-sftp gem provides an SFTP library, which lets you upload, delete, and otherwise manipulate files and directories via over the SSH File Transfer Protocol, or *SFTP*. FTP is a widely used protocol to transferring files between systems. FTP servers and clients can be found on nearly every platform. However, that FTP does not provide secure authentication— it's possible to intercept a username and password, since the username and password are sent unencrypted. The data is sent unencrypted as well, so it's conceivable for sensitive data transmitted over FTP to be intercepted by a third party. SFTP, on the other hand, is based on SSH, which provides both secure authentication and encryption for any transferred data. Additionally, SFTP works over SSH, so it doesn't use multiple ports like FTP—you only need to have the SSH port open in your firewall, and SFTP should work fine.

The net-sftp gem can be used for file transfers in a variety of situations. For example, you could use it to transfer user data uploaded to your website—image files or video files, for example. You could also use net-sftp to make a regular backup of a project you are working on—you could transfer it every night (or even every hour!) to a Web server, and since net-sftp is encrypted, you won't need to worry about sensitive data being intercepted (assuming, of course, that your Web server is reasonably secure).

How Does It Work?

The net-sftp library provides a host of functions for manipulating remote filesystems via SFTP. You can read an FAQ that provides more details on the different net-sftp operations at the following URL:

```
http://net-ssh.rubyforge.org/sftp/faq.html
```

Note Confusingly, there are two other protocols that use the name SFTP. The first is traditional FTP over SSH; it's possible to implement FTP over SSH, but it's difficult and uncommon. Simple File Transfer Protocol is another uncommon—and unsecure—file-transfer protocol. Here, however, we're discussing only the SSH File Transfer Protocol—it's the most common of the three, and the only one the net-sftp gem supports.

For example, suppose we wanted to transfer the file very_important_financial_data.xls to the remote host BigImportantCompany.com, using the username ImportantVIP and password BigSecret. We could use the following code to do so:

```
Net::SFTP.start('BigImportantCompany.com',
                :username=>'ImportantVIP',
                :password=>'BigSecret') do |sftp_connection|
  sftp_connection.put_'very_important_financial_data.xls',
   "some_secret_directory/very_important_financial_data.xls"
end
```

■**Note** You can find an additional example of the net-sftp gem in action in Chapter 21.

■**Note** You may also want to execute arbitrary commands using SSH—if so, look into the net-ssh gem, which the net-sftp gem uses. You can learn more about net-ssh in Chapter 19.

You can use the following command to install the net-sftp gem:

```
gem install net-sftp
```

Sending Files via SFTP Using net-sftp

Listing 18-1 demonstrates sending files over SFTP using the net-sftp gem. It will take a number of command-line options, such as hostname, username, password, and so forth, as well as a list of files to send.

Listing 18-1. *Sending Files via SFTP (net-sftp_upload.rb)*

```
require 'net/sftp'
require 'optparse'

options = {}
opt=OptionParser.new do |opts|
  opts.banner = "Usage: netsftpput.rb [options] hostname.com file1 file2 file3..."

  opts.on("-u", "--username USERNAME", "username") { |u|    options[:username] = u }
  opts.on("-p", "--password PASSWORD", "password") { |p|    options[:password] = p }
  opts.on("-o", "--port PORT", "port") { |p|    options[:port] = p }
  opts.on("-d", "--director DIRECTORY", "directory") { |d|
                                        options[:directory] = d }
  opts.on_tail("-h", "--help", "Show this message") { puts opts.help; exit }

end
```

```
opt.parse!

options[:hostname] = ARGV.shift
options[:username] ||= 'root'
options[:password] ||= ''
options[:port] ||= 25
options[:directory] ||= '/tmp'

Net::SFTP.start(options[:hostname],
                :port=>options[:port],
                :username=>options[:username],
                :password=>options[:password]) do |sftp_connection|
  ARGV.each do |filename|
    sftp_connection.put_file filename, "#{options[:directory]}/#{filename}"
  end
end
```

Save the code as net-sftp_upload.rb. You can run the example as follows:

```
ruby net-sftp_upload.rb yourhostname.com -u yourusername
                   -p password your_file_1.txt your_file_2.txt
```

Note that you'll need to type the above command onto just one line. Of course, change the italicized values to the appropriate values for the machine you'd like to send your files to. The files will be placed in the /tmp directory by default, which is probably not where you want them; you can override that with the -d option.

Dissecting the Example

First we use the optparse library to read our various options. You can get the details on exactly how optparse works at http://www.ruby-doc.org/stdlib/libdoc/optparse/rdoc/index.html. The script has a few defaults, which kick in only if you don't specify the options on the command line. Specifically, it will default to root as the username, a blank password, port 25, and /root as the output directory. Of course, you'll likely have a root directory set on your machine, so you'll typically have to set this option to have the command work.

The optparse library will strip all of the options from the ARGV array. This means, for example, that the -H hostname part of the command will be stripped—so will all of the other options and their arguments. All that will be left in the ARGV array are the hostname and the files to send. The shift call removes the first argument remaining in the ARGV array and places it in the options[:hostname] variable.

The following chunk of code connects to the server and actually transfers the file:

```
Net::SFTP.start(options[:hostname],
                :port=>options[:port],
                :username=>options[:username],
                :password=>options[:password]) do |sftp_connection|
  ARGV.each do |filename|
    sftp_connection.put_file filename, "#{options[:directory]}/#{filename}"
  end
end
```

The Net::SFTP.start call opens a connection to the remote server. We then loop through the ARGV array—which, at this point, contains only files—and we call put_file for each file. This will send the file to the remote server. As you can see, the put_file function is fairly straightforward—it takes two parameters, the first being the local filename and the second being the remote filename. As you can imagine, there's a corresponding get_file function that retrieves a file from the server, which might be useful depending on your exact circumstance. There is a host of other methods, too—such as rename, which renames a file on the remote machine.

Conclusion

net-sftp is a powerful way to transfer files. In many cases, SFTP can be an excellent choice for transferring files between two systems. When you have a choice, it's more secure to send files via SFTP than via traditional FTP, so net-sftp can be an excellent choice.

## CHAPTER 19

Executing Commands on Remote Servers with net-ssh

The net-ssh gem lets you connect to remote servers via the SSH protocol and then execute commands. SSH, short for Secure Shell, is a widely used protocol that lets you securely connect to remote servers and, among other features, execute commands. You can also forward arbitrary TCP ports so that you can send packets from your machine through the remote machine and onto a third machine. SSH is encrypted, so usernames and passwords are protected against eavesdropping.

Since you can execute any shell command via SSH, you can use net-ssh to perform a wide range of tasks. For example you could stop and restart a database server or Web server, or you could check the current server-CPU usage. You could also perform system-administration or security tasks, like listing the logged-in users or checking for rootkits.

How Does It Work?

net-ssh supports both of the SSH features I just mentioned—command execution and port forwarding. You can execute programs either interactively or non-interactively—that is, you can send a command and just let it run, or you can feed data to it as it runs. There are two versions of the SSH protocol available—SSH1 and SSH2. net-ssh supports SSH2, which is the newer version.

Of course, net-ssh is more useful on Unix-like operating servers such as Linux and OS X than it is on Windows machines, since you are severely constrained as to what you can do from the command line under Windows. The examples in this chapter all use Linux/OS X shell commands. (Note that the client can be running on any operating system.)

You can use the following command to install net-ssh:

```
gem install net-ssh
```

Note Ruby versions earlier than 1.8.2 don't work with the net-ssh gem—you'll need to get a patched version of OpenSSL to use net-ssh. For further details visit http://net-ssh.rubyforge.org/api/.

Here's an example of a regular SSH command:

```
ssh user@example.com ls -al
user@example.com's password: some_password
```

```
total 96356
drwxr-xr-x  23 user user    12288 Jan 24 14:32 .
drwxr-xr-x   5 root root     4096 Jan  4 18:46 ..
-rw-r--r--   1 user user      414 Mar 30  2006 .bash_profile
-rw-r--r--   1 user user     2273 Dec 18 12:15 .bashrc
drwxr-xr-x   5 user user     4096 Oct  3 10:21 .cpan
drwx------   2 user user     4096 Jan  6 11:31 .elinks
…snip…
```

That command connects via SSH; it runs the command ls -al via SSH and prints the results. (Of course, your results may vary and you'll have to substitute user@example.com for your username, followed by an at sign, followed by your hostname.)

We can do the same thing using net-ssh as follows:

```
require 'net/ssh'

Net::SSH.start('example.com', :port=>13110,
               :username=>'some_user',
               :password=>'some_password') do |ssh_connection|
  ssh_connection.open_channel do |channel|
    channel.on_data do |data|
      puts data
    end
    channel.exec "ls -al "
  end
  ssh_connection.loop
end
```

The results of running that snippet are identical to running the ssh script; however, the net-ssh snippet can be used as part of a larger Ruby program, so you can use it to automate many different tasks.

The open_channel call creates a channel—this is, an input/output channel on the remote machine. (You can have more than one channel open at once, so you could have multiple commands running at the same time.) The on_data call specifies what code should run when data is sent from the server to the client—in this case, it just uses puts to print it. Next, the ls -al command is run using the channel's exec method, and because of the on_data call, the output of the ls -al command is printed to the screen. Finally, the ssh_connection.loop line waits for the command to finish—otherwise our program might exit before the ls -al command is done executing.

Editing Remote Files with net-ssh and Vim

To demonstrate net-ssh, we'll build a script (Listing 19-1) that logs into a remote server via
SSH and then uses Vim to edit a text file. Specifically, the example opens the file and replaces
one string with a different string, and then saves the file. This could be used to change a configuration line on the server, such as a Web-server configuration or a MySQL configuration
—this is especially useful if you are managing a number of servers, since you can just run the
command once for each server.

You'll need a few things to run this example: a Linux or OS X machine with SSHD running
and Vim installed, plus some familiarity with accessing that machine via an SSH client, and
some basic familiarity with editing text files on Linux/OS X.

Listing 19-1. *Remote File Editing with net-ssh (netssh_replace.rb)*

```ruby
require 'net/ssh'
require 'optparse'

# This use of OptionParser lets the user
# specify the username, password, and port
# options on the command line.

options = {}
opt=OptionParser.new do |opts|
  opts.banner = "Usage: net_ssh_replace.rb [options] " <<
                "hostname.com file search_string replacement_string"

  opts.on("-u", "--username USERNAME", "username") { |u|   options[:username] = u }
  opts.on("-p", "--password PASSWORD", "password") { |p|   options[:password] = p }
  opts.on("-o", "--port PORT", "port") { |p|   options[:port] = p }
  opts.on_tail("-h", "--help", "Show this message") { puts opts.help; exit }

end
opt.parse!

# Exit if the user didn't specify enough
# command line arguments.

( puts opt.help; exit ) unless ARGV.length == 4

options[:hostname] = ARGV.shift
options[:filename] = ARGV.shift
options[:search_string] = ARGV.shift
options[:replacement_string] = ARGV.shift

options[:username] ||= 'root'
options[:password] ||= ''
options[:port] ||= 22
```

```
# Create a new SSH connection.

Net::SSH.start(options[:hostname],
    :port=>options[:port],
    :username=>options[:username],
    :password=>options[:password]) do |ssh_connection|
# Open a channel for I/O.

  ssh_connection.open_channel do |channel|

  # Execute our command.

  channel.exec "vim #{options[:filename]} -c '%s/#{options[:search_string]}/" <<
               "#{options[:replacement_string]}/g' -c 'wq!' "
  end

  # Wait for our command to finish.

  ssh_connection.loop
end
```

Save this example as `netssh_replace.rb`. The example itself can be run from a Linux, OS X, or Windows machine—you just need an Linux/OS X machine running SSHD to point the script toward. You'll also need to create a text file on the server with the following text in it:

```
ServerSignature On
```

This is the same line you might find in an Apache `httpd.conf` file—it's a default setting that specifies that error pages have the full version number of the server on them. That can reveal potentially damaging information to attackers, so that default setting is a bad idea from a security perspective. (Of course, you can also try this listing on a real `httpd.conf` file if you have one handy.)

You can run the example using the following Windows command prompt or Linux/OS X shell command:

```
ruby netssh_replace.rb hostname.com /complete/path/to/test/file/
    "ServerSignature On" "Server Signature Off" -u username -p password
```

Note that although this command is printed on two lines, you should type it on one line; additionally, you'll need to replace the italicized parameters with the appropriate filename, hostname, username, and password for your test machine. You can then log into your remote machine via SSH and execute the following command:

```
cat /complete/path/to/test/file/
```

```
ServerSignature Off
```

As you can see, our file had our unsecure line replaced with a more secure version. Of course, you can use this for any other text-configuration option as well. There are myriad other ways to do this, such as using Sed or manually editing the file with Vim, but net-ssh served us well in this case. It lets us access remote machines easily and execute arbitrary commands, which, as you can imagine, can be very useful for automated system administration or system-monitoring tasks.

Dissecting the Example

The first half or so of our script fills our options array with various options we'll need: the hostname of the remote server, the SSH port number, the username, and so forth. Several of these have defaults: the SSH port number, for example, is standard, but is often changed for security reasons. We use the optparse library to parse the command-line arguments—you can see another excellent example of this in Chapter 18, and you can find the optparse documentation online at the following URL:

http://www.ruby-doc.org/stdlib/libdoc/optparse/rdoc/index.html

Let's take a quick look at the core of Listing 19-1. First we create the connection to the remote server as follows:

```
Net::SSH.start(options[:hostname],
    :port=>options[:port],
    :username=>options[:username],
    :password=>options[:password]) do |ssh_connection|
```

This code snippet essentially passes our various options as named parameters to the Net::SSH.start method—it creates a new connection for us. Note that this line passes a block to this method—the block contains all of the code that manipulates this connection, and automatically closes the connection when the block is finished. In some languages, this would be implemented with start and stop methods, but the block idiom is clearer and more elegant.

Next, we use the open_channel method to open a new channel, which is an input/output connection within our SSH session. You can have multiple channels open at once—for example, you could open several tail -f commands to watch log files, and then perform some action whenever one changed. In this example, though, we are using just one channel, and we'll use it to execute only one command.

```
ssh_connection.open_channel do |channel|
channel.exec "vim #{options[:filename]} -c '%s/#{options[:search_string]}/" <<
"#{options[:replacement_string]}/g' -c 'wq!' "
end
```

Tip If you'd like more details on channels with net-ssh, or on any other part of the net-ssh gem, consult the online net-ssh documentation at http://net-ssh.rubyforge.org/.

Note that the call to `vim` has a number of arguments—first we specify the file we want to edit, which was passed from the command line. Second we use the `-c` option to execute two different ex commands: a `%s` command that will replace all instances of our search string with the replacement string, and a `wq!` command that will write the file to the disk and then quit. The ex editing engine, which comes with Vim, has a great deal of flexibility—you can get the online documentation at

`http://vimdoc.sourceforge.net/`

Finally, we need to call one more method:

```
ssh_connection.loop
```

This command waits until our single channel is finished, and then our program continues. Without this line of code, our script would exit without waiting for the channel to open and then execute the routine; the call to `.loop` ensures that our replacement code gets executed.

Conclusion

`net-ssh` is an easy-to-use gem that lets you manipulate any remote machine running SSHD. It makes virtually any kind of operation easier, from starting and stopping services to reconfiguring a server or patching an application.

■ ■ ■

## CHAPTER 20

Validating Credit Cards with creditcard

The creditcard gem lets you verify credit-card numbers; it does not run the card, but rather checks only its numerical validity. This can be useful in a variety of situations; for example, Web applications that process credit cards need to know if a credit card is valid. Of course, when your credit-card gateway is called, it will verify that the card number is correct. However, this is typically at the very end of the checkout, since you can't run the card through the gateway until the shopper has confirmed that he wishes to purchase the item. The creditcard gem can be used at any stage of the process, such as on the Payment Details page to catch typing mistakes—in fact, it can be used even without an Internet connection, which could be useful in bulk card-processing applications. The creditcard gem can give instant feedback on the validity of a card—it could even autoselect the appropriate type of card for the user based on the card number.

How Does It Work?

The creditcard gem lets you validate credit cards in a Ruby script, such as in a Rails or Camping Web application. (See Chapters 7 and 23 for more details on Rails and Camping, respectively.) The creditcard gem doesn't actually check that a given card is valid and has credit available—it simply checks if the card is self-consistent according to the formula for each credit-card company.

However, if you use the creditcard gem to verify credit cards on your site, you'll have to be very careful about storing the information properly—after all, your server logs may contain credit-card information, which could be a significant problem. It unsafe and likely illegal in some areas to store unencrypted credit cards; in addition, your merchant account provider or credit-card processor likely places additional restrictions on the storage and security of credit cards, and your local government may have additional restraints as well. You should check with a lawyer for applicable laws and regulations regarding an ecommerce application that handles credit-card data.

Essentially, the creditcard gem adds two valuable functions to the String class: creditcard? and .creditcard_type. The creditcard? function returns true if the credit card is valid, and false otherwise—the .creditcard_type function returns the card type (Visa, MasterCard, or another card type).

You can use the following Linux/OS X shell or Windows command-prompt command to install the creditcard gem:

```
gem install creditcard
```

Verifying Credit-Card Numbers in Batch with creditcard

The example script in Listing 20-1 uses the creditcard gem to read a CSV file, verify every credit card in the file, and then print a new CSV file with a field that indicates whether the card is valid. Essentially, the script will act as a filter, taking in data from a file, processing data, and outputting the new data.

Specifically, the script will be passed a few arguments—first the name of a CSV file, and then a field number that specifies which field has the credit-card number in it. It will then print a new CSV file, but with an extra field—containing either valid or invalid depending on the card's validity. The extra field will be immediately after the credit-card field, and the remainder of the fields will be left as is.

■**Note** We also use the creditcard gem as an example in Chapter 3; you can see more code using the creditcard gem there.

Listing 20-1. *Verifying Credit-Card Numbers from CSV (creditcard_csv_filter.rb)*

```
require 'creditcard'
require 'fastercsv'

# Exit if the user didn't pass at least one argument.

(puts "#{$0} - a batch creditcard validator\n" <<
     "usage: #{$0} csv_file record_number"; exit) unless ARGV.length>0

filename      = ARGV[0]
option_number = ARGV[1].to_i - 1

# Use FasterCSV to read the CSV from the file.
# Chapter 15 covers FasterCSV in detail.

lines=FasterCSV.read(filename)

# At times, CSV files may have blank lines -
# particularly if they are generated by hand.
# The following call deletes all of the blank lines.

lines.delete_if do |line|
    line == []
end
```

```
lines.each do |line|
  # Here we insert a new field at user-specified location -
  # it indicates whether the card is valid or not.
  line.insert(option_number+1, (line[option_number].creditcard? ?
            'valid' : 'invalid'))
end

# Finally, we write out the completed CSV file to the screen.

lines.each do |line|
  puts line.to_csv
end
```

Save this script as `creditcard_csv_filter.rb`. We'll need to create a test CSV file, so save the following text as `test.csv`:

```
Test Name,Test Address,Testville,TX,4111-1111-1111-1111,$399.00,Test Order
Test Name,Test Address,Testville,TX,not-a-number,$99.00,Test Order
Test Name,Test Address,Testville,TX,5431-1111-1111-1111,$35.35,Test Order
Test Name,Test Address,Testville,TX,5001-1000-1000-0000,$29.00,Test Order
Test Name,Test Address,Testville,TX,341-1111-1111-1111,$19.99,Test Order
Test Name,Test Address,Testville,TX,6011-6011-6011-6611,$9.35,Test Order
```

We can then run a test using the following Linux/OS X shell or Windows command-prompt command:

```
ruby creditcard_csv_filter.rb test.csv 5
```

```
Test Name,Test Address,Testville,TX,4111-1111-1111-1111,valid,$399.00,Test Order

Test Name,Test Address,Testville,TX,not-a-number,invalid,$99.00,Test Order
Test Name,Test Address,Testville,TX,5431-1111-1111-1111,valid,$35.35,Test Order
Test Name,Test Address,Testville,TX,5001-1000-1000-0000,invalid,$29.00,Test Order
Test Name,Test Address,Testville,TX,341-1111-1111-1111,valid,$19.99,Test Order
Test Name,Test Address,Testville,TX,6011-6011-6011-6611,valid,$9.35,Test Order
```

As you can see, this script will print out a new version of the CSV file with one new field—the validity field. If we wanted to, we could have exported the data into a CSV file with a different format, or used `ActiveRecord` to export it into a MySQL database. (See Chapter 5 for more detail.)

Dissecting the Example

First the program reads the CSV file into the lines array. After that, the program essentially works in three parts: the first loop deletes all of the empty lines. The second loops through all of the lines and adds a new field for each line—the `valid`/`invalid` field. The last part prints each line.

```
lines.delete_if do |line|
    line == []
end

lines.each do |line|
  line.insert(option_number+1, (line[option_number].creditcard? ?
    'valid' : 'invalid'))
end

lines.each do |line|
  puts line.to_csv
end
```

The call to `delete_if` deletes all of the elements for which the block evaluates to true–in other words, all elements that are equal to [ ], or all elements that are an empty array.

The first loop through the lines array uses the `insert` method of the array to add a new element at `option_number+1`— right after our credit-card field. The value we insert into the array is based on a call to the `.creditcard?` function—this function returns true if it is a valid card, and false otherwise. We use the ? (ternary) operator to make this value `valid` if the function returns `true` and `invalid` otherwise.

Conclusion

The `creditcard` gem verifies credit cards easily and efficiently, and it is an easy way to check cards for validity before they are processed. If your application calls for checking credit cards, the `creditcard` gem is an excellent choice.

■■■

## CHAPTER 21

Writing PDFs with pdf-writer

pdf-writer is a Ruby library for producing PDF files. PDF (Portable Document Format) documents are ubiquitous and flexible. Typically, they are read-only and have the advantage of appearing exactly the same on the screen as they do when they are printing; other document formats designed for the screen, such as HTML, often appear vastly different in print. Often businesses use PDFs for certain type of presentations, such as proposals or press releases. By using the pdf-writer library, you can programmatically create PDFs in Ruby.

How Does It Work?

pdf-writer creates PDF documents. Specifically, it provides you with a set of methods to draw text, places images, and so forth, as well as a method to save the resulting document as a PDF file. pdf-writer is written in pure Ruby, so there are no external dependencies. (In Chapter 6 we used the external programs html2ps and ghostscript to produce a PDF—that method also works, but it requires external programs. pdf-writer will work on any Ruby environment.)

One of the great benefits of PDF documents is that they are highly portable—they will look very similar whether viewed on a Mac, or a PC, or whether printed onto paper. Additionally, PDF documents are compact—they can contain multiple pages, hyperlinks, and other features and still be saved and emailed easily. This is different from HTML pages, which typically involve multiple files and are awkward for the average computer user to redistribute.

The pdf-writer library provides us with an entire library of methods for displaying text, images, tables, and graphs in PDF documents. Listing 21-1 will provide a more detailed example, but let's first consider a simple demonstration:

```ruby
require 'pdf/writer'

pdf_document = PDF::Writer.new

pdf_document.select_font "Times-Roman"
pdf_document.text "Hello world!"
pdf_document.save_as "out.pdf"
```

This example simply creates a new PDF::Writer object, prints out the string Hello world! in Times-Roman font, and finally, writes the PDF to the file out.pdf. As you can see, it's reasonably straightforward to create PDF documents using pdf-writer. Note that Times-Roman is one of the 14 standard fonts available to any PDF reader. You can find the complete list of fonts—and the other details on pdf-writer—from the online documentation:

http://ruby-pdf.rubyforge.org/pdf-writer/

You can use the following command to install pdf-writer:

```
gem install pdf-writer
```

Creating Reports with pdf-writer and Net/SFTP

Often, programming involves creating reports. Reports can take many forms, but frequently you'll find that PDFs are a very convenient output format; PDFs can be easily displayed, printed, or emailed to coworkers, and that makes them an excellent choice for report formatting.

Of course, the source of data for such reports varies widely; one common source is files. Files can be anything from proposals to sales data to invoices; often you'll find that you need statistics on files, such as a list of files in a directory or a comprehensive list of how much space is being used by which files. The example in Listing 21-1 will do just that; it will demonstrate using pdf-writer by creating a PDF with a report of files and their disk usage in remote directories on a remote server. You can also specify multiple directories.

You'll need the Net/SFTP gem installed; if you don't have it installed, you can install it via the Windows command prompt or OS X/Linux shell command gem install net-sftp. You can find out more information on net-sftp in Chapter 18.

Additionally, you'll need access to a remote Linux or OS X machine with sshd installed to run this example. The example itself, though, can be run from a Linux, OS X, or Windows machine—you just need an equipped Linux/OS X machine to point the script at.

■**Note** You'll also need a PDF viewer, such as Adobe Acrobat Reader (http://www.adobe.com/products/ acrobat/readstep2.html) or Ghostscript Ghostview (http://www.cs.wisc.edu/~ghost/), to see the output.

Listing 21-1. *Writing File Reports to a PDF File (sftp_2_pdf.rb)*

```ruby
require 'pdf/writer'
require 'net/sftp'
require 'optparse'

options = {}
opt=OptionParser.new do |opts|
  opts.banner = "Usage: #{$0} [options] hostname.com " <<
                "directory1 directory 2 directory3..."

  opts.on("-u", "--username USERNAME", "username") { |u|   options[:username] = u }
  opts.on("-p", "--password PASSWORD", "password") { |p|   options[:password] = p }
  opts.on("-o", "--port PORT", "port") { |p|   options[:port] = p }
  opts.on("-O", "--order FIELDNAME", "fieldname") { |f|
                                          options[:sortcolumn] = f }
```

```ruby
    opts.on("-s", "--sort ASC_OR_DESC", "sort") { |s|    options[:sortorder] = s }
    opts.on_tail("-h", "--help", "Show this message") { puts opts.help; exit }

end
opt.parse!

options[:hostname] = ARGV.shift
options[:directories] = ARGV
options[:username] ||= 'root'
options[:password] ||= ''
options[:sortcolumn] ||= 'filename'
options[:port] ||= 25

pdf_document = PDF::Writer.new

# Connect to the server specified on the command line.

Net::SFTP.start(options[:hostname],
    :port=>options[:port],
    :username=>options[:username],
    :password=>options[:password]) do |sftp_connection|

  options[:directories].each do |directory|
    pdf_document.select_font "Times-Roman"
    pdf_document.text "Directory #{directory} on " <<
                      "host #{options[:hostname]}", :font_size->32
    directory = sftp_connection.opendir(directory)
    files = sftp_connection.readdir(directory)

    # Build the table of data from the remote directory.

    table_data = []
    files.each do |file|
      table_data << {"filename"=>file.filename,
                     "size"=> file.attributes.size,
                     "mtime"=> file.attributes.mtime
                    } unless file.filename =~ /^\.+$/
    end

    # Sort the data according to the options
    # specified on the command line.

    table_data.sort! do   |row1, row2|
      if options[:sortorder] == 'ASC'
        row1[options[:sortcolumn]] <=> row2[options[:sortcolumn]]
```

```
      else
        row2[options[:sortcolumn]] <=> row1[options[:sortcolumn]]
      end
    end

    # Format all of the dates.

    table_data.collect do |row|
      row["mtime"] = Time.at(row["mtime"]).strftime('%m/%d/%y')
    end

    pdf_document.move_pointer 20


    # Create the table.

    require 'PDF/SimpleTable'

    table= PDF::SimpleTable.new
    table.shade_color = Color::RGB::Grey90
    table.position = :left
    table.orientation = 30
    table.data = table_data
    table.column_order = ["filename", "size", "mtime"]
    table.render_on pdf_document

    pdf_document.move_pointer 50

  end
end

pdf_document.save_as "out.pdf"
```

Save this as sftp_2_pdf.rb. To test the example, you can use the following Windows command prompt or Mac OS X/Linux shell command:

```
ruby sftp_2_pdf.rb yourhost.com /var/log -u username -p password
```

The argument to the script—*yourhost.com*—specifies the host name you'd like to connect to, and the /var/log argument specifies the path. You'll also need to put your username and password in place of *username* and *password*, respectively. Figure 21-1 shows the resulting PDF document.

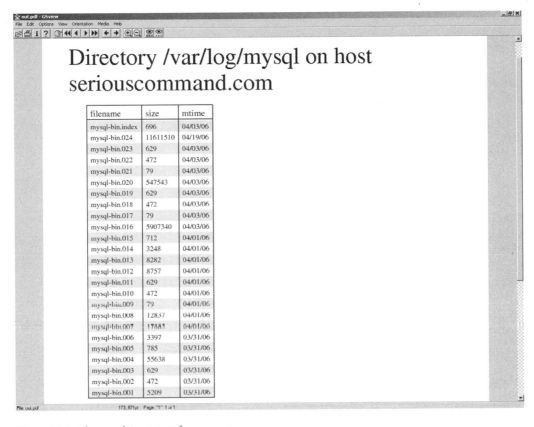

Figure 21-1. *The resulting PDF document*

Dissecting the Example

Let's examine Listing 21-1. First we use optparse to parse the command-line arguments—you can see another excellent example of this in Chapter 18, and you can find the optparse documentation online at the following URL:

```
http://www.ruby-doc.org/stdlib/libdoc/optparse/rdoc/index.html
```

Next we create a new PDF::Writer object, as follows:

```
pdf_document = PDF::Writer.new
```

We'll use this object to create our PDF file. We'll then loop through each directory specified on the command line, and print a header for each of them; the following code does just that:

```
pdf_document.select_font "Times-Roman"
pdf_document.text "Directory #{directory} on " <<
                "host #{options[:hostname]}", :font_size=>32
```

The call to select_font specifies which font we'll use, and the call to the text method actually prints the text. The text method has a number of optional parameters—you can see the full documentation at http://ruby-pdf.rubyforge.org/pdf-writer/.

Next we create an array containing the data for the files—it will contain filenames, file sizes, and file timestamps. It will also be sorted and the timestamp column will be formatted properly. The code which does that is as follows:

```
directory = sftp_connection.opendir(directory)
files = sftp_connection.readdir(directory)

table_data = []
files.each do |file|
  table_data << {"filename"=>file.filename,
                 "size"=> file.attributes.size,
                 "mtime"=> file.attributes.mtime
                 } unless file.filename =~ /^\.+$/
end
table_data.sort! do  |row1, row2|
  if options[:sortorder] == 'ASC'
    row1[options[:sortcolumn]] <=> row2[options[:sortcolumn]]
  else
    row2[options[:sortcolumn]] <=> row1[options[:sortcolumn]]
  end
end

table_data.collect do |row|
  row["mtime"] = Time.at(row["mtime"]).strftime('%m/%d/%y')
end
```

As you can see, the first block of code populates the table_data array with the data retrieved from the net-sftp connection. The second block sorts by the column and order specified by the command line. (Ascending order, specified by ASC, means that the values ascend—earlier dates followed by later dates, A followed by Z, and so forth.)

Next, we draw a table with all of this data—the filenames, sizes, and timestamps. Let's take a look at that code:

```
pdf_document.move_pointer 20

require 'PDF/SimpleTable'

table= PDF::SimpleTable.new
table.shade_color = Color::RGB::Grey90
table.position = :left
table.orientation = 30
table.data = table_data
table.column_order = ["filename", "size", "mtime"]
table.render_on pdf_document

pdf_document.move_pointer 50
```

The first and last lines call the move_pointer method, which increments the pointer that specifies the current vertical location on the page—in other words, it creates some blank space for us. The units of distance are in points, and a point is 1/72 of an inch, so the first blank space will be 20/72 of an inch. Note that you can use scaling options to redefine how big a point is; also note that since it's a physical measurement, and not a measurement in pixels, it may appear differently on different screen sizes, zoom levels, and so forth.

Next we create a PDF::SimpleTable object. We set the shade_color to Color::RGB::Grey90—this is a gray color roughly equal to #E6E6E6 in hex notation. This color will be used to shade every other row to make the rows easy to distinguish from each other.

The next step is to set the position to :left, and the orientation equal to 30—the position value sets the origin of the orientation value, meaning that the table will be drawn 30 points away from the left margin of the page. If position had been set to :right, then the table would be drawn 30 points from the right of the page.

We then set the data property to the table_data variable—that's the data we carefully retrieved, sorted, and formatted earlier. We set the column_order variable to set the order of the columns we want to display. Finally, we use the render_on method to actually place the table in our PDF.

There's just one step left:

```
pdf_document.save_as "out.pdf"
```

This simple call writes our completed PDF document to the file out.pdf.

Conclusion

The pdf-writer gem is a powerful way to write PDFs using pure Ruby code. In some cases the pdf-writer code can be complex, but the flexiblity and power it affords to create portable, printable documents is quite useful.

CHAPTER 22

■ ■ ■

Handling Recurring Events with runt

The runt gem is a library for creating temporal expressions—expressions that describe date recurrence. For example, you can create a temporal expression that represents the first Monday of each month, or one that represents every 28th day; you could also, for instance, create a temporal expression that represents the first day of a particular accounting period—like a quarter year. You can use runt in a variety of ways; for example, you could use it if you had to run a special report every Monday, or you could run a backup script every other day.

How Does It Work?

With runt, you can create regular expressions that represent recurring events—even fairly complex ones. You could create a schedule with an event that repeats every ten days, except for weekends or holidays. You could also create an event that repeats once a month on the third Monday or the last Thursday of the month. runt can handle these kinds of events and then match them against a range of dates—it can retrieve all of the first Thursdays in every month in a given year, for example.

Once you've created an expression, you can do a few things with it. First, you can test a date against it—basically, "Is this date one of these?" The following code creates an expression for "Every last Thursday " and checks if 5/28/2020 is within that timeframe:

```
require 'runt'
include Runt

date_expression = DIMonth.new(Last, Thursday)

puts "It's a last Thursday." if date_expression.include?(Date.new(2020,5,28))
```

The result of running the code is as follows:

```
It's a last Thursday.
```

The class DIMonth performs the bulk of the work here—the constants Last and Thursday and defined by runt, and the DIMonth.new call returns a date expression matching every last Thursday. After that, the .include? call checks if the specified date, 5/28/2020, is the last Thursday of the month, and if so, prints out a brief message.

You can check time, as well—you could, for example, have part of your website that is
available only from 8AM–10AM on the last Thursday of the month. The following code creates a
date expression for the time 8 AM–10 AM on the last Thursday, and checks a few times against it:

```
require 'runt'
include Runt

date_expression = DIMonth.new(Last, Thursday) & REDay.new(8,0,10,0)

puts '7am on 5/28/2020 Included!' if date_expression.include?(
                                        DateTime.new(2020,5,28,7,0))
puts '8am on 5/28/2020 Included!' if date_expression.include?(
                                        DateTime.new(2020,5,28,7,0))
```

Running this code produces the following results:

```
8am on 5/28/2020 Included!
```

The call to REDay.new produces a date regular expression matching any time from 8AM
to 10PM; the & operator is used to combine it with the results of the DIMonth.new call, which
matches the last Thursday of each month, and as a result of the & operator combining the two
expressions, we get a combined temporal expression that matches any time variable from 8AM
to 10PM on the last Thursday of each month. In other words, we can compare this date regular
expression with a DateTime object and find out whether the DateTime object falls within 8 AM to
10 PM on the last Thursday of the month.

You can also apply a time expression to a range of dates and find all of the dates that lie
within that range—we'll use this in Listing 22-1. Here's a brief example that lists all of the last
Thursdays in 2020:

```
require 'runt'
include Runt

date_expression = DIMonth.new(Last, Thursday)

date_expression.dates( DateRange.new(PDate.day(2020,1,1),
                PDate.day(2020,12,31)) ).each do |date|
  puts date.strftime('%m-%d-%Y')
end
```

Running this example produces the following result:

```
01-30-2020
02-27-2020
03-26-2020
04-30-2020
05-28-2020
06-25-2020
```

```
07-30-2020
08-27-2020
09-24-2020
10-29-2020
11-26-2020
12-31-2020
```

The call to `.dates` takes two dates—in this case, the first and the last day of 2020—and returns an array of dates that match that criteria. The `PDate` class used to create those two arguments is much like the `Date` class that is built into Ruby, but allows you to specify precision; in this case, we used the `.day` method, which specifies that our dates are accurate only to the day—they have no hour, minute, or second component.

You can find the full details on `runt` at the `runt` homepage:

```
http://runt.rubyforge.org/
```

You can use the following Linux/OS X shell or Windows command-prompt command to install the `runt` gem:

```
gem install runt
```

Planning User-Group Meetings with runt

Our sample script (Listing 22-1) will use the `runt` gem to generate a schedule for a theoretical Ruby user group. It will take options like `3rd Monday 2026`, which will generate a schedule for all of the third Mondays in every month of 2026.

You'll also need the `linguistics` gem to use this example; we'll use it to generate ordinals and pluralize day names. You can install it via the following command:

```
gem install linguistics
```

■**Note** The linguistics gem isn't discussed specifically in this book—it's a very short gem, with just a few self-explanatory methods—but you can find out more about it at its homepage:

```
http://www.deveiate.org/code/Linguistics/
```

Listing 22-1. *Group Meeting Planner with runt (group_planner.rb)*

```
require 'runt'
include Runt

require 'linguistics'
Linguistics::use( :en )

require 'date'
```

```
(puts "#{$0} - plans monthly gatherings\nusage: #{$0} day_number day_name year\n";
       exit ) if ARGV.length != 3

day_number= ARGV.shift.dup.gsub(/(st|nd|rd|th)$/,'').to_i

day_names= Date::DAYNAMES.collect { |day| day.downcase }
day_name_argument = ARGV.shift.dup
day_name_value= day_names.index(day_name_argument.downcase)

year = ARGV.shift.dup.to_i

header= "All of the #{day_number.en.ordinal} " <<
        "#{day_name_argument.en.plural} of #{year}"

puts header
puts "=" * (header.length)

date_expression = DIMonth.new(day_number, day_name_value)

date_expression.dates( DateRange.new(PDate.day(year,1,1),
                       PDate.day(year,12,31)) ).each do |date|
    puts date.strftime('%m-%d-%y')
end
```

Save this script as group_planner.rb. You can test it using the following command:

```
ruby group_planner.rb 3rd Monday 2026
```

```
All of the 3rd Mondays of 2026
==============================
01-19-2026
02-16-2026
03-16-2026
04-20-2026
05-18-2026
06-15-2026
07-20-2026
08-17-2026
09-21-2026
10-19-2026
11-16-2026
12-21-2026
```

As you can see, the script printed out a list of every third Monday in 2026, and we could pass it any arrangement we wanted—every second Thursday, every third Wednesday, and so forth.

Dissecting the Example

Let's take a look at a few important lines from Listing 22-1:

```
day_number= ARGV.shift.dup.gsub(/(st|nd|rd|th)$/,'').to_i

daynames= Date::DAYNAMES.collect { |day| day.downcase }
day_name_argument = ARGV.shift.dup
day_name_value= daynames.index(day_name_argument.downcase)

year = ARGV.shift.dup.to_i
```

This code pulls various arguments from the command line. `ARGV.shift.dup` pulls one argument off of the command-line options. We use this to grab our three options—day number, day name, and year. Specifically, the call to `.shift` pulls the element off, and then the call `.dup` duplicates the object for us. (This is useful because strings from the `ARGV` array are frozen—that is, they can't be modified, but a duplicate of them can be modified since it does not copy the "frozen or not frozen" setting.)

We then process each argument—for the day number, we strip off any trailing ordinal elements. This means that 3rd becomes 3, 4th becomes 4, and so on. (However, this is optional; you can also pass in a literal 3 instead of 3rd.)

For the day name, we first use `.collect` on the `Date::DAYNAMES` array to create a copy of the array, which is all lowercase. We can then use the `.index` function—which returns the index number of a value in an array—to find the appropriate index for the day name we've been passed. (Note that this would be simpler if there were a case-insensitive version of the `.index` function. We could use a `.each` block, but the `.collect` method is a bit simpler.)

Next, the following chunk of code prints a header for our output—it uses the `linguistics` gem to make the label look nicer:

```
header= "All of the #{day_number.en.ordinal} " <<
        "{day_name_argument.en.plural} of #{year}"

puts header
puts "=" * (header.length)
```

The first line uses the `.en.ordinal` method to insert the ordinal—it transforms 1 into 1st, for example, and 2 into 2nd; the `.en` part specifies the language as English, since other languages follow other ordinalization rules. The second call uses the `.en.plural` method to create the plural of our day name. (Of course, in this particular case, we could have simply tacked an s onto the end, since all of the English day names end in -day, but it is a nice demonstration of what you can do with the `linguistics` gem.)

The last two lines print the header line and then a line of equals signs the same length as the header line.

Finally, the last chunk of code uses the `DIMonth` class to match our chosen day for each month. Note that the class name `DIMonth` stands for *Day In Month*—`DIWeek`, likewise, is a runt class name meaning *Day In Week*.

```
date_expression = DIMonth.new(day_number, day_name_value)

date_expression.dates( DateRange.new(PDate.day(year,1,1),
```

```
                        PDate.day(year,12,31)) ).each do |date|
      puts date.strftime('%m-%d-%Y')
end
```

The first line here creates a date expression using `DIMonth.new`. `DIMonth.new` takes a day number and a weekday number—that is, `DIMonth.new(1, 1)` means the first Monday, `DIMonth.new(2, 3)` means the second Wednesday, and so forth.

Next we call the `.dates` method on the date expression. We pass it a newly created `DateRange` object, which specifies a range between the 1st of January and the 31st of December. (A `PDate` object is much like a regular `Date` object, except that `PDate` can have precision, from as short a time as a millisecond to as long as a year.)

The `.dates` method returns an array of dates that match our date expression, so we use `.each` to iterate through each one, and then we print it out using `puts`.

Executing Commands on a Recurring Schedule

Suppose you needed to perform a backup on the first Monday of every month. The script in Listing 22-2 will let you do just that, as well as run any arbitrary command on a similar schedule.

■Note Both Windows Task Scheduler and cron—the automatic schedulers for Windows and OS X/Linux, respectively—have fairly similar facilities to `runt`'s, and it may be easier in some cases to use them instead. Of course, `runt`'s recurring-event facilities are available to you for any purpose, not just for running commands. Note that cron can schedule events on a weekly basis—every Monday, for example—but not every *first* Monday, so this particular script may be useful in adding that capability to Linux machines. (Of course, `runt` can be used inside of a larger application, unlike Windows Task Scheduler, so in general it's also useful under Windows.)

Listing 22-2. *Running Commands on a Recurring Schedule with runt (run_on.rb)*

```
require 'runt'
include Runt

(puts "#{$0} - runs commands on the indicated Nth weekday of the month\n" <<
    "usage: #{$0} day_number day_name command\n";
    exit ) if ARGV.length <= 3

day_number= ARGV.shift.dup.gsub(/(st|nd|rd|th)$/,'').to_i

daynames= Date::DAYNAMES.collect { |day| day.downcase }

day_name_argument = ARGV.shift.dup
day_name_value= daynames.index(day_name_argument.downcase)
```

```
date_expression = DIMonth.new(day_number, day_name_value)

if(date_expression.include?(Date.today))
  puts `#{ARGV.join(' ')}`
end
```

Save this script as run_on.rb. You can execute it as follows:

```
ruby run_on.rb 1st Monday echo 'Time to do a backup!'
```

```
Time to do a backup!
```

Of course, your result will vary depending on the day—if it's not the first Monday of the month, the script will print nothing. The echo 'Time to do a backup!' command could be replaced with an actual backup command instead of a reminder, and you'd still need a way to get this command to run recurrently; you could create a crontab entry, for example. You can get more information on crontab here:

```
http://www.adminschoice.com/docs/crontab.htm
```

Dissecting the Example

The first portion of the script in the Listing 22-2 is the same as Listing 22-1, so you can see the dissection of Listing 22-1 for details on how to construct the date expression. Here we'll look at the last three lines of Listing 22-2:

```
if(date_expression.include?(Date.today))
  puts `#{ARGV.join(' ')}`
end
```

The .include? method returns true if the date expression includes the specified date—in this case, it's checking whether the date expression specified on the command line matches the current date. If it does, then backticks are used to run the command specified on the command line, and puts is used to print the output to the screen.

Conclusion

Managing complex recurring dates can be very complicated, but runt lets you use familiar idioms to simply manage even very complex date expressions; as a result, runt is an excellent choice for any Ruby project that involves recurring dates.

## CHAPTER 23

Building Websites with Rails

Rails—often called Ruby on Rails—is a very popular Ruby Web framework. Web frameworks make writing Web applications easier. Ruby on Rails is a particularly popular Web framework. It won a Jolt "Web Development Tools" product excellence award in 2006, and quite a few tech start-ups have been created with a business plan centered on Ruby on Rails.

Ruby on Rails offers quite a few advantages to a Web developer. It uses ActiveRecord for data access, which is a very popular ORM (object-relational mapping) library, and ActiveRecord can make relational database development much easier. (You can find out more about ActiveRecord in Chapter 5.) Rails has numerous other features, including a powerful templating system, a wide variety of plugins, automated testing and deployment, and more.

Ruby on Rails is a great choice for Web applications of almost any variety. For example, you could use Rails to develop an ecommerce site—CDBaby.com sells CDs, and the site runs Rails. You could also use Ruby on Rails to digitize your office's paper trail, like CastingFrontier.com does for actors, or you could use it to develop virtually any other Web application you might need to develop.

How Does It Work?

Because Rails uses ActiveRecord as its data source, it's able to use a number of different database backends, such as MySQL and PostgreSQL.

Ruby on Rails is an MVC framework. MVC stands for Model View Controller, which are the three parts of the framework. The first, the model, represents the database structure and data, as well as associated logic—validation and so forth. The view represents the actual presentation of the data—how it appears on the Web browser. Finally, the controller represents the actual business logic—it controls what can be done where, and how the view and the model are used. This is very beneficial for development speed and maintainability; it means that each component needs to worry about only a designated area so that, say, the presentation can be changed without worrying about changing the backend logic. This can make development much faster and easier, and is one of the great benefits of Rails in particular and MVC frameworks in general. You can learn more about MVC frameworks at the following URL:

http://en.wikipedia.org/wiki/Model-view-controller

Ruby on Rails is arguably more than just a Web framework—it's a phenomenon. A remarkable number of technology start-ups are switching to Ruby on Rails or are starting with Ruby on Rails software as a cornerstone of their business plan.

Ruby on Rails is also remarkable because of the wide availability of plugins for it—they are available for a great many purposes, ranging from automatically resizing image uploads to entire user-authentication systems. A Rails plugin differs from a regular gem in that it's intended to run only inside a Rails application, and so it's installed into a particular Ruby on Rails application and not into your system as a whole. (Confusingly enough, many general-purpose Rails plugins are also available as gems, giving you a choice of how to install and use the plugin.)

For example, we'll use the AjaxScaffold plugin in Listing 23-1 to create a database interface. There are tons of other plugins, many of which can make complex tasks simple. Of course, you can use Ruby gems in your Rails applications as well. You can find the official list of plugins at the following URL:

```
http://wiki.rubyonrails.org/rails/pages/Plugins
```

You can get links to Ruby on Rails sites, mailing lists, wikis, and tutorials on the Ruby on Rails homepage:

```
http://api.rubyonrails.org/
```

You can use the following command to install Rails:

```
gem install rails
```

A Simple Database Application with Rails

Our example will be a small database application. We'll create a simple database, and then use Rails, along with the Rails plugin AjaxScaffold, to manage the database. Specifically, we're going to create a tiny application to manage a collection of sports cars. We'll use MySQL as the database backend, so if you don't have the mysql gem installed, you'll need to install it using the command gem install mysql.

First let's create a MySQL database using the SQL source shown in Listing 23-1.

Listing 23-1. *Sportscar Database Schema (schema.sql)*

```
CREATE DATABASE sportscar_development;
USE sportscar_development;
CREATE TABLE sportscars(
  id INT(11) AUTO_INCREMENT NOT NULL PRIMARY KEY,
  model VARCHAR(30),
  make VARCHAR(30),
  year INT(11),
  description TEXT,
  purchase_price DECIMAL(9,2));

CREATE DATABASE sportscar_test;
USE sportscar_test;
CREATE TABLE sportscars(
  id INT(11) AUTO_INCREMENT NOT NULL PRIMARY KEY,
  model VARCHAR(30),
```

```
  make VARCHAR(30),
  year INT(11),
  description TEXT,
  purchase_price DECIMAL(9,2));

CREATE DATABASE sportscar_production;
USE sportscar_production;
CREATE TABLE sportscars(
  id INT(11) AUTO_INCREMENT NOT NULL PRIMARY KEY,
  model VARCHAR(30),
  make VARCHAR(30),
  year INT(11),
  description TEXT,
  purchase_price DECIMAL(9,2));
```

Save the code file as schema.sql. Next use the following command to build the structure of the database:

```
mysql < schema.sql
```

Now that we've created the database, let's create a Ruby on Rails frontend for it. Instead of listing all of the code, let's walk through the application-creation process, since Ruby on Rails creates a number of files for you automatically. You can use the following command to begin creating the application:

```
rails sportscar
```

This command will create a large number of files and directories for us automatically; the exact files and directories will vary depending on your Rails version, but it should look similar to the following:

```
    create    app/controllers
    create    app/helpers
    create    app/models
    create    app/views/layouts
    create    config/environments
    create    components
    create    db
    create    doc
    create    lib
    create    lib/tasks
    create    log
    create    public/images
    create    public/javascripts
    create    public/stylesheets
    create    script/performance
    create    script/process
    create    test/fixtures
    create    test/functional
```

```
create   test/integration
create   test/mocks/development
create   test/mocks/test
create   test/unit
create   vendor
create   vendor/plugins
create   tmp/sessions
create   tmp/sockets
create   tmp/cache
create   Rakefile
create   README
create   app/controllers/application.rb
create   app/helpers/application_helper.rb
create   test/test_helper.rb
create   config/database.yml
create   config/routes.rb
create   public/.htaccess
create   config/boot.rb
create   config/environment.rb
create   config/environments/production.rb
create   config/environments/development.rb
create   config/environments/test.rb
create   script/about
create   script/breakpointer
create   script/console
create   script/destroy
create   script/generate
create   script/performance/benchmarker
create   script/performance/profiler
create   script/process/reaper
create   script/process/spawner
create   script/runner
create   script/server
create   script/plugin
create   public/dispatch.rb
create   public/dispatch.cgi
create   public/dispatch.fcgi
create   public/404.html
create   public/500.html
create   public/index.html
create   public/favicon.ico
create   public/robots.txt
create   public/images/rails.png
create   public/javascripts/prototype.js
create   public/javascripts/effects.js
create   public/javascripts/dragdrop.js
create   public/javascripts/controls.js
```

```
create  public/javascripts/application.js
create  doc/README_FOR_APP
create  log/server.log
create  log/production.log
create  log/development.log
create  log/test.log
```

Next we'll need to configure our application to access our database. Edit the sportscar\
config\database.yml file, which was created by the rails sportscar command, and replace it
with the following text:

```
development:
  adapter: mysql
  database: sportscar_development
  username: your_user_name
  password: your_password
  host: localhost

test:
  adapter: mysql
  database: sportscar_test
  username: your_user_name
  password: your_password
  host: localhost

production:
  adapter: mysql
  database: sportscar_production
  username: your_user_name
  password: your_password
  host: localhost
```

You'll have to replace your_user_name and your_password with the appropriate MySQL
username and password, of course. Additionally, note that the default username is root and
the default password is a blank password; if these settings are correct for your system, you
won't need to change the file.

At this point, our Rails application is connected to the database, but we don't have any
code in it. We need to create a model—this is a class that uses ActiveRecord to represent a
table in our database. Since we have only one table, sportscars, we need to create only one
model. You can create that single model using the following command:

```
cd /path/to/your/rails/application
ruby script/generate model sportscar
```

```
exists  app/models/
exists  test/unit/
exists  test/fixtures/
```

```
create  app/models/sportscar.rb
create  test/unit/sportscar_test.rb
create  test/fixtures/sportscar.yml
create  db/migrate
create  db/migrate/001_create_sportscar.rb
```

We are going to use the AjaxScaffold plugin to generate code to access our database. We first need to install the AjaxScaffold plugin via the following command:

```
ruby script/plugin install svn://rubyforge.org/var/svn/ajaxscaffoldp/trunk
```

```
A  C:\path\sportscar\vendor\plugins\ajaxscaffoldp
A  C:\path\sportscar\vendor\plugins\ajaxscaffoldp\test
A  C:\path\sportscar\vendor\plugins\ajaxscaffoldp\test\ajax_scaffold_test.rb
A  C:\path\sportscar\vendor\plugins\ajaxscaffoldp\app
...
Exported revision 90.
```

At this point we need to create a new controller—that's the controller part of the MVC Web framework. We then need to add a few lines of code to access our AjaxScaffold plugin from our controller.

```
ruby script/generate controller sportscar_scaffold
```

```
exists  app/controllers/
exists  app/helpers/
create  app/views/sportscar_scaffold
exists  test/functional/
create  app/controllers/sportscar_scaffold_controller.rb
create  test/functional/sportscar_scaffold_controller_test.rb
create  app/helpers/sportscar_scaffold_helper.rb
```

Next we need to add the code. Edit the file sportscar\app\controllers\sportscar_scaffold_controller.rb file, and place the following code in it:

```
class SportscarScaffoldController < ApplicationController
  ajax_scaffold :sportscar
end
```

Finally, let's create the file sportscar\app\views\layouts\application.rhtml with the following code:

```
<html>
  <head>
    <title>Sportscar Inventory Tracker</title>
    <%= ajax_scaffold_includes %>
```

```
    </head>
    <body>
      <%=@content_for_layout%>
    </body>
</html>
```

This file controls the look of our application. It's an HTML template; the HTML output from our application is inserted into it. It has only two dynamic components: first it calls the helper function `ajax_scaffold_includes`, which inserts links to the various CSS and JavaScript files that the Ajax scaffolding needs; and second, it includes the `@content_for_layout` variable, which is the actual HTML output from our application.

Our application is now ready to run; we have an Ajax Web interface with the ability to view add, delete, edit, and sort records. Let's take it for a spin using the following shell command:

```
ruby script/server
```

You should be able to see the application (as in Figure 23-1) with a Web browser at the following URL:

```
http://localhost:3000/sportscar scaffold
```

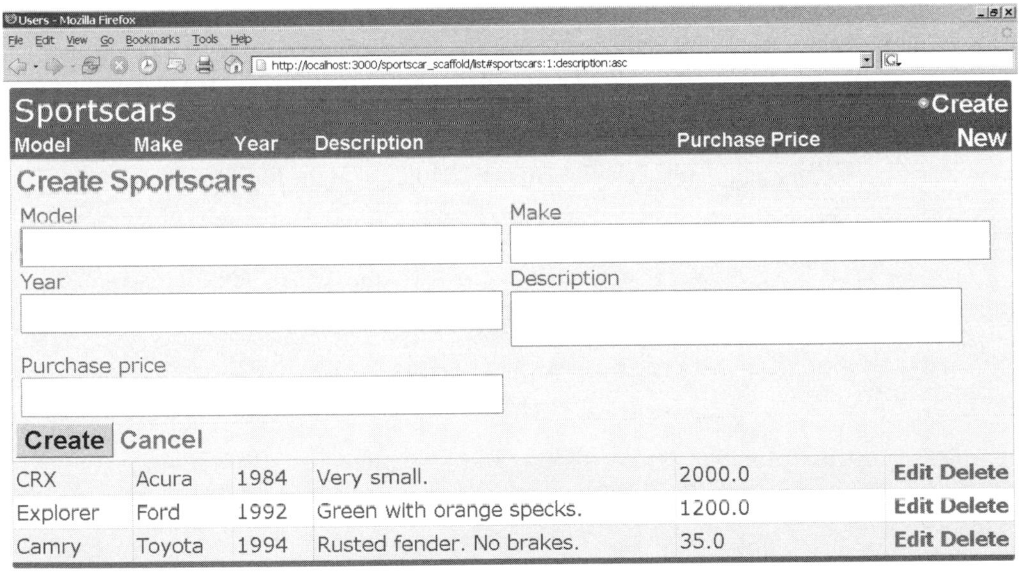

Figure 23-1. *The completed Web application*

Dissecting the Example

As you've likely noticed, there wasn't much code involved in creating a great deal of functionality. In fact, most of our application was invoked with the following line in the controller:

```
ajax_scaffold :sportscars
```

Essentially, this line passes control for the controller to the AjaxScaffold plugin. Note that if you replaced the method ajax_scaffold with scaffold, you'd use the default Rails scaffolding and not the AjaxScaffold scaffolding—the default is considerably less attractive, but doesn't require software besides Rails to be installed. Incidentally, there are a number of other scaffolding plugins available—Streamlined, for instance, is another powerful scaffolding system for Rails. You can obtain it at the following URL:

http://streamlined.relevancellc.com/

Although scaffolding is a powerful technique, it's not always appropriate (it's often an excellent fit for the backend of the application, such as an administration area). Nonetheless, scaffolding is both a powerful starting point and a great example of how quickly you can develop with Rails. It's also a great example of how you can write code in Rails—if you examine the sportscar\vendor\plugins\ajaxscaffoldp directory, you can see all of the code that the plugin uses to create our interface. (The AjaxScaffold plugin detects the fields and field types via the ActiveRecord gem, which is an integral part of Rails—check out Chapter 5 for more details.)

Conclusion

Ruby on Rails is a complex subject—one that could (and does) fill several books. Most Ruby on Rails applications will be much more complex than our example, and will include many controllers and views. Fortunately, there's a wealth of information available to help you learn Rails quickly—a good start would be http://rubyonrails.org; you can also get Ruby on Rails news at the meta-news-blog-job site I run, http://coolruby.com. If you'd like to try a more complex application, examine the Ruby on Rails wiki tutorial at the following URL:

http://sl33p3r.free.fr/tutorials/rails/wiki/wiki-en.html

Ruby on Rails is a great way to develop websites—whether you're developing a small internal site or a large-scale Internet site, you'd be wise to consider using Rails.

■ ■ ■

## CHAPTER 24

Automating Development Tasks with rake

rake is a Ruby utility that can automate software-development tasks of virtually any variety. Often, of course, software development involves text files—source code, documentation, and so forth—and rake excels at manipulating such files. It lets you develop "tasks" that can be called easily from the command line using the rake utility.

For example, you can use rake to run tests on source code, to generate documentation from source, to upgrade a database to the latest, or for many other tasks; often you'll need to create files from other files—compile code, for example—and rake works great for that. You may also need to perform housekeeping of other kinds—for example, the default session store in Rails creates a great many temporary files, so you could create a rake task that deletes them for you.

How Does It Work?

rake helps you automate development tasks, such as transforming files into other files, running SQL commands, or virtually any other simple repetitive task. There are a number of other tools that do this—ant and make, for example. However, rake, like RubyGems, requires only Ruby. It's also more flexible, since tasks in rake are written in Ruby—a full programming language, and not just a configuration file. It also provides some additional help for writing tasks, so it's not only flexible, but it also has the power that both of the aforementioned tools have.

Specifically, rake has two types of tasks: file tasks and regular tasks. *File tasks* transform files into other files, and *regular tasks* perform arbitrary tasks. File tasks, for example, are the kinds of tasks that a makefile would use to transform a C source-code file into an object file, or that you could use to automatically transform an XML source file into an output file.

In any case, it's pretty straightforward to create a rake task. Here's a simple example:

```
task :test do
  puts "I'm alive!"
end
```

Save that as rakefile. You can use the following commands:

```
cd /path/to/rakefile
rake test
```

```
I'm alive!
```

You can put virtually any kind of Ruby code in a rake task. You can get the full rake documentation here:

```
http://rake.rubyforge.org/
```

To install rake, use the following command:

```
gem install rake
```

Easy Documentation with BlueCloth and rake

Projects of all kinds often involve digital documentation; a well-managed project will have everyone involved contributing to the documentation, so that it covers the full range of the available knowledge. However, because writing documentation takes time, it's important to get documentation created and updated quickly. One way to do this is by writing in an easy-to-use format; in fact, the BlueCloth gem (introduced in Chapter 6) allows us to use MarkDown, which is an easy-to-use markup language designed for easily and quickly writing textual documents. (Many Ruby projects use RDoc, which is a common and easy-to-use way to include documentation in Ruby code; however, BlueCloth may be easier to use for nontechnical personnel, like graphic designers or even clients.)

The sample script in Listing 24-1 uses the rake gem to take a directory full of BlueCloth files and convert them into output files in HTML. Using this scheme, you could keep an entire tree of BlueCloth documentation and use rake to keep a directory full of HTML files up-to-date with the source BlueCloth files; you can have publicly accessible HTML files, which are easy to view with the HTML, but you also get the benefit of having easy-to-edit BlueCloth documentation.

You'll need the BlueCloth gem to use this example; we'll use that gem to convert the source files into the output HTML files. You can install the BlueCloth gem using the following command:

```
gem install bluecloth
```

Listing 24-1 contains the code for our example.

Listing 24-1. *Convert BlueCloth Documentation to HTML (rakefile)*

```
input_dir='documentation'
output_dir='public'

task :default => [:build_directories, :build_html]

task :build_directories do |t|
   mkdir output_dir unless File.exists?(output_dir)
   mkdir input_dir unless File.exists?(input_dir)
end
```

```ruby
# Loop through all of the BlueCloth files and create
# HTML documentation from them.

task :build_html do |t|
  require 'bluecloth' # Note that this is here,
                      # and not at the top of the file;
                      # that way, we can add tasks later
                      # that don't require bluecloth,
                      # and developers can run those tasks
                      # without having bluecloth installed.

  cd input_dir

  files=FileList["*.bc"].to_a

  cd ".."

  files.each do |filename|
    input_file="#{input_dir}/#{filename}"

    output_file= "#{output_dir}/" <<
      filename.gsub(/^(.*)\.bc$/,'\1') << ".html"

    File.open(output_file,'w').puts BlueCloth::new(
              File.open(input_file).read
              ).to_html

    puts "processing #{input_file} into #{output_file}"

  end

end
```

Save this example as rakefile. Use the following command to run the example:

```
rake build_directories
```

```
(in /path/to/your/directory)
mkdir documentation
mkdir public
cd public
cd ..
```

You'll see that rake created two directories: documentation and public. Next we'll create a BlueCloth file with some sample documentation in it (a justification for our project being written in Ruby). In the input directory, create a new text file called language_justification.bc, and save the following text into it:

```
Project Language Justification
==============================

Ruby is an open source, powerful programming language. It's
a scripting language, much like Perl or Python. However,
it's surprisingly elegant; complex techniques can be
implemented in just a few lines of code. It's also
harmonious, in that things - even complex things - work the
way you might expect them to, even when used in surprising
ways.

Additionally, there are Ruby libraries - called "gems" -
that are available to perform a wide variety of tasks.
These libraries can be used to automate tasks such as
the following:

  - Authenticating users
  - Processing credit cards
  - Manipulating images
  - And much more.
```

Now let's run the rake command:

```
rake build_html
```

```
(in /path/to/your/directory)
cd input
cd ..
processing documentation/language_justification.bc into
```

```
public/language_justification.html
```

If we now open language_justification.html with a text editor, we can see the following result:

```
<h1>Project Language Justification</h1>

<p>Ruby is an open source, powerful programming language. It's a scripting
language, much like Perl or Python. However, it's surprisingly elegant; complex
techniques can be implemented in just a few lines of code. It's also harmonious,
 in that things - even complex things - work the way you might expect them to,
even when used in surprising ways.</p>
```

```
<p>Additionally, there are Ruby libraries - called "gems" - that are available
to perform a wide variety of tasks. These libraries can be used to automate
tasks such as the following:</p>

<ul>
<li>Authenticating users</li>
<li>Processing credit cards</li>
<li>Manipulating images</li>
<li>And much more.</li>
</ul>
```

As you can see, our file was run through BlueCloth and turned into an output file. If you create more test files in the documentation directory, they'll be automatically converted via BlueCloth into HTML files in the public directory when you run the rake command. Figure 24-1 shows what the example HTML file will look like when viewed in a Web browser.

Note In our example, we process only files ending in .bc, so you could have multiple file types, each with a different action.

Note If you wanted to use this rakefile with a Ruby on Rails application, you could just paste it onto the end of the Ruby on Rails default rakefile; it'll work fine.

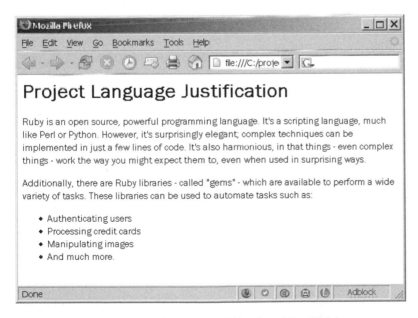

Figure 24-1. *Language_justification.html displayed in a Web browser*

Dissecting the Example

Let's take a look at a few important lines from Listing 24-1.

```
task :default => [:build_directories, :build_html]
```

This line specifies the default task—the task that will run if rake is called from the command line with no arguments. In this case, it simply runs the build_directories and build_html tasks.

```
task :build_directories do |t|
   mkdir output_dir unless File.exists?(output_dir)
   mkdir input_dir unless File.exists?(input_dir)
end
```

This task creates the output_dir and input_dir directories, which we specify at the top of the script. Of course, we use File.exists? to verify that each directory doesn't already exist.

```
task :build_html do |t|

  cd input_dir

  files=FileList["*.bc"].to_a

  cd ".."

  files.each do |filename|
    input_file="#{input_dir}/#{filename}"

    output_file= "#{output_dir}/" << filename.gsub(/^(.*)\.bc$/,'\1') << ".html"

    require 'bluecloth'

    File.open(output_file,'w').puts BlueCloth::new(
              File.open(input_file).read
              ).to_html

    puts "processing #{input_file} into #{output_file}"

  end

end
```

This task enters the input_dir directory and gets a list of all of the files ending in bc. Note that FileList is a facility provided by rake; it automatically skips text-editor backups and source control files, which is convenient. The build_html task opens each file, converts it into HTML using BlueCloth, and then writes the new version into a similarly named file in the output directory. The output file is named according to a fairly simple convention: the line that calls gsubs strips the .bc extension and adds an .html extension. You could have a more complicated naming convention if your application required it, of course.

Conclusion

rake is an excellent way to automate repetitive tasks; it can make virtually any time-consuming and uncreative development task easier.

■ ■ ■

## CHAPTER 25

Manipulating Images with RMagick

RMagick is a Ruby interface to the ImageMagick image-manipulation libraries. You can use RMagick to perform virtually any operation on an image from within a Ruby script. You could, for example, resize a directory full of images for a Web photo gallery. You could also use this feature to add a "watermark" to a directory full of images on a Web store so that competitors can't steal your product images to use on their sites.

How Does It Work?

RMagick is a Ruby interface to ImageMagick, which lets you create and edit images from within a Ruby script. You can resize, crop, composite, and perform a variety of effects on images in a number of formats. You can, for example, double the size of an image and then use a filter, such as Gaussian blur. You can also crop images, resample images, increase and decrease color depth, and more.

You can read an image from any file that ImageMagick supports, and then write to any file that ImageMagick supports—you can, therefore, read an image supplied by a user in any size and a variety of formats and then output it in a standardized size and format.

A variety of tasks are fairly easy using RMagick. For example, it's pretty effortless to resize images with RMagick. The following code resizes an image called example.png and writes it to the file example_resized.png:

```
require 'rmagick'

image= Magick::Image.read('example.png').first

image.change_geometry(
  "64x64") do |cols, rows, img|
  img.resize!(cols, rows)

  img.write 'example_resized.png'
end
```

The `Magick::Image.read` method returns an array; if we opened, say, a GIF animation with multiple frames, we could step through this array to manipulate each frame of the image. However, our image has just a single frame, so the `.first` call returns the first element of the array, which is an object that represents our image.

The `change_geometry` method takes a new size as an argument and passes a set of new dimensions to the associated block. The size it passes to the block might be different than the size we initially passed to the `change_geometry` method. This is because the `change_geometry` method takes into account the aspect ratio of the image in question, so that a square image resized will stay a square image. (You can add exclamation points to one or more of the dimensions to fix that dimension, so if you passed the size 64!x64! to the `change_geometry` call, you'd get 64×64 image every time, even if the image needed to be distorted to do so.)

Finally, the call to `.resize!` resizes our image, and the call to `.write` actually writes it to the file.

It's also easy to change image formats with RMagick. For example, the following code reads an image called `example.png`, converts it into `.jpg` format, and writes it to the file `example_converted_to_jpeg.jpg`:

```
require 'rmagick'
```

```
image= Magick::Image.read('example.png').first.write 'example_converted_to_jpeg.jpg'
```

RMagick automatically detects the format of the file extension and writes the file appropriately, so the above example needs only to specify a file ending in `.jpg` to convert the file to our new format.

Of course, there are many other operations RMagick is capable of. You can get the full details about the RMagick gem API at the following URL:

```
http://rmagick.rubyforge.org/
```

You can use the following command to install RMagick

```
gem install rmagick
```

Note that RMagick requires either ImageMagick or GraphicsMagick to be installed, since it uses either of those to perform the actual image manipulation. You can find out the details on ImageMagick and GraphicsMagick at the following URLs:

```
http://www.imagemagick.org/script/download.php
http://www.graphicsmagick.org/www/download.html
```

Creating Thumbnails with RMagick

The example in Listing 25-1 is a small application to create an index for a directory full of pictures. We'll create a thumbnail for each picture, and then create an HTML document that we can use to view all of them at once.

Note that this example requires Markaby to produce the output HTML. You can install Markaby with the following command:

```
gem install markaby
```

Listing 25-1. *Creating Thumbnails with rmagick (create_thumbnails.rb)*

```ruby
require 'rmagick'
require 'markaby'
require 'optparse'

options = {}
opt=OptionParser.new do |opts|
  opts.banner = "Usage: #{$0}.rb [options] image_directory"

  opts.on("-u", "--thumbnail_directory directory",
                "thumbnail_directory") { |u|
                 options[:thumbnail_directory] = u }
  opts.on("-h", "--thumbnail_height HEIGHT",
                "thumbnail_height") { |h|
                 options[:thumbnail_height] = h.to_i }
  opts.on("-w", "--thumbnail_width WIDTH",
                "thumbnail_width") { |w|
                 options[:thumbnail_width] = w.to_i }
  opts.on("-c", "--background_color COLOR",
                "background_color") { |c|
                 options[:background_color] = c }

  opts.on("-t", "--crop_top HEIGHT", "crop_vertical") { |ct|
                 options[:crop_top] = ct.to_i }
  opts.on("-b", "--crop_bottom HEIGHT", "crop_bottom") { |cb|
                 options[:crop_bottom] = cb.to_i }

  opts.on("-l", "--crop_left WIDTH", "crop_left") { |cl|
                 options[:crop_left] = cl.to_i }
  opts.on("-r", "--crop_right WIDTH", "crop_right") { |cr|
                 options[:crop_right] = cr.to_i }

  opts.on_tail("-h", "--help", "Show this message") { puts opts.help; exit }

end
opt.parse!


( puts opt.help; exit ) unless ARGV.length==1
options[:directory] = ARGV.shift
options[:thumbnail_directory] ||= "#{options[:directory]}/thumbnails"
options[:thumbnail_height] ||= 64
options[:thumbnail_width] ||= 64
options[:background_color] ||= 'black'
```

```ruby
background = Magick::Image.new(options[:thumbnail_height],
                              options[:thumbnail_width]) do
  self.background_color=options[:background_color]
end

Dir.mkdir(options[:thumbnail_directory]) unless
         File.exists?(options[:thumbnail_directory])

html=Markaby::Builder.new

html.html do
  html.head do
    html.title "Picture Index for #{options[:directory]}"
  end
  html.body do

    Dir.foreach(options[:directory]) do |file|

      # Manipulate the files only if they are images.

      if file =~ /.*\.(jpg|gif|bmp|png|tif|tga)$/i

        full_filename= "#{options[:directory]}/#{file}"
        thumbnail_filename= "#{options[:thumbnail_directory]}/#{file}"

        # Read the image from the disk.

        image= Magick::Image.read(full_filename).first

        # Crop the image if any of the crop options were specified
        # on the command line.

        image.crop!(Magick::SouthGravity, image.columns, image.rows -
                    options[:crop_top]) unless options[:crop_top].nil?
        image.crop!(Magick::NorthGravity, image.columns, image.rows -
                    options[:crop_bottom]) unless options[:crop_bottom].nil?

        image.crop!(Magick::WestGravity, image.columns - options[:crop_right],
                    image.rows) unless options[:crop_right].nil?
        image.crop!(Magick::EastGravity, image.columns - options[:crop_left],
                    image.rows) unless options[:crop_left].nil?
```

```ruby
    # Perform the actual resizing.

    image.change_geometry(
      "#{options[:thumbnail_width]}x" <<
      "#{options[:thumbnail_height]}") do |cols, rows, img|

        img.resize!(cols, rows)

        composite= background.composite(img, Magick::CenterGravity,
                                        Magick::OverCompositeOp )
        composite.write thumbnail_filename
    end

    # Add a div to our output HTML which
    # displays our new thumbnail.

    html.div :style=>"padding:1em; float:left; text-align:center" do
      a :href=>full_filename do
        html.img :src=>thumbnail_filename, :align=>:center
      end
      p   do
        small file
      end
    end

      end
    end
  end
end

print html.to_s
```

Save the code file as create_thumbnails.rb. Next, create a directory named thumbnails underneath where you saved the file. Copy some images in JPEG or GIF format into the directory. Finally, let's create our thumbnail index using the following command:

```
ruby create_thumbnails.rb thumbnails > test.html
```

If you view the file `test.html` in a Web browser, you can see the completed thumbnail index (see Figure 25-1).

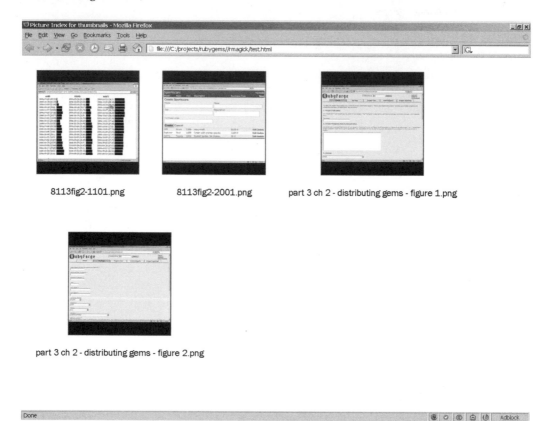

8113fig2-1101.png   8113fig2-2001.png   part 3 ch 2 - distributing gems - figure 1.png

part 3 ch 2 - distributing gems - figure 2.png

Figure 25-1. *The Web browser showing our thumbnails*

Dissecting the Example

The first chunk of code in our example parses the command line using `optparse`—that lets the user specify options like the thumbnail size, the directory to create thumbnails for, and so forth. After that, we create a background image for our thumbnails:

```
background = Magick::Image.new(options[:thumbnail_height],
                               options[:thumbnail_width]) do
  self.background_color=options[:background_color]
end
```

This `RMagick` code creates a single-color background image that is the height of our thumbnail. This will be used as a backdrop so that if the thumbnail is not the same aspect ratio (width-to-height ratio) as the source image, the remainder of the thumbnail will be colored the background color. (The thumbnail height, width, and background color are all part of the `options` array, which can be overridden from the command line.)

```
Dir.mkdir(options[:thumbnail_directory]) unless
        File.exists?(options[:thumbnail_directory])
```

This line creates a directory for our thumbnails to be stored in—unless, of course, the directory already exists.

Next the code creates a `Markaby` builder object, which is used to create our output HTML page. Each method call on the `Markaby` object corresponds to an HTML tag; you can find out more in Chapter 14.

Our script then loops through each of the directory's files that have any of a few extensions: JPG, PNG, and so forth. (The script doesn't have an exhaustive list of formats that RMagick supports—it covers only the most common ones. See http://RMagick.rubyforge.org/ for more details.)

Finally, let's take a look at the code that actually manipulates each image. Note that this code is called in a loop—once for each file in our directory:

```
image= Magick::Image.read(full_filename).first

image.crop!(Magick::SouthGravity, image.columns, image.rows -
    options[:crop top]) unless options[:crop_top].nil?
image.crop!(Magick::NorthGravity, image.columns, image.rows -
    options[:crop_bottom]) unless options[:crop_bottom].nil?

image.crop!(Magick::WestGravity, image.columns - options[:crop_right],
    image.rows) unless options[:crop_right].nil?
image.crop!(Magick::EastGravity, image.columns - options[:crop_left],
    image.rows) unless options[:crop_left].nil?

# Perform the actual resizing.

image.change_geometry(
                    "#{options[:thumbnail_width]}x" <<
                    "#{options[:thumbnail_height]}") do |cols, rows, img|

  img.resize!(cols, rows)

  composite= background.composite(img, Magick::CenterGravity,
    Magick::OverCompositeOp )
  composite.write thumbnail_filename
end
```

The first line reads the image using RMagick's `.read` method; we then call `.first` on it, which gives us the first layer. (Of course, if we had multiple layers in our image we might want to manipulate each differently, but for our example we're assuming that each picture has just one layer.) We don't have to specify the file format—RMagick can automatically determine the format for each image.

The next four lines, each of which starts with `image.crop!`, apply optional cropping. If the user uses the option `--crop_top 30` on the command line, for example, the program will crop 30 pixels off the top of each image before resizing it for thumbnails. Note that the program doesn't actually modify the source image—it only changes the thumbnail. This may be useful, for example, if you have a watermark or other artifact that is of a fixed size and has a specific location.

The final block of code—starting with `image.change_geometry`—might be a bit confusing at first, but it's very helpful. The `change_geometry` code takes an ImageMagick size specifier and returns a width and a height. This automatically respects aspect ratios, which means that your image won't be distorted. For example, if you had a 100×200 source image that you want to resize to 100×100, the `change_geometry` method would calculate a new size of 50×100—if you resized to 100×100 directly, you'd stretch the image to twice the proper width.

Once we are inside the block, we resize our image using the `.resize!` method; note that we used the calculated `cols` and `rows` (in other words, width and height) values.

Next we composite the image with our background image into one single image—we use the `CenterGravity` option, which dictates that if the new image is smaller than our background image, it will be centered on the background.

Conclusion

There is an almost infinite variety of operations you might want to perform on an image, and you can use `RMagick` from your Ruby scripts to easily automate nearly any of them.

CHAPTER 26

■ ■ ■

Speeding Up Web Applications with memcache-client

memcache-client is a Ruby interface to memcached; memcached is a distributed caching system. Originally, memcached was developed for LiveJournal.com, which was one of the earliest popular blogging communities. It is reported that the newly developed memcached was able to decrease LiveJournal's database load to nearly nothing using only existing hardware. For a site that at the time handled over 20 million page views a day and had over a million different users, that's very significant. A number of other popular sites use memcached, including Slashdot and Wikipedia.

Of course, to use memcached you need an interface, and memcache-client is a powerful, easy-to-use memcached interface for Ruby. For example, you could use memcache-client as a way to speed up an ecommerce site by caching slow database queries, and the faster your application is, the cheaper it will be to scale to handle more users.

How Does It Work?

memcache-client lets you access memcached from a Ruby program; typically, memcached would be used to supplement a database server or database-server clusters, although memcached could be used to implement virtually any kind of caching. The model works like this: When you have a complicated read-only query, you first check if the value is stored in the memcached cache, and if it is you use the value from the cache, saving time and CPU power. However, if it's not present you run the query and cache the result.

Note that memcached doesn't replace a database, since it is only a cache. However, it's a very useful cache: You can have as many memcached servers as you'd like, and they can fail as necessary—when you can't contact a memcached server, you can simply pull the result from the database. Additionally, since memcached works over TCP/IP, different processes on different machines can use the same memcached server transparently.

Here's a simple example of setting and then retrieving a value on a memcached server using memcache-client:

```
require 'memcache'
mem = MemCache.new '127.0.0.1'
mem[:test_key] = 'Hello world!'
puts mem[:test_key]
```

As you can see, it's pretty easy to set and retrieve values using memcache-client; the first line loads the memcache library, the second line creates our connection, and the last two lines simply use the memcached connection as if it were a hash.

You can get the full memcache-client documentation here:

```
http://dev.robotcoop.com/Libraries/memcache-client/index.html
```

The following command lets you install memcache-client:

```
gem install memcache-client
```

■**Note** You'll need to run a memcached server on your machine to follow the examples in this chapter. You can get a Linux/OS X version at the memcached homepage:

```
http://www.danga.com/memcached/
```

You can get a Windows verison of memcached at the following URL:

```
http://jehiah.com/projects/memcached-win32/
```

Speeding Up the Ruby on Rails Session Cache with memcached

Suppose you are creating an ecommerce site that sells audio-visual equipment. You're implementing your site in Ruby on Rails (see Chapter 23 for more details), and want to have a very full set of features. Unfortunately, you have a limited budget, so you need to make the most of your Web-server resources. memcache-client can help with this, and an excellent place to start is by replacing the rails built-in session cache; session caches store information like a user's login info and shopping cart, but unfortunately, Ruby on Rails's built-in session cache is file-based and very slow. However, memcache-client offers a fast, easy-to-use alternative.

To demonstrate the speed of memcache-client, we'll build a short test Rails application that simulates a user logging in; we'll then build a simple test rig, which will time 10,000 logins, and then we'll time both the memcache-client version and the unmodified test version.

First let's create a test Rails application, which simulates a user signing into the site. You'll need to have Rails installed; you can install it with the command gem install rails. (Ruby on Rails is covered in detail in Chapter 23.) You can create the frame of our test application using the following command:

```
rails default_store_test
cd default_store_test
ruby script/generate controller user
```

Now place the code from Listing 26-1 into the file app/controllers/user_controller.rb.

Listing 26-1. *User Controller for Test Application (user_controller.rb)*

```
class UserController < ApplicationController
  def login
    referring_page = session['referring_page']
    session['user_id'] = 33
    session['cart_contents']= [
                  { :id=>1,
                    :quantity=>3,
                    :description=>'23 inch Television'},
                  { :id=>2,
                    :quantity=>1,
                    :description=>'Misc DVD Lot'},

                  { :id=>3,
                    :quantity=>1,
                    :description=>'Digitial Video Recorder'}
                             ]
    render :text=>'Thank you for signing in!'
  end
end
```

The following commands will create a second Rails application, which will be the version of our test application that uses memcached:

```
rails memcached_store_test
cd memcached_store_test
ruby script/generate controller user
```

Copy the code from Listing 26-1 into the memcached_store_test/app/controllers/ user_controller.rb file, just like you did for the default_store_test application.

Finally, add the code from Listing 26-2 to the end of the memcached_store_test/ config/environment.rb file, which was created for us by Ruby on Rails.

Listing 26-2. *Memcache Session Store Connection (memcache_session_store.rb)*

```
MEMCACHE_CONNECTION = MemCache.new(['localhost:17898'],
                      :namespace=>"memcached-store-test-#{RAILS_ENV}")
ActionController::Base.session_options[:cache] = MEMCACHE_CONNECTION
```

At this point, you should have two applications in two different directories: The default_ store_test directory has the default session store example, and the memcached_store_test has the memcached version.

Now that we have the two examples, we need to test them to compare their speeds. Listing 26-3 contains a brief tester that uses the rwb gem to test the speeds.

■Note rwb stands for Ruby Web Bench; it's a small gem that runs performance tests on Web applications. You'll need it installed to test the speed of your applications. You can install it using the following command:

```
gem install rwb
```

You can find out more about rwb at the following URL:

```
http://www.red-bean.com/~pate/
```

Listing 26-3. *Application Speed Tester (performance_tester.rb)*

```
require 'rwb'

number_of_runs=ARGV.shift.to_i

url_list = RWB::Builder.new()
url_list.add_url(1, 'http://localhost:3000/user/login')

tester = RWB::Runner.new(url_list, number_of_runs, 50)
tester.run

tester.report_header
tester.report_overall
```

Save the code from Listing 26-3 as `performance_tester.rb`. To determine the speed of the two applications, let's first test them both. Execute the following command:

```
cd /path/to/default_store_example
ruby script/server
```

We need to be running the `Rails` server in the background, so open a new window to execute the next command. (You can also use a different terminal or SSH connection under Linux or OS X, depending on whether you are running this example locally.) The command to test this server is as follows:

```
ruby performance_tester.rb 10000
```

```
completed 1000 runs
completed 2000 runs
completed 3000 runs
completed 4000 runs
completed 5000 runs
completed 6000 runs
completed 7000 runs
completed 8000 runs
completed 9000 runs
completed 10000 runs
```

```
Concurrency Level:      1
Total Requests:         10000
Total time for testing: 687.969 secs
Requests per second:    14.5355386652596
Mean time per request:  68  msecs
Standard deviation:     35
Overall results:
        Shortest time:  31 msecs
        50.0%ile time:  62 msecs
        90.0%ile time:  110 msecs
        Longest time:   406 msecs
```

As you can see, it took 687.969 seconds to run this example. Note that the example used 10,000 requests, but you could just as easily use 1000 or 100 requests, which would be much faster—and less accurate, of course, but you may not wish to wait ten minutes for each test to run. To make the test faster, simply replace the number 10000 in the command ruby performance_tester.rb 10000 with a lower number.

Next, let's try the memcached optimized version; if you have the previous server still running, stop it. Run the following command:

```
cd /path/to/memcached_store_example
ruby script/server
```

In a different window, run this command:

```
ruby performance_tester.rb 10000
```

```
completed 1000 runs
completed 2000 runs
completed 3000 runs
completed 4000 runs
completed 5000 runs
completed 6000 runs
completed 7000 runs
completed 8000 runs
completed 9000 runs
completed 10000 runs
Concurrency Level:      1
Total Requests:         10000
Total time for testing: 459.157 secs
Requests per second:    21.7790428981808
Mean time per request:  45  msecs
Standard deviation:     31
Overall results:
        Shortest time:  15 msecs
        50.0%ile time:  32 msecs
        90.0%ile time:  78 msecs
        Longest time:   625 msecs
```

Whereas the default version ran in a total of 687.969 seconds, the memcached-client version ran in 459.157 seconds. That means that the unoptimized version took roughly 50 percent longer. Of course, your exact results will vary depending on your application, operating system, computer speed, and many other factors, but in any case memcached-client is an excellent choice for a Rails session store.

Dissecting the Example

Let's take a look at a few relevant lines from Listings 26-1, 26-2, and 26-3. First, a few lines from 26-1:

```
def login
  referring_page = session['referring_page']
  session['user_id'] = 33
  session['cart_contents']= [
                 [ :id=>1,
                   :quantity=>3,
                   :description=>'23 inch Television'],
                 [ :id=>2,
                   :quantity=>1,
                   :description=>'Misc DVD Lot'],
                 [ :id=>3,
                   :quantity=>1,
                   :description=>'Digitial Video Recorder']
                           ]
  render :text=>'Thank you for signing in!'
end
```

This single action simulates the storing and reading of the kinds of session data you have in an ecommerce application. Of course, this example isn't connected to a database, and you can't actually buy anything, but it is an accurate enough test to show the speed differences between memcached and the default Rails session store.

Next, let's take a look at the code from Listing 26-2; this code is added to the end of the config/environment.rb file to enable our memcached session store:

```
MEMCACHE_CONNECTION = MemCache.new(['localhost:17898'],
                   :namespace=>"memcached-store-test-#{RAILS_ENV}")
ActionController::Base.session_options[:cache] = MEMCACHE_CONNECTION
```

As you can see, it's fairly straightforward to attach the memcached session store to the Rails application; it involves only two lines of code. The first line creates a connection; note that the array ['localhost:17898'] contains the address and port number for our single server, and that you could add more elements into that array if necessary.

Also note that the second parameter to the MemCache.new call, :namespace, sets a namespace according to the current environment—this separates the session store for the different environments: the development environment, the production environment, and the test environment. The advantage of this separation is that if you have data stored in, say, the development environment, it won't be used in either the production or testing environment.

The last line sets the `ActionController::Base.session_options[:cache]` variable to our connection to our `memcached` server, and that's all we need to have a `memcache-client` session store in `Rails`.

Finally, let's take a look at a few lines from Listing 26-3; these don't relate directly to `memcache-client`, but it's useful to know how you can use `rwb` to benchmark Web applications.

```
url_list = RWB::Builder.new()
url_list.add_url(1, 'http://localhost:3000/user/login')

tester = RWB::Runner.new(url_list, number_of_runs, 50)
tester.run

tester.report_header
tester.report_overall
```

The first line creates an `RWB::Builder` object; this lets us create a list of URLs to visit. The second line adds a single URL into our list; it specifies the URL to our test login action, and it specifies that it has a weight of 1. In this case, the weight doesn't have any effect, but if we had multiple URLs, we could use the weight parameter to make one URL be visited more often than another.

The third line creates an `RWB::Runner` object that will run our tests and report the results. The first argument to the `RWB::Runner.new` call will specify the list of URLs; the second argument is the number of times to run the test ,which was specified on the command line. The third argument to the `RWB::Runner.new` call is the concurrency: how many open connections are permitted at once.

The call to `tester.run` on the fourth line begins the tests; once they are finished, report_ header is called—this outputs some statistics like total time elapsed, total number of connections, and so forth. Next report_overall is called, which gives some statistics about the 50th-percentile connection time, the longest time, and so forth. (Technically the 50th-percentile time is slightly different than the average time, but the difference isn't important in this case, so if you aren't familiar with statistics you can consider it an average.)

Accessing memcached Servers with a Graphical Client

The script in Listing 26-4 uses the `fxruby` gem (see Chapter 11) to create a graphical interface to a `memcached` server. You'll be able to set a key and a value; you can also select a key and retrieve the value. This serves as a debugging tool for `memcached` servers, and also demonstrates how easy it is to use `memcache-client`.

Listing 26-4. *Graphical memcached Interface (graphical_memcached_client.rb)*

```
require 'memcache'
require 'fox16'

(puts "usage: #{$0} server1 server2..."; exit) unless (ARGV.length >= 1)
```

```
server_addresses=ARGV

mem = MemCache.new server_addresses

include Fox

fox_application=FXApp.new

main_window=FXMainWindow.new(fox_application, "Memcached Client",
                            nil, nil, DECOR_ALL )
control_matrix=FXMatrix.new(main_window,3, MATRIX_BY_COLUMNS)
controls={}

#first row of controls:  the 'get value' row.

FXLabel.new(control_matrix, 'Get:')
controls[:get_key] = FXTextField.new(control_matrix, 30)
FXButton.new(control_matrix, 'Get').connect(SEL_COMMAND) do
  controls[:get_key_result].text = mem[controls[:get_key].text].to_s
end

#second row of controls: the 'results of get value' row

FXLabel.new(control_matrix, 'Result:')
controls[:get_key_result] = FXLabel.new(control_matrix, '')
FXFrame.new(control_matrix, 0)

#third row of controls: the 'set value' row

FXLabel.new(control_matrix, 'Set:')

textbox_matrix=FXMatrix.new(control_matrix,3, MATRIX_BY_COLUMNS, 0, 0, 0, 0, 0)
controls[:set_key]= FXTextField.new(textbox_matrix, 15)

FXLabel.new(textbox_matrix,'Value:')
controls[:set_value] = FXTextField.new(textbox_matrix, 15)

FXButton.new(control_matrix, 'Set').connect(SEL_COMMAND) do
  mem[controls[:set_key].text] = controls[:set_value].text
end


fox_application.create

main_window.show( PLACEMENT_SCREEN )

fox_application.run
```

Save this example as `graphical_memcached_client.rb`. Use the following command to run the example:

```
ruby graphical_memcached_client.rb 127.0.0.1
```

You should see a screen with a few options. (If not, did you start your memcached server?) The first text box lets you retrieve a value from the memcached server; the second lets you set it.

To test the client, enter an example key next to the Set label, and then enter any value in the Value box. Hit Set to set a value in the memcached server. Enter the same key under the Get option, and then hit Get.

Feel free to use multiple clients on the same server—it will work fine. You can also easily use multiple servers—just specify multiple IP addresses on the command line.

■**Caution** Keep in mind that memcached servers don't have authentication, so your memcached deployment should not be accessible from the Internet.

Dissecting the Example

Let's look at a few important lines from Listing 26-4.

```
mem = MemCache.new server_addresses
```

This first line opens connections to the memcached servers specified on the command line. Generally, there is more than one memcached server in an environment—for example, if you have a number of Web servers and a few database servers, you'd typically run memcached on the Web servers—which often have memory to spare. That way, you'd offload work off of the database server so that even noncached queries run faster.

```
controls[:get_key_result].text = mem[controls[:get_key].text].to_s
```

This line retrieves a result from the database when you click the Get button. The call, as you can see, is pretty simple—the mem object works like a hash, and we access it like one, using the [ ] method.

```
mem[controls[:set_key].text] = controls[:set_value].text
```

This line sets the key by using the [ ]= method. As you can see, assigning values to a memcached server is straightforward.

Conclusion

memcache-client is a fast, easy way to connect to memcached servers, and is a great choice any time you want to use memcached servers from a Ruby site or application.

## CHAPTER 27

Managing Zip Archives with rubyzip

The rubyzip gem is a library for manipulating Zip archives. The Zip file format is a compressed archive format that is very popular on Windows systems. However, there is support for it on nearly all major operating systems; tools that uncompress Zip files are now distributed with Windows, OS X, and most Linux distributions. Zip files can contain multiple files, like tar archives, and are compressed, so in many ways they are similar to tar.gz files. The Zip format shows up in some surprising places; for example, OpenOffice.org documents consist of a number of XML files and other files stored in a Zip archive. They don't have .zip extensions, but you can verify this by renaming an OpenOffice document to have the .zip extension and then viewing it with a Zip archiver.

Many times the Zip format is used as a container for data formats of other kinds, and when you encounter such formats, you can use the rubyzip gem to extract the data before you can process it. For example, data from a financial or ecommerce site might come to you as a CSV file inside of a Zip file; you can use rubyzip to pull the CSV file out of the Zip container and then you could process it using the fastercsv gem. (Chapter 15 has more details on fastercsv.)

How Does It Work?

rubyzip provides a familiar object-oriented interface for Zip files. You can use the zipfilesystem class to access Zip files as if they were regular filesystems—you can read files, write to files, read the contents of directories, and so forth.

For example, we could create a new Zip file named a_new_zip_file.zip and create a new file in it with the following code:

```
require 'zip/zipfilesystem'

Zip::ZipFile.open('a_new_zip_file.zip', Zip::ZipFile::CREATE) do |zipfile|
  zipfile.file.open("a_file_in_the_archive", "w") do |filehandle|
    filehandle.puts "The contents of this file are "
    filehandle.puts "extremely important and "
    filehandle.puts "should not be taken lightly."
  end
end
```

As you can see from this example, the interface is very similar to Ruby's built-in File class, and you can use the puts method on a file in the archive just like you would for a regular file.

You could also list the contents of that same Zip file as follows:

```
require 'zip/zipfilesystem'

Zip::ZipFile.open('a_new_zip_file.zip') do |zipfile|
  zipfile.dir.foreach('/') do |file|
    print file
  end
end
```

This code uses the foreach method to iterate through all of the filenames in the Zip file's top-level directory and prints out the name of each file.

You can find the full details on rubyzip here:

```
http://rubyzip.sourceforge.net/
```

The following command lets you install the rubyzip gem:

```
gem install rubyzip
```

Reading Text from a Zip File

Listing 27-1 uses the rubyzip gem to display text from a Zip file. This is useful because often Zip files are used as packaging for other types of files; for example, OpenOffice.org documents are XML documents packed inside of Zip files. Suppose you store invoices in OpenOffice.org format. You can use this example to extract the meta information for all of the documents in a directory, then read the XML to produce a list of document titles and authors—this summary would be a useful reference. In fact, you could even use OpenOffice.org meta info to store application-specific information—say, invoice numbers or client numbers.

Listing 27-1. *Displaying Text from a Zip File (rzipcat.rb)*

```
require 'zip/zipfilesystem'

(puts "usage: #{$0} zipfile [filename]
prints out one file or all files from a zip file"; exit) unless ARGV.length

zipfile=ARGV.shift
filename=nil
filename=ARGV.shift unless ARGV.length==0

def print_file(filename, fs)
    puts filename
    puts "=" * filename.length
    puts fs.file.read(filename)
end
```

```
# Open the zip file.

Zip::ZipFile.open(zipfile) do |fs|
  # If the user specified just one file,
  # print only that file.
  if filename
      print_file filename, fs
  else
    # If not, print all of the files.

    fs.dir.foreach('/') do |filename|
      print_file filename, fs
    end
  end

end
```

Save this script as `rzipcat.rb`. Create a few text files with text of any kind in them, and place them in a Zip file. Run the following command to test the script:

```
ruby rzipcat name_of_your_zipfile.zip
```

---

first_text_file.txt
```
--==================
contents of first text file...
```

second_text_file.txt
```
====================
contents of second text file...
```

The script should display the contents of the text files you placed in the Zip archive. You can also pick out just one Zip file using our script:

```
ruby rzipcat name_of_your_zipfile.zip first_text_file.zip
```

---

first_text_file.txt
```
====================
contents of first text file...
```

As you can see, we've created a utility that reads from Zip files with just a few lines of code. Incidentally, as mentioned above, OpenOffice.org documents are Zip files—you can verify this by running the following command on an OpenOffice.org document of your choice:

```
ruby rzipcat.rb your_file_name.sxw meta.xml
```

```
meta.xml
========
<?xml version="1.0" encoding="UTF-8"?>
<!DOCTYPE office:document-meta PUBLIC "-//OpenOffice.org//DTD OfficeDocument 1.0
//EN" "office.dtd"><office:document-meta xmlns:office="http://openoffice.org/200
0/office" xmlns:xlink="http://www.w3.org/1999/xlink" xmlns:dc="http://purl.org/d
c/elements/1.1/" xmlns:meta="http://openoffice.org/2000/meta" office:version="1.
...snip...
```

The file listed here, meta.xml, is just one of many files in an OpenOffice.org document; it specifies meta information about the document, such as author information, the document title, and so forth.

Dissecting the Example

Let's look at a few important lines from Listing 27-1:

```
def print_file(filename, fs)
    puts filename
    puts "=" * filename.length
    puts fs.file.read(filename)
end
```

The function here is used to print out the contents of each file; it's called by the code later in the script. It is passed two arguments—our filesystem object and a filename. The function then does three things—it prints the filename, it prints a line of equal signs below the filename, then it prints out the contents. The expression fs.file.read(filename) reads the file from the Zip filesystem.

The following lines open the original Zip file and process each filename we've specified on the command line:

```
Zip::ZipFile.open(zipfile) do |fs|

  if filename
     print_file filename, fs
  else
    fs.dir.foreach('/') do |filename|
      print_file filename, fs
    end
  end

end
```

The first line here contains a call to the Zip::ZipFile.open function. This opens the Zip file, and creates a ZipFileSystem object. This function has a number of methods, all of which you can find at the online documentation at http://rubyzip.sourceforge.net/, but there are two that concern us here: the file and dir methods. Each returns an object that is similar to Ruby's built-in File and Dir classes; we use this functionality to loop through all of the files in the Zip file's root directory. The specific call that loops through the files is `fs.dir.foreach('/')`; we then call our `print_file` function for each filename, which then prints out the file.

Conclusion

Zip files are a very common way to compress and contain multiple files; they're used in a variety of settings. `rubyzip` is a fast and easy way to both read and write Zip files.

■ ■ ■

## CHAPTER 28

Speeding Up Function Calls with memoize

memoize is an easy way to speed up function calls. It does this by caching the return value of the function for each set of arguments—a process called *memoization*. This can dramatically speed up the function, and it can be particularly helpful for calculations involving recursion. It's also very useful for functions that are repetitive and involve reading data from a hard drive. For example, you could use this to speed up a photo gallery that retrieves EXIF data from JPEGs, or a media player that reads ID3 tags.

How Does It Work?

memoize caches function calls by intercepting those calls, checking if the value is contained in the cache, and substituting the result if the cache has a match. If not, the original function is called and that value is stored in the cache for the next time. As you can imagine, this can speed up some types of calculations by quite a bit. You can get the full details about memoize at the following URL:

```
http://www.gemjack.com/gems/memoize-1.2.2/index.html
```

For example, Listing 28-1 calculates factorials; it first calculates without memoize, and then with memoize speeding up the process. The factorial of a given number is the product of all positive integers smaller than or equal to that number; in other words, the factorial of 4 is equal to $1 \times 2 \times 3 \times 4$. As you can imagine, this can be time-consuming to calculate for very large numbers; Listing 28-1 calculates the factorial of a relatively small number, but we'll do it quite a few times.

■**Note** Ruby's built-in benchmark module is used in Listing 28-1 to produce timing statistics; you can find more details here:

```
http://www.ruby-doc.org/core/classes/Benchmark.html
```

Listing 28-1. *Factorial Calculations with and without memoize (fast_factorial.rb)*

```
require 'memoize'
require 'benchmark'

(puts "usage: #{$0} number_of_times_to_calculate_factorial " <<
              "factorial_to_calculate " ;
      exit) unless ARGV.length==2

runs = ARGV.shift.to_i
factorial_number = ARGV.shift.to_i

include Memoize  # This brings the Memoize module into the
                 # current object namespace.

def factorial(n)
    return 1 if n==0
    return factorial(n-1) * n
end

Benchmark.bm(11) do |bm|
    bm.report("without memoize") { runs.times { factorial(factorial_number) } }

    memoize :factorial
    bm.report("with memoize    ") { runs.times { factorial(factorial_number) } }
end
```

Save this as fast_factorial.rb. You can run our demo using the following command:

```
ruby fast_factorial.rb 10000 200
```

	user	system	total	real
without memoize	22.031000	0.016000	22.047000	(23.187000)
with memoize	0.140000	0.000000	0.140000	(0.141000)

Note that the total column shows the total time for the function to calculate the factorial; as you can see, the memoize version of the function is quite a bit faster—specifically, it's around 157.5 times faster. (Your results will vary significantly—your machine may be slower or faster, but the memoize version should always be much faster than the non-memoize version.) Of course, this is a dramatic example since it involves a huge number of calls with identical parameters, but nonetheless it illustrates how caching can help significantly. (Keep in mind that this works well only when you have multiple calls to the same function with the same parameters.) The more repeat calls that you have, the more memoize can speed up your calculations. However, currently you can't expire results in the cache, so if you have rapidly changing data, memoize may not work well for you.

You can use the following command to install memoize:

```
gem install memoize
```

Organizing a List of MP3s

memoize can speed up any function call that is called repeatedly with the same parameters, not just those that perform calculations. For example, suppose you wanted to create a graphical list of an MP3 collection sorted by an arbitrary criteria, such as track length, artist, title, and so forth. You can do this with the id3lib-ruby gem (which is detailed in Chapter 29). However, looking up the id3 tag information is fairly time-consuming, and without the memoize gem, it'd be very slow on a large collection of MP3 files. Listing 28-2 uses both the id3lib-ruby gem and memoize to sort a collection of MP3s very quickly.

Listing 28-2. *Sorting an MP3 collection (id3list.rb)*

```
require 'id3lib'
require 'optparse'
require 'memoize'

include Memoize

$options = {}
$options[:set]={}

opt=OptionParser.new do |opts|
    opts.banner = "Usage: #{$0} directory_name OPTIONS... "

    opts.on("-s", "--sort OPTION=VALUE", "Sorts by the given ID3.") do |sort|
      $options[:sort] = sort

    end
    opts.on("-d", "--do-not-memoize", "Turns off memoization.") do |sort|
      $options[:do_not_memoize] = true

    end
    opts.on_tail("-h", "--help", "Show this message") { puts opts.help; exit }

end
opt.parse!

(puts "Please specify a directory of mp3 files to work with.";
      exit) unless ARGV.length == 1

def get_file_id3_value(file, tag_name)
  tag = ID3Lib::Tag.new(file)
  tag.send(tag_name)
end
```

```
def get_file_display_name(file)
  tag = ID3Lib::Tag.new(file)
  return "<p><i>#{tag.title}</i> from <i>#{tag.album}</i> by " <<
         "#{tag.artist}<br><small><a href='#{file}'>#{file}</a></small></p>"
end

list_of_mp3_files = Dir.glob("#{ARGV[0]}/*.mp3")


memoize :get_file_id3_value unless $options[:do_not_memoize]

list_of_mp3_files.sort! do |a,b|
  get_file_id3_value(a, $options[:sort] ).to_s <=>
      get_file_id3_value(b, $options[:sort] ).to_s
end

puts "<html><body>"

list_of_mp3_files.each do |file|
  puts get_file_display_name(file)
end

puts "</html></body>"
```

Save the code from Listing 28-2 as id3list.rb. You can run the example as follows—note that you'll have to substitute */path/music* with the correct path to your music collection:

```
time ruby id3list.rb -s artist "/path/music" --do-not-memoize > without.html
```

```
real    1m8.462s
user    0m0.015s
sys     0m0.000s
```

```
time ruby id3list.rb -s artist "/path/music"  > memoized.html
```

```
real    0m26.267s
user    0m0.015s
sys     0m0.015s
```

Note These two commands use the `time` utility, which is available only under Linux or OS X. You can run the example with the following commands under Windows:

```
ruby id3list.rb -s artist "C:\music"  --do-not-memoize > without.html
ruby id3list.rb -s artist "C:\music"  > memoized.html
```

You'll need to replace `C:\music` with the appropriate path to your music collection. Although you won't get precise statistics without having the `time` utility, you should see that the first command is much slower than the second.

As you can see, the first run—which did not use `memoize`—took 1 minute 8 seconds, whereas the second run—which did use `memoize`—took just 26 seconds. Of course, the results will vary depending on the size of your music collection, the speed of your computer, and so forth.

You can open either of the two result documents (`without.html` or `memozied.html`) in a Web browser, and you'll get a result similar to the one in Figure 28-1. (Note that the two documents are identical; they were both created in Listing 28-2 only to show that memoizing does not affect the output.)

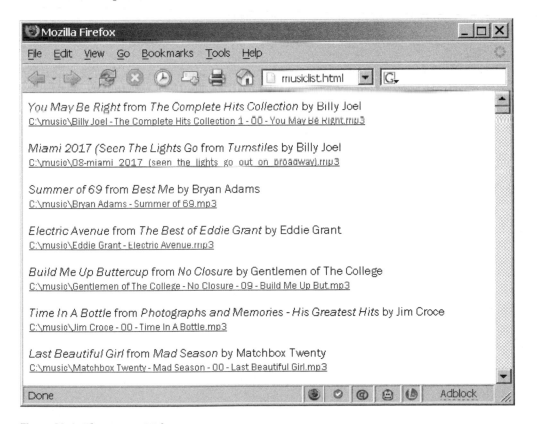

Figure 28-1. *The output Web page*

Dissecting the Example

There is essentially one function call you need to understand to use memoize, and it is named, unsurprisingly enough, memoize. Our example calls it using the following code:

```
memoize :factorial
```

That single line replaces our factorial function with the memoize wrapper—which, of course, calls the original the first time a particular set of parameters is encountered. As a result, it behaves just like the original version of the factorial function, but with one crucial difference: it won't do unnecessary work.

Note that the memoize function takes an optional parameter: a filename. If we used the following line, for example, we'd store our cache on disk instead of in memory:

```
memoize :factorial, 'cache_file_name'
```

That version of the memoize call is identical to the first except for the location of the cache, so you can use it the same way as we did in Listing 28-2.

Note Unlike the memory cache, the file cache sticks around between sessions—which could speed up performance quite considerably in the long run. On the other hand, this may be a problem if your results change from run to run—you can, of course, delete the cache file if you'd like.

Incidentally, the code behind the memoize gem is fairly short—which says quite a bit about the flexibility of the Ruby programming language. You can read the actual memoize source on RubyForge at the following URL:

```
http://raa.ruby-lang.org/gonzui/markup/memoize
```

Conclusion

memoize isn't for all types of functions or for all caching needs, but it can easily speed up computation-heavy problems—while keeping your code easy to read and to maintain. (If you need a more powerful caching solution, check out the memcached gem in Chapter 26.)

■ ■ ■

## CHAPTER 29

Tagging MP3 Files with id3lib-ruby

id3lib-ruby is a Ruby library for manipulating ID3 tags, which are embedded audio descriptors found in MP3 files. When an MP3 file is played in an MP3 player—such as an iPod, a car stereo, or a software audio player—ID3 tags provide the data that allows you too see the artist, track, and album information. You can learn more about them at http://en.wikipedia.org/wiki/ID3.

Because MP3 is such a commonplace compression and encoding scheme for digital music, any application that uses MP3 files will find this library useful. For example, you could use this library to create an organizer for MP3 files or a digital jukebox. You could also use it to create a mass tagger, which is a program that sets the attributes of a number of MP3 files at once, so if you have a number of incorrectly tagged files, you could correct a great many of them at once. Since poorly tagged MP3 files are quite common, this can be important, so an MP3 mass tagger is the prime example for this chapter.

How Does It Work?

id3lib-ruby provides a set of tools for reading and writing ID3 tags to and from MP3 files; you specify an ID3 tag to load using the ID3Lib::Tag.new method, and then you can access the ID3 attributes using intuitively named methods. For example, you could print out the artist and album from example.mp3 using the following code:

```
require 'id3lib'
example_tag=ID3Lib::Tag.new('example.mp3')
puts "#{example_tag.artist} #{example_tag.album}"
```

Your output might look like this:

```
A Fresh New Artist  - A Popular Song
```

It's reasonably easy to set the tags, as well:

```
require 'id3lib'
example_tag=ID3Lib::Tag.new('example.mp3')
example_tag.artist='This Is A Band'
example_tag.update!
```

The call to .update! writes the updated information to the file. Note that the method is update! and not update—this is perhaps because the method modifies the file in place, although that is slightly against the normal Ruby convention, which reserves the ! suffix for methods that modify the receiver in place.

ID3lib-ruby also provides support for less-commonly used tasks, such as for attaching album-cover art to MP3 files; you can get the full details about id3lib-ruby at the following URL:

http://www.gemjack.com/gems/id3lib-ruby-0.4.1-mswin32/index.html

You can use the following command to install id3lib-ruby:

gem install id3lib-ruby

Under Windows, you can choose to install the Win32 gem when prompted. Under other operating systems, choose the Ruby gem. Under non-Win32 operating systems, you'll need the id3lib library installed; you can get it at the following URL:

http://id3lib.sourceforge.net/

Changing MP3 Tags with ID3 Mass Tagger

Listing 29-1 shows a small command-line utility to view and set ID3 tags. By default, the program will view the ID3 tags of the MP3 files it receives as arguments on the command line. You can also pass it an option to set one or more ID3 attributes, so if you had a number of mistagged files—for instance, a misspelled artist or album name—you could correct them all at once.

Listing 29-1. *Creating a Mass ID3 Tagger (id3tool.rb)*

```ruby
require 'id3lib'
require 'optparse'

$options = {}
$options[:set]={}

opt=OptionParser.new do |opts|
    opts.banner = "Usage: #{$0} file1 file2 file3... "

    opts.on("-s", "--set OPTION=VALUE",
    "Sets the ID3 option OPTION to VALUE.") do |options|
      option, value = options.split(/=/)
      (puts 'Please set the ID3 in the format option=value.';
        exit) unless option and value
      $options[:set][option] = value

    end
    opts.on_tail("-h",
                 "--help", "Show this message") {
                     puts opts.help; exit }
```

```
end
opt.parse!

# IF they didn't specify at least one file,
# display a brief message and exit.

(puts "Please specify one or more mp3 files to work with.";
       exit) unless ARGV.length > 0
# Loop through all of the files on the command
# line...
ARGV.each do |file|
  # .. read their tags...
  tag = ID3Lib::Tag.new(file)
  # ... display the info we found...
  display= "#{file} - #{tag.title} from #{tag.album} by #{tag.artist}"

  # ... update the info if necessary...
  if $options[:set].length>0
    $options[:set].each { |key, value| tag.send("#{key}=",value) }
    tag.update!
    display << " ...updating... "
  end

  # ... and finally print out the result.
  puts display
end
```

Save this file as id3tool.rb. Next we'll need to get an MP3 file to test it—download the file test.mp3 from the following URL:

```
http://practicalrubygems.com/test.mp3
```

Next let's test our tool by displaying the ID3 tag from this file:

```
ruby id3tool.rb test.mp3
```

```
test.mp3 - Demo Song from Test Album by Test Band
```

As you can see, it will display the ID3 tag information—in this case, the file is "Demo Song" from *Test Album* by Test Band. If you'd like, you can also try it on other MP3 files.

Next let's try setting an attribute using the following command:

```
ruby id3tool.rb test.mp3 -s "artist=John Doe"
```

```
test.mp3 - Demo Song from Test Album by Test Band ...updating...
```

```
ruby id3tool.rb test.mp3
```

```
test.mp3 - Demo Song from Test Album by John Doe
```

As you can see, our program will successfully update the ID3 tag. In this case, our demo only sets tags, but you could perform any substitutions—for example, you could have a database with a list of common artist misspellings, and automatically load each MP3, check for misspellings, and replace them as necessary.

You can also use this program on more than one MP3 at a time; if you have multiple files on your hard drive, you can retag multiple files at once. For example, suppose you had a number of files whose name started with test_artist, and which were tagged with the artist Test Artist, but should be tagged Example Artist. You can fix the files as follows:

```
ruby id3tool.rb test_artist_*.mp3 -s "artist=Example Artist"
```

```
test_artist_first_song.mp3 - Test Song from Example Album by Test Artist
..updating...
test_artist_second_song.mp3 - Test Song from Example Album by Test Artist
...updating...
```

This example won't rename the files—it will just redo the tags, so they will still have the name test_artist in the filename. Of course, you could use id3lib-ruby to modify the script to rename the files based on their ID3 tags.

Dissecting the Example

Let's take a look at a few important lines from Listing 29-1.

```
tag = ID3Lib::Tag.new(file)
```

This line loads the tag information from each file we're processing; afterward, we can access the various attributes as methods, as we do next:

```
display= "#{file} - #{tag.title} from #{tag.album} by #{tag.artist}"
```

This line places a short description of the file and its ID3 attributes in the display variable —we'll print it at the end of the loop:

```
if $options[:set].length>0
    $options[:set].each { |key, value| tag.send("#{key}=",value) }
    tag.update!
    display << " ...updating... "
end
puts display
```

First, this block of code checks if any attributes need to be set; if so, we'll loop through each of the options and set them. (The technique used to set them is somewhat tricky: it's calling the method named after the option name and an equals sign, so that if you are setting the `artist` attribute, it calls the `artist=` method.)

Next we call the `tag.update!` method—this writes our changes out to the file.

Finally, we print out the `display` variable, which contains the name of the file, a few of its ID3 attributes, and whether the file was updated.

Conclusion

id3lib-ruby is a powerful, easy-to-use way to manipulate ID3 tags. Of course, you won't always need to use it, but when you are dealing with MP3 files—particularly with large numbers of them—it's an invaluable tool.

## CHAPTER 30

Shortening URLs with shorturl

Shorturl is an easy-to-use Ruby library for accessing URL-shortening services such as TinyURL.com, which can take long URLs and map them into smaller ones. For example, the following is a link to this book's Amazon.com page:

```
http://www.amazon.com/o/ASIN/1590598113/ref=pd_rvi_gw_1/105-4006969-0930819
```

The following is an equivalent TinyURL.com link:

```
http://tinyurl.com/yk4che
```

As you can see, the second link is much shorter; it's easier to paste into chat rooms, e-mails, and so forth. Additionally, some e-mail clients don't correctly handle URLs longer than a single line—they erroneously split up the URL so they won't work correctly.

You can use the shorturl functionality in a variety of ways. For example, you could have a message board that automatically replaces complicated URLs with much shorter ones. You could do much the same for a blog, photo gallery, or virtually any other kind of site. You can use shorturl for outside sites too; for example, if you had a site that aggregates news from a variety of other sites, you could use shorturl to give a short version of the URL for every news story—that way, your visitors could easily share the stories with their friends and coworkers. In fact, that's a particularly good example; since you have no control of the format of the links of the external sites, they may be extremely long and complicated.

How Does It Work?

shorturl allows you to use UR- shortening services through a Ruby interface. Normally you'd use these services via a Web browser, so shorturl uses the Ruby standard library Net/HTTP to simulate a Web browser. It supports a number of services, including http://tinyurl.com, http://shortify.com, and http://rubyurl.com. You can get the list of supported services by calling the WWW::ShortURL.valid_services function.

As a brief example, we could use the following Ruby code to shorten a URL:

```
require 'shorturl'
puts WWW::ShortURL.shorten('http://example.com/somelongpath?someparameters=true')
```

That will print out a shortened version of the http://example.com/… URL. We could add an additional parameter to the call to .shorten that would specify the service we'd like to use. By default it uses rubyurl, but we could use a different service such as TinyURL like so:

```
require 'shorturl'
puts WWW::ShortURL.shorten('http://example.com/somelongpath?someparameters=true',
    :tinyurl)
```

The services are very similar, and the biggest difference between them is the resulting domain name—rubyurl URLs start with rubyurl.com, tinyurl URLs start with tinyurl.com, and so forth.

In any case, it's pretty straightforward to use the shorturl gem. You can get the full documentation here:

```
http://www.gemjack.com/gems/shorturl-0.8.3/index.html
```

The following shell command lets you install shorturl:

```
gem install shorturl
```

Shortening RSS Feeds with shorturl

Our example script will use the shorturl gem to create shortened links for an entire RSS feed —specifically, an RSS feed with the Google Blog Search results for the phrase "Ruby on Rails."

It will also use the Camping gem as the Web framework, and the feedtools gem for retrieving the results—see Chapters 7 and 10, respectively, for more details. You can install them with the following two commands:

```
gem install feedtools
gem install camping
```

Listing 30-1 provides the code for this example.

Listing 30-1. *Blog Search with shorturl (shortblogs.rb)*

```
require 'camping'
require 'feed_tools'

# URI is a module built into Ruby for manipulating URIs;
# we'll use it for encoding our data into our
# Google search URL. You can get more details here:
#
# http://www.ruby-doc.org/stdlib/libdoc/uri/rdoc/index.html
#

require 'uri'
require 'shorturl'

Camping.goes :ShortBlogs
```

```
# This module contains our single view, frontpage.

module ShortBlogs::Controllers
  class Frontpage < R '/'
    def get
      render :frontpage
    end
  end
end

module ShortBlogs::Views

  @@search_term= 'ruby on rails'
  @@number_of_results = 15

  def frontpage
    h1 "Blogs about #{@@search_term.titlecase}"

    # Create a Google blog search URL from our
    # search term, and then pull the RSS items
    # from it.

    url =  "http://blogsearch.google.com/blogsearch_feeds?"
    url << "hl=en&q=#{URI.encode(@@search_term)}&ie=utf-8"
    url << "&num=#{@@number_of_results}&output=rss&scoring=d"

    feed=FeedTools::Feed.open(url)

      # Loop through each item, and
      # print out a shortened link to it.

      feed.items.each do |feed_item|
        url=WWW::ShortURL.shorten(feed_item.link)
        div do
          a(:href=>url) {feed_item.title} << ' - ' << url
        end
      end

    end
end
```

Save this example as shortblogs.rb. You can use the following command to run the example:

```
camping shortblogs.rb -h 127.0.0.1
```

```
** Camping running on 127.0.0.1:3301.
```

Note The -h 127.0.0.1 argument is not required, but it makes Camping bind only to our loopback address; this means that only we can access our application. (Omit the -h 127.0.0.1 argument if you want other hosts to be able to access this or any other Camping application.)

At this point, you should be able to point your Web browser at http://127.0.0.1:3301 and see the application.

Dissecting the Example

Let's take a look at a the core of this application—the lines that actually loop through the results, shorten the URLs, and display them to the user:

```
feed.items.each do |feed_item|
  url=WWW::ShortURL.shorten(feed_item.link)
  div do
    a(:href=>url) {feed_item.title} << ' - ' << url
  end
end
```

The feed.items array contains all of the items for our RSS feed; we then use the WWW::ShortURL.shorten method to shorten the link. The next three lines create a div element with a link it in, followed by a line that contains a dash and then the URL repeated as text so that it can be copied and pasted easily.

Note that we have parentheses around the arguments to the a method—specifically, (:href=>url). Otherwise the block {feed_item.title} would be interpreted as belonging to the keyword url—which would make it a method, not a variable. Since there isn't a url method, it will raise a *method not found* error.

Conclusion

As you can see, the shorturl gem is an easy way to reduce the length of links by using external link-shortening services. Often, you can't control the format of outside links, and using shorturl can make painfully long links manageable.

■ ■ ■

## CHAPTER 31

Creating Standalone Ruby Applications with rubyscript2exe

rubyscript2exe is a utility that creates standalone Ruby applications for the Windows, OS X, and Linux platforms.

Ruby programs require a Ruby interpreter; with rubyscript2exe, you can include the Ruby interpreter and your script in a single file, which can be executed by the end user just like any other program. It can also include Ruby libraries, such as the gems covered in this book—as a result, you can use it as a complete solution for distributing complex Ruby scripts.

Additionally, since rubyscript2exe uses your local copy of Ruby and of all of your gems, you can be sure that your Ruby script will run as intended—a newer or later version of Ruby installed on the end user's machine won't break your code, since it's running your Ruby interpreter.

As you can imagine, rubyscript2exe can be quite useful; you could use rubyscript2exe to distribute packaged software written in Ruby, for example; you could also use it to create a simple script to perform an administrative task—say, patching a security hole—on a number of users workstations and then distribute it via CD-R media. The end users could then easily run it by double-clicking on an icon. Because of rubyscript2exe, neither example would require that the end users have Ruby or any gems installed.

How Does It Work?

rubyscript2exe creates a single, combined executable consisting of your script, the Ruby interpreter and standard libraries, and any Ruby code you use, such as Ruby gems or other libraries. Note that it is not a compiler—when you run the combined executable, it extracts the Ruby interpreter, libraries, your code, and its dependencies into a temporary directory and runs it from there.

Additionally, it uses the version of the gems, libraries, and Ruby interpreter that you have installed on your development computer—it can't create, say, a Linux executable on a Windows machine or vice versa. Also, even if there is a newer version of Ruby or of a given gem on the end user's machine, a rubyscript2exe executable will use the version it was created with.

Finally, since rubyscript2exe isn't a compiler, it will be a larger executable than would be produced by a Ruby-to-bytecode compiler—it includes all of the files rather than producing only what's necessary. However, this is also a strength: a Ruby compiler would possibly introduce bugs and inconsistencies, but when you run a rubyscript2exe script, you are running the program as the author intended—in fact, you are running it with the exact version of Ruby he used to develop it.

In any case, you can get the full rubyscript2exe gem documentation here:

```
http://www.erikveen.dds.nl/rubyscript2exe/index.html
```

You can use the following command to install rubyscript2exe:

```
gem install rubyscript2exe
```

Note You'll need to take an additional step under Mac OS X; you'll either need to compile eee_darwin or download a precompiled version. (Typically, the precompiled route is easier.) You can find out the details at the rubyscript2exe homepage:

```
http://www.erikveen.dds.nl/rubyscript2exe/index.html#toc_6.1.0
```

Packaging the id3tool Script with rubyscript2exe

For this example, we're going to package the id3tool mass-tagging MP3 script found in Chapter 29 into a standalone executable. This has the advantage of not needing Ruby installed on the system that is running the executable. We're going to make a small alteration to the code—modifying the script so that it won't run fully when it is being compiled—so we'll use the code provided in Listing 31-1 rather than the code from Chapter 29.

Listing 31-1. *Standalone ID3 Retagger (id3tool_rs2e.rb)*

```ruby
require 'id3lib'
require 'optparse'
require 'rubyscript2exe'

exit if RUBYSCRIPT2EXE.is_compiling?

$options = {}
$options[:set]={}

opt=OptionParser.new do |opts|
    opts.banner = "Usage: #{$0} file1 file2 file3... "

    opts.on("-s", "--set OPTION=VALUE",
            "Sets the ID3 option OPTION to VALUE.") do |options|
      option, value = options.split(/=/)
```

```
      (puts 'Please set the ID3 in the format option=value.';
            exit) unless option and value
      $options[:set][option] = value

    end
    opts.on_tail("-h", "--help",
                  "Show this message") { puts opts.help; exit }

end
opt.parse!

(puts "Please specify one or more mp3 files to work with.";
      exit) unless ARGV.length > 0
ARGV.each do |file|
  tag = ID3Lib::Tag.new(file)

  display= "#{file} - #{tag.title} from #{tag.album} by #{tag.artist}"

  if $options[:set].length>0
    $options[:set].each { |key, value| tag.send("#{key}=",value) }
    tag.update!
    display << " ...updating... "
  end

  puts display
end
```

Save this example as id3tool_rs2e.rb. Next we'll need to convert this into a standalone executable using the following command:

```
rubyscript2exe id3tool_rs2e.rb
```

```
Tracing id3tool_rs2e ...
Gathering files...
Copying files...
Creating id3tool_rs2e.exe ...
```

Next let's test our new executable—note that your command will be different depending on your environment: Your executable will be named id3tool_rs2e.exe for Windows, id3tool_rs2e_darwin for OS X, and id3tool_rs2e_linux for Linux; of course, you can always rename the executable after it's created. (The name of the executable is listed on the last line of the output of the rubyscript2exe command.)

We need a test MP3 file to verify that the program is working, so download the file test.mp3 from the following URL:

```
http://practicalrubygems.com/test.mp3
```

Next use one of the following commands.
Use this command under Windows:

```
id3tool_rs2e.exe test.mp3
```

Use this command under Linux:

```
./id3tool_rs2e_linux test.mp3
```

Use this command under OS X:

```
./id3tool_rs2e_darwin test.mp3
```

You should get this result on all platforms:

```
test.mp3 - Test from test by test
```

You can now copy the executable to a machine without Ruby or id3lib installed—it will still work.

Dissecting the Example

Let's take a look at a few important lines from Listing 31-1.

```
require 'id3lib'
require 'optparse'
require 'rubyscript2exe'

exit if RUBYSCRIPT2EXE.is_compiling?
```

When we use the rubyscript2exe command to create the executable, this is the only code that actually runs; the exit if RUBYSCRIPT2EXE.is_compiling? line causes the script to exit at that point if it's a rubyscript2exe trial run. (In a trial run rubyscript2exe runs our program as a test; when it does so, it checks all of the require statements to find all of the gems and other libraries that our program uses.)

■**Caution** During a trial run, rubyscript2exe really only needs to see the require statements; the rest of the program just wastes CPU cycles, and in some cases may even be dangerous—for example, you might want to use rubyscript2exe on a program that empties a database, but you might not want to actually empty the database when you create the executable. In that case, you can use the exit if RUBYSCRIPT2EXE.is_compiling? line of code to prevent that from happening. In other words, the exit if RUBYSCRIPT2EXE.is_compiling? line exits the program early during the compilation of the executable. (Note that you don't need the require 'rubyscript2exe' line if you don't need the ability to exit during the compilation of the executable; in that case, you can safely omit the last two lines in Listing 31-1.) Additionally, the RUBYSCRIPT2EXE module provides you with a few other flags—check out the rubyscript2exe homepage at http://www.erikveen.dds.nl/rubyscript2exe/index.html for more details.

Special rubyscript2exe Command-Line Options

When our compiled executable is run, rubyscript2exe will perform some argument processing before our compiled script receives the arguments; there are three special arguments that
have special behavior. If rubyscript2exe detects one of these arguments, rubyscript2exe will
intercept it. (Other arguments—just like the ones we used in Listing 31-1 when we passed the
name of the MP3 file—work fine, though.)

For example, the following command will list the contents of our executable:

```
id3tool_rs2e --eee-list
```

```
d bin
f bin\digest.so (20557)
f bin\etc.so (20551)
f bin\fcntl.so (20555)
f bin\id3lib_api.so (690688)
f bin\LIBEAY32.dll (842752)
f bin\msvcrt-ruby18.dll (905276)
f bin\MSVCRT.DLL (290869)
f bin\openssl.so (180303)
f bin\ruby.exe (20531)
f bin\rubyw.exe (20532)
f bin\sha2.so (28752)
f bin\SSLEAY32.dll (148992)
..snip...
```

This example is for Windows—your files will vary on other operating systems, and your
command will be different (./id3tool_rs2e_linux --eee-list for Linux and
./id3tool_rs2e_darwin --eee-list for OS X).

You can also use the --eee-just-extract option to extract all of these files into the current
directory; the --eee-info option displays information about the executable—size, number of
files, and so forth. Most of the time, you won't need to use these special options, but they are
available for debugging purposes. You can find out more about these command-line options
at the following URL:

```
http://www.erikveen.dds.nl/rubyscript2exe/index.html#3.2.0
```

> **■Note** The eee part of the --eee... options stands for Environment Embedding Executable; this is the
> part of rubyscript2exe that actually packs and unpacks the executable. It can also be used for other pur-
> poses, such as distributing scripts in other languages or for creating standalone Ruby installations; you can
> find out more about it here:
>
> ```
> http://www.erikveen.dds.nl/eee/index.html
> ```

Conclusion

As you can see, it's easy to produce a standalone application using `rubyscript2exe`—even if that application has external dependencies. Although the Ruby world is large and varied, you will often have to interface with non-developers and others without Ruby installations; when that happens, `rubyscript2exe` can be a powerful tool.

■ ■ ■

## CHAPTER 32

Cleaning Dirty HTML with tidy

HTML is a standard file format for pages that can be viewed in a Web browser. There are a great many ways to create HTML pages, ranging from graphical editors such as Dreamweaver to text editors such as Notepad, Emacs, or Vim. Unfortunately, graphical editors generally do not work well with most Web frameworks, including Rails, and HTML produced with text editors may not be standards-compliant; it may lack closing tags or use invalid tag combinations or attributes. Additionally, some graphical editors produce bad HTML; the problem is exacerbated by the fact that modern browsers are very tolerant of HTML that is not standards-compliant, so very incorrect HTML will often still display properly.

Unfortunately, if you are writing tools that need to read HTML files, you may not have the same flexibility—you might need to have well-formed HTML. tidy can help you with this. For example, if you have to read handcrafted HTML from the Internet, you can't be sure it will be standards-compliant, but you can use tidy to deal with badly formatted HTML. tidy has other applications as well—for example, if you had a Rails application that let the user enter his own HTML, you can't be sure he'll format his tags properly. You could use tidy to reformat the user's HTML—ensuring that your site produces proper HTML, which lets you have support for the widest audience possible, since not all browsers can handle bad HTML easily. Bad HTML can also cause problems with your layout—an extra ending tag can prematurely end a container, which can seriously damage your page's appearance.

tidy is a Ruby library for handling improperly formatted HTML. It can also be used to make HTML source easier to read; for example, you can take a long HTML file without line breaks and use tidy to spread them out over multiple lines.

How Does It Work?

The tidy gem uses an external library, called HTML Tidy, to clean the HTML. Specifically, it provides an object-oriented Ruby wrapper around HTML Tidy; all of the options that you can pass to HTML Tidy you can also pass to tidy. This includes the ability to correct HTML mistakes, thereby hopefully making a non-standards-compliant HTML page standards-compliant and therefore more compatible; it also includes purely visual formatting options, such as automatically indenting the code, which can make the HTML code much easier to read.

In particular, HTML Tidy fixes a number of common mistakes automatically. For example, `<li>` tags without a closing `</li>` are automatically closed and DOCTYPE declarations are automatically added. It can also make quite a few other changes. You can find out more about the particular changes that HTML Tidy can make for you at the following URL:

```
http://www.w3.org/People/Raggett/tidy/
```

■**Note** For the following examples, you'll need to change the `Tidy.path` = line to reflect the path to your tidy `.dll` or `.so` file.

Consider the following code, which you could use to turn an HTML fragment into a full page:

```
require 'tidy'

Tidy.path = './tidy.dll'
dirty_html_fragment='<h1>This is a very important business header</h2> ' <<
                    '<p>"Quite  important," said a leading businessman ' <<
                    'when asked about this paragraph. "I never leave ' <<
                    'home without it." '
clean_html_page= Tidy.open() { |tidy|  tidy.clean(dirty_html_fragment)}

puts clean_html_page
```

Running this code produces the following result:

```
<!DOCTYPE html PUBLIC "-//W3C//DTD HTML 3.2//EN">
<html>
<head>
<meta name="generator" content=
"HTML Tidy for Windows (vers 14 February 2006), see www.w3.org">
<title></title>
</head>
<body>
<h1>This is a very important business header</h1>
<p>"Quite important," said a leading businessman when asked about
this paragraph. "I never leave home without it."</p>
</body>
</html>
```

Note how `tidy` added the `<!DOCTYPE>` declaration and the `<head>` and `<body>` tags, and how it closed our unclosed paragraph tag. It also detected that the `<h1>` tag was incorrectly closed with an `</h2>` tag and replaced the `</h2>` with the appropriate `</h1>` tag.

You can also pass optional parameters like this:

```
require 'tidy'

Tidy.path = './tidy.dll'
dirty_html_fragment='<h1>This is a very important business header</h2> ' <<
                    '<p>"Quite  important," said a leading businessman ' <<
                    'when asked about this paragraph. "I never leave ' <<
                    'home without it." '
```

```ruby
clean_html_page= Tidy.open('indent'=>'auto',
                           'uppercase-tags'=>'yes') do |tidy|
  tidy.clean(dirty_html_fragment)
end

puts clean_html_page
```

Running this code produces the following result:

```html
<!DOCTYPE html PUBLIC "-//W3C//DTD HTML 3.2//EN">

<HTML>
<HEAD>
  <META name="generator" content=
  "HTML Tidy for Windows (vers 14 February 2006), see www.w3.org">

  <TITLE></TITLE>
</HEAD>

<BODY>
  <H1>This is a very important business header</H1>

  <P>"Quite important," said a leading businessman when asked about
  this paragraph. "I never leave home without it."</P>
</BODY>
</HTML>
```

Note that in this example, we use two options: 'indent'=>'auto' and 'uppercase-tags'=>'yes'. The first lets tidy use automatic indenting; the second directs it to use uppercase HTML tags. (Some people prefer uppercase tags stylistic reasons, but they are discouraged in the W3C HTML 4 standard and not permitted in XHTML.)

There are various other formatting options; you can find out more about HTML Tidy at the following URL:

```
http://tidy.sourceforge.net/
```

You can use the following command to install tidy:

```
gem install tidy
```

This requires you to have the HTML Tidy library installed on your system; you can get it at http://tidy.sourceforge.net/.

Under Windows, you'll need to the install the DLL version of the HTML Tidy library; make a note of where you unzip it, since you'll need it to use tidy.

Under Mac OS X and Linux, you'll need to compile the HTML Tidy library from source; once you've done so, you can get the path to the HTML Tidy library using the following command:

```
locate tidylib.so
```

You can learn more about the `tidy` gem at the following URL:

```
http://tidy.rubyforge.org/
```

Tidying Up HTML on the Web with tidy

Our example (Listing 32-1) will be a small Web application that will let us paste HTML code into a text box, press a button, and have it display the resulting clean HTML.

Our application will use the `Camping` Web framework; this framework provides us with support for easily creating Web applications. Chapter 7 has more details on how the `Camping` Web framework works. You can install the `Camping` gem as follows:

```
gem install camping
```

Listing 32-1. *A Web Application to Clean HTML (webtidy.rb)*

```ruby
%w(rubygems camping tidy).each { |lib| require lib }


#
# Set the path for our Tidy DLL or .so file.
#
# The default here is for a DLL in the current directory under Windows;
# If you've put it elsewhere, you'll need to enter the value in the line below.
#
# Under Linux or Mac OS X, you can use the command 'locate libtidy.so'
# to retreieve the path to Tidy.
#

Tidy.path = './tidy.dll'


Camping.goes :WebTidy


module WebTidy::Controllers

  #
  # Homepage for the application.
  #
  class Index < R '/'
    def get
      if @input[:html]
        @html_output= Tidy.open('indent'=>'auto') do |tidy|
          tidy.clean(@input[:html])
        end
      end
      render :homepage
    end
  end
```

```
end

#
# Contains all of the views for the application.
#

module WebTidy::Views
  TIME_FORMAT="%H:%M:%S"

  #
  # View which shows the homepage.
  #

  def homepage
    p 'Input Text:'
    form do
      textarea  @input[:html], :cols=>45, :rows=>5, :name=>:html
      br :clear->:left
      input :type=>:submit, :value=>'Send'
    end

    if @html_output
       textarea @html_output, :cols=>45, :rows=>5, :name=>:html
    end
  end

  def layout
    html do
      head do
        title 'WebTidy'
      end
      body do
        h1 "welcome to webtidy"
        div.content do
          self << yield
        end
      end
    end
  end
end
```

Save this file as webtidy.rb. You can run the application as follows:

```
camping webtidy.rb
```

You should be able to see the application at the following URL:

```
http://localhost:3301/
```

Next, enter the following HTML into the Input HTML box:

```
<h2>List Of Things I Don't Have</h2>
<ul>
<li>A moon rock
<li>A firm grasp of Spanish
<li>An orangutan
```

Click the Tidy button. You should get the following HTML response:

```
<!DOCTYPE html PUBLIC "-//W3C//DTD HTML 3.2//EN">

<html>
<head>
  <meta name="generator" content=
  "HTML Tidy for Windows (vers 14 February 2006), see www.w3.org">

  <title></title>
</head>

<body>
  <h2>List Of Things I Don't Have</h2>

  <ul>
    <li>A moon rock</li>

    <li>A firm grasp of Spanish</li>

    <li>An orangutan</li>
  </ul>
</body>
</html>
```

As you can see, tidy fixed the various mistakes: it added the ending </li> tags and the ending </ul> tag, and made a number of other changes. In fact, the output is valid HTML 3.2; if you'd like, you can test it using the W3C validator at the following URL:

```
http://validator.w3.org/
```

Dissecting the Example

One of the lines at the top of Listing 32-1 is very important:

```
Tidy.path = './tidy.dll'
```

This line tells the tidy gem where the HTML Tidy library can be found; if you are running Windows and your DLL file is not in the same directory as the script from Listing 32-1, you'll need to change this line.

If you are running Linux or Mac OS X, you'll need to change this line; the library will be called libtidy.so, so you can locate it using the following command:

```
locate libtidy.so
```

Let's take a look at the portion of our example that does the actual HTML cleaning:

```
@html_output= Tidy.open('indent'=>'auto') do |tidy|
  tidy.clean(@input[:html])
end
```

This line creates a Tidy object using the .open call, and then inside of the block we call the .clean method of the Tidy object. That's essentially the bulk of the typical use of tidy.

There are other options—for example, tidy produces an error log with all details on the errors it has changed, and you can retrieve these errors with the .errors method, but typically that won't be particularly important. If you'd like more details on such options, consult the tidy site:

```
http://tidy.sourceforge.net/
```

Conclusion

tidy is a powerful utility for fixing and visually formatting HTML, and, fortunately, it's easy to use. Whether you are filtering the output from a Web application or scraping HTML sites with questionable HTML, tidy can make your life much easier.

## CHAPTER 33

Parsing XML with xml-simple

XML is a standard file format for exchanging data. It's an SGML-based markup language, and it appears similar to HTML. xml-simple is a Ruby library for parsing XML. It's a port of the Perl xml-simple library, and it has a similar interface, which is easier to use than Ruby's built-in REXML library. (You can get more information on REXML at http://www.germane-software.com/software/rexml/.)

You can use xml-simple to work with any program or site that can use XML as a data-exchange format. For example, RSS, which is a format for exchanging news, is an XML-based file format, and you could parse RSS with xml-simple. Microsoft Access and Microsoft Excel can both import and export XML; additionally, all OpenOffice documents are stored as XML compressed in a ZIP file. XML is also commonly available from a wide variety of websites, as it's commonly used to transfer information pertinent to products, affiliates, and other commerce-related data.

How Does It Work?

xml-simple is, as the name implies, a very simple XML parser. It provides just two methods: xml_in and xml_out. The former reads XML from either a file or from a string and returns a hash that represents the XML file. The latter does the opposite: it takes a hash and returns a string of XML that represents the hash.

Reading an XML File with xml_in

Consider the following XML file:

```
<items>
  <item>
    <description>Dangerous Stingray Holding Tank</description>
    <price>$45,000.00</price>
  </item>

  <item>
    <description>Perilous Stingray Holding Tank</description>
    <price>$35,000.00</price>
  </item>

  <item>
```

```
    <description>Pacifistic Stingray Holding Tank</description>
    <price>$20,000.00</price>
  </item>

</items>
```

The xml_in method would return a hash that looks like this:

```
{"item"=>
    [
      {"price"=>["$45,000.00"],
  "description"=>["Dangerous Stingray Holding Tank"]},

      {"price"=>["$35,000.00"],
       "description"=>["Perilous Stingray Holding
 Tank"]},

      {"price"=>["$20,000.00"],
       "description"=>["Pacifistic Stingray Holding
Tank"]}
    ]
}
```

If we saved the sample XML file to input.xml, we could run the following code:

```
require 'xmlsimple'

XmlSimple.xml_in('input.xml')['item'].each do |item|
  puts "#{item['description']}, #{item['price']}"
end
```

Running this code produces this result:

```
Dangerous Stingray Holding Tank, $45,000.00
Perilous Stingray Holding Tank, $35,000.00
Pacifistic Stingray Holding Tank, $20,000.00
```

As you can see, the xml_in method turns XML into a very easy-to-use hash. You can use the following shell command to install xml-simple:

```
gem install xml-simple
```

For the full details about the xml-simple gem, visit the following URL:

```
http://xml-simple.rubyforge.org/
```

Converting a Hash to XML with xml_out

The xml_out method does the opposite of the xml_in method—it takes a hash like the one we just looked at and turns it into an XML string. You could use xml_out as follows:

```
require 'xmlsimple'

hash= {:items=>{"item"=>
    [
      {"price"=>["$45,000.00"],
  "description"=>["Dangerous Stingray Holding Tank"]},

      {"price"=>["$35,000.00"],
       "description"=>["Perilous Stingray Holding
 Tank"]},

      {"price"=>["$20,000.00"],
      "description"=>["Pacifistic Stingray Holding
 Tank"]}
  ]
}}


puts XmlSimple.xml_out(hash, 'keeproot' => true)
```

Running that code produces this result:

```
<items>
  <item>
    <price>$45,000.00</price>
    <description>Dangerous Stingray Holding Tank</description>
  </item>
  <item>
    <price>$35,000.00</price>
    <description>Perilous Stingray Holding
 Tank</description>
  </item>
  <item>
    <price>$20,000.00</price>
    <description>Pacifistic Stingray Holding
 Tank</description>
  </item>
</items>
```

As you can see, the xml_out method is an easy way to produce valid XML from a Ruby hash. Note that the keeproot option prevents XmlSimple from adding an additional root node; the advantage of this behavior is that since the document can have only one root node, you don't need to add a root node to use xml_out on any arbitrary array.

Tracking OpenSSL Vulnerabilities with xml-simple

OpenSSL.org publishes vulnerability advisories in XML format. These can be important—if you are running a vulnerable version of OpenSSL, you might end up with security breach that is likely to cost you headaches at best and significant amounts of money at worst.

Since the data is in XML format, it includes not only a brief textual description of the vulnerability, but also a machine-readable list of version numbers. Therefore, our example (Listing 33-1) will take a version number on the command line, connect to http://www.openssl.org/, see if any of the vulnerabilities apply to our version, and print any that apply. The source XML file looks like this:

```
<security updated="20060928">

    <issue public="20020730">
      <cve name="2002-0656"/>
      <affects base="0.9.6" version="0.9.6"/>
      <affects base="0.9.6" version="0.9.6a"/>
      <affects base="0.9.6" version="0.9.6b"/>
      <affects base="0.9.6" version="0.9.6c"/>
      <affects base="0.9.6" version="0.9.6d"/>

      <fixed base="0.9.6" version="0.9.6e" date="20020730"/>
      <advisory url="http://www.openssl.org/news/secadv_20020730.txt"/>

      <reported source="OpenSSL Group (A.L. Digital)"/>
      <description>
A buffer overflow allowed remote attackers to execute
arbitrary code by sending a large client master key in SSL2 or a
large session ID in SSL3.
    </description>
</issue>
...
```

Essentially, our code wants to find all of the issue elements—which are contained in a parent security element—and determine whether each one has an affect element with a version attribute equal to our version of OpenSSL.

Listing 33-1. *Checking for OpenSSL Vulnerabilities (check_openssl_vulnerabilities.rb)*

```
require 'xmlsimple'
require 'net/http'
require 'yaml'

# If they did not specify a version to search
# for, exit with a brief message.
(puts "usage: #{$0} version" ; exit ) if ARGV.length!=1

my_version=ARGV[0]
```

```ruby
# This is the URL where we are going to
# download the vulnerability list.

url='http://www.openssl.org/news/vulnerabilities.xml'

# Next, we actually download the file
# and save the results in the data variable.

xml_data = Net::HTTP.get_response(URI.parse(url)).body
data = XmlSimple.xml_in(xml_data)

data['issue'].each do |vulnerability|
  outstring=''
  affected=false
  # If the vulnerability affects at least one
  # openSSL version - which should always
  # be true, but we check just in case.

  if vulnerability['affects']
    vulnerability['affects'].each do |affected|
      if affected['version']==my_version
        affected=true
        # If it affects our version, we'll
        # print it out below.
      end
    end
  end

  if affected
    (outstring <<
      "from #{vulnerability['reported'][0]['source']} "
    ) unless vulnerability['reported'].nil?

    (outstring <<
      "at #{vulnerability['advisory'][0]['url']} "
    ) unless vulnerability['advisory'].nil?
  end

  # If we have something to print out, then
  # print it out.

  puts "Advisory #{ outstring}" unless outstring==''
end
```

Save this file as check_openssl_vulnerabilities.rb. You can run the application as follows:

```ruby
ruby check_openssl_vulnerabilities.rb 3.0
```

Executing this command produces the following output:

```
Advisory from OpenSSL Group (A.L. Digital) at http://www.openssl.org/news/secadv
_20020730.txt
Advisory from OpenSSL Group (A.L. Digital) at http://www.openssl.org/news/secadv
_20020730.txt
Advisory at http://www.openssl.org/news/secadv_20030219.txt
Advisory at http://www.openssl.org/news/secadv_20030319.txt
Advisory at http://www.openssl.org/news/secadv_20030317.txt
Advisory from NISCC at http://www.openssl.org/news/secadv_20030930.txt
Advisory from NISCC at http://www.openssl.org/news/secadv_20030930.txt
Advisory from NISCC at http://www.openssl.org/news/secadv_20030930.txt
Advisory from Novell at http://www.openssl.org/news/secadv_20031104.txt
Advisory from OpenSSL group at http://www.openssl.org/news/secadv_20040317.txt
Advisory from OpenSSL group at http://www.openssl.org/news/secadv_20030317.txt
Advisory from OpenSSL group (Stephen Henson) at http://www.openssl.org/news/
secadv_20040317.txt
Advisory from researcher at http://www.openssl.org/news/secadv_20051011.txt
Advisory from openssl at http://www.openssl.org/news/secadv_20060905.txt
Advisory from openssl at http://www.openssl.org/news/secadv_20060928.txt
Advisory from openssl at http://www.openssl.org/news/secadv_20060928.txt
Advisory from openssl at http://www.openssl.org/news/secadv_20060928.txt
Advisory from openssl at http://www.openssl.org/news/secadv_20060928.txt
```

As you can see, our application connected to openssl.org, retrieved the results that affected our version of OpenSSL, and displayed them.

Dissecting the Example

Let's look at the code that iterates through all of the issue elements, each of which represents one security vulnerability.

```
data['issue'].each do |vulnerability|
```

As you can see, it's pretty easy to do—we use the hash returned by xml_in just like any other hash. The expression data['issue'] returns an array that contains all of the elements named issue; we then use the .each method to iterate through it. Note that the top-level element— security—is excluded automatically because XML documents always contain a top-level container.

For each issue we find, we need to check if the vulnerability affects our particular version:

```
affected = false

if vulnerability['affects']
  vulnerability['affects'].each do |affected|
    if affected['version']==my_version
      affected=true
```

```
      end
    end
end
```

Note the second line here—it checks if the XML element contains an `affects` element. All of the `issue` elements should contain an `affects` element, but we want to ensure our program can proceed even if there is an invalid `issue` element; otherwise, it may crash upon encountering the invalid `issue` element and not catch an important vulnerability later.

```
if affected
    (outstring << "from #{vulnerability['reported'][0]['source']} "
      ) unless vulnerability['reported'].nil?

    (outstring << "at #{vulnerability['advisory'][0]['url']} "
      ) unless vulnerability['advisory'].nil?

    puts "Advisory #{outstring}"
end
```

The first line here checks if our `affected` flag was set to true; if so, we need to construct a warning message and print it. First we try to print the source of the information if there isn't a reported element; afterward, we print the URL of the advisory—assuming that one is provided, of course.

Note that the expression `vulnerability['reported'][0]['source']` refers to the source element or attribute in the first `reported` element; typically, we have only one, but `xml-simple` will always place it in an array in any case—it has no way of knowing the structure of our data.

Conclusion

`xml-simple` is an easy-to-use library for reading and writing XML. It's not always appropriate—it does not offer XPath support, for example—but code written using `xml-simple` is easy to read and maintain. As a result, `xml-simple` can simplify complex XML parsing routines, leaving you to concentrate on the unique part of your application.

PART 3

■ ■ ■

Creating Gems

All applications involve custom code. By creating and packaging your custom code, you'll have access to the power of the RubyGems system for deployment and dependency resolution, combined with the debugging power of the thriving Ruby community.

■ ■ ■

## CHAPTER 34

Creating Our Own Gems

In this chapter, you'll learn how to create your own RubyGems. This can be useful for a variety of reasons: It gives you access to the gem-dependency system, it helps reusability between multiple programs, and more. For example, suppose you ran an ecommerce site that sold CDs, and the custom code you wrote to calculate shipping costs was used by several in-house programs; you could package the code as a gem, and then you could reuse it easily among the different programs.

This chapter covers how to create a gemspec, what the various fields mean, how to use the gem build command to create a gem package, and what you can do when things go wrong.

What Is Inside a Gem?

In Chapter 1 I covered installing gems; we used the gem utility to automatically download and set them up. However, to create our own gems, we'll need to know what the gem files themselves consist of. Specifically, gems are .gem files; .gem files are essentially archives, like a Zip or TAR file. This archive contains all of the files the gem uses. Typically, the archive contains subdirectories: a lib/ directory containing the library source, a test/ directory containing tests, and so forth. The structure of the gem is up to the developer. At the very least, there'll also be a README file with a short description and licensing information. A gem also contains some metadata, like the name of the developer, the homepage of the gem, and so forth. Both the list of files used in the gem and the metadata come from a gemspec.

What's a Gemspec?

Before we create our own gem, we must create a custom *gem specification*, commonly called a gemspec. The gemspec specifies various things about the gem: what it's called, its version number, what files are inside of it, who wrote it, what platforms it runs on, and so forth. This specification comes in the form of a Ruby script that creates a Gem::Specification object. Once you have this gemspec, you can use the gem build command to create a .gem file from it.

The Gem::Specification object has a number of attributes that describe the gem. These include the name of the gem, the author name, the dependencies, and so forth. This description also includes a list of all the files in the project.

Incidentally, you can find the RubyGems documentation for gemspecs at the following URL:

http://docs.rubygems.org/read/chapter/20

Building a Gem Package from a Gemspec

Often, preexisting software needs to be redistributed; gems are a great way to do that. To redistribute your software as a gem package, you'll need to create a gemspec file and then pack it, along with your source code and documentation, into a .gem file. As an example of doing just that, let's modify the TrackTime example we created in Chapter 7 to run in gem form. The TrackTime server is a small Web app, based on Camping; however, most gems are libraries, so for the sake of the example we'll create a shell class around TrackTime. This shell class will launch TrackTime instances, and we'll package the shell class in a gem. This allows us to redistribute to code as we wish, so that anyone with Ruby and RubyGems installed can install our software from the gem file.

■**Note** Our naming conventions will be different here than in Chapter 7; in that chapter, we named the TrackTime application `TrackTime.rb`. In this chapter, the TrackTime application will be saved in a file named `TrackTime_app.rb` and the shell class, which uses the TrackTime application, will be saved in `tracktime.rb`; as a result, when the end user employs the statement `require 'tracktime'`, she'll get the shell class and not the original code.

Our gem will use a simple flat directory structure with just three files. Place the code from Listing 34-1 in a file called `tracktime.rb`.

Listing 34-1. *Class That Starts Tracktime Instances (tracktime.rb)*

```
# This file contains a single class that will let you
# start a TrackTime server easily.
#
# You can use this file as follows:
#
# require 'tracktime'
# TrackTimeServer.start
#
# You can also use it in a Ruby one-liner:
#
# ruby -e "require 'tracktime'; TrackTimeServer.start"
#

require "tracktime.rb"
require "mongrel"

class TrackTimeServer

  # Starts a TrackTime server on the specified interface,
  # port, and mountpoint.
  #
```

```
# Note that since this joins the server thread to the current thread,
# no code after this call will be executed.
#
def TrackTimeServer.start(interface='0.0.0.0', port=3000, mountpoint='tracktime')

  TrackTime::Models::Base.establish_connection :adapter => 'sqlite3',
                                               :database => 'tracktime.db'
  TrackTime::Models::Base.logger = Logger.new('tracktime.log')
  TrackTime.create

  @server = Mongrel::Camping::start(interface, port, "/#{mountpoint}", TrackTime)
  puts "**TrackTime is running on Mongrel - " <<
      "check it out at http://localhost:#{port}/#{mountpoint}"
  @server.run.join
  end
end
```

The code produces a very simple class: It has just one method, which will start a
TrackTime server using mongrel. It uses sqlite3 to host the database, just like the camping
command, which we looked at in Chapter 7. It logs all errors to a tracktime.log file. For more
details on hosting Camping apps using mongrel, see Chapter 17.

Next, copy the TrackTime example from Chapter 7 into tracktime_app.rb; this will contain the actual code that our shell class calls to run the server.

Next we'll create a gem-specification file called gemspec.rb. It will specify two things: what
files are part of our gem, and the metadata (who wrote the gem, what it's named, its version,
the gems it depends on, and so forth). This code is presented in Listing 34-2.

Listing 34-2. *Gem Specification for the TrackTime Gem (gemspec.rb)*

```
SPEC = Gem::Specification.new do |spec|

  # Descriptive and source information for this gem.
  spec.name = "TrackTime"
  spec.version = "1.0.0"
  spec.summary = "A small web application to manage billable hours"

  spec.author = "David Berube"
  spec.email = "djberube@berubeconsulting.com"
  spec.homepage = "http://www.berubeconsulting.com/TrackTime"

  spec.add_dependency("camping", ">1.0.0")
  spec.add_dependency("sqlite3-ruby", ">1.0.0")
  spec.add_dependency("mongrel", ">0.3.0")

  require 'rake'

  unfiltered_files =   FileList['*']
  spec.files = unfiltered_files.delete_if do |filename|
```

```
            filename.include?(".gem") || filename.include?("gemspec")
    end

    spec.has_rdoc = true
    spec.extra_rdoc_files = ["README"]

    spec.require_path = "."
    spec.autorequire = "tracktime.rb"
end
```

This code creates a new Gem::Specification object and sets a few descriptive parameters: name, version, and so forth. It then uses the add_dependency method to add two dependencies—camping and mongrel.

It then uses rake's FileList function to create a list of files in the current directory; this is convenient since this automatically excludes a number of files we don't want to include: backups from editors, version-control files, and so forth. (rake comes with Ruby on Rails, but if you don't have rake installed, you can install it easily via gem install rake. You will only need rake to *build* this gem, though, not to install it. For more on rake, see Chapter 24.)

Tip If you're unsure that the correct files are being grabbed, you can add the following lines to print them to the screen:

```
spec.files.each do |file|
  puts file
end
```

The next property set is the has_rdoc method, which controls whether the gem has RDoc documentation. (RDoc is a document generator that works from Ruby source code; you can find out more at http://rdoc.sourceforge.net/.) The next line, extra_rdoc_files, tells the RDoc generator to include our README file—that means you can view our README file as the first page of the documentation.

The final two statements specify the path and name of the file on which RubyGems should automatically execute a require statement whenever a require statement is executed on our gem.

Next let's make a README file—it'll contain a short description and a few pieces of metadata, such as the author and license. The practice of including a short overview of the gem in a text file named README is very common for gems, and will be included in the RDoc documentation automatically. Put the text from Listing 34-3 in a file named README.

Listing 34-3. *README File for the TrackTime Server (README)*

```
TRACKTIME
---------


TrackTime is a simple web application to track billable hours.
```

It's written using Camping and Mongrel.

You can run it as follows:

ruby -e "require 'tracktime'; TrackTimeServer.start"

Author::   David Berube (mailto:djberube@berubeconsulting.com)
Copyright:: Copyright (c) 2006 David J Berube
Homepage:: http://practicalRubyGems.com
License:: GNU GPL - http://www.gnu.org/copyleft/gpl.html

At this point, you should have four files in a directory: tracktime_app.rb, tracktime.rb, README, and gemspec.rb. Next we can build our gemspec into a .gem file as follows:

```
>gem build gemspec.rb
  Successfully built RubyGem
  Name: TrackTime
  Version: 1.0.0
  File: TrackTime-1.0.0.gem
```

We now have a .gem file: TrackTime-1.0.0.gem. Now we can install it like this:

```
>gem install tracktime-1.0.0.gem
Successfully installed TrackTime, version 1.0.0
Installing ri documentation for TrackTime-1.0.0...
Installing RDoc documentation for TrackTime-1.0.0...
```

Note that we use the fully qualified filename; if our gem were on RubyForge, we could simply execute gem install tracktime. However, since it's available only locally, we have to tell the gem command where to find it.

We've created a gem specification and a gem from that specification. We've even installed the gem we created. Now let's test it as follows:

```
>ruby -e "require 'tracktime'; TrackTimeServer.start"
-- create_table(:tracktime_client_times, {:force=>true})
   -> 0.0310s
**TrackTime is running on Mongrel - check it out at http://localhost:3000/tracktime
```

The first line of output is from ActiveRecord (see Chapter 5 for more details on ActiveRecord)—it's telling us that it created the single table that TrackTime uses, tracktime_client_times, for us. (It's a sqlite3 table, so you won't need to do any configuration; it'll be created in the same directory you run the code from; sqlite is a tiny database system—you can find out more at http://sqlite-ruby.rubyforge.org/.) The second is from our TrackTimeServer class, notifying us that it has started correctly.

If you open a Web browser and go to http://localhost:3000/tracktime, you'll find that you can, indeed, use the TrackTime app—it's being served via our gem.

Conclusion

There is a number of options for packing gems we didn't use in our small example—it doesn't include test files or a directory tree, for example, but creating both of those is straightforward. You can find the complete reference to all the available options at the gemspec documentation: `http://docs.rubygems.org/read/chapter/20`.

However, creating a gem isn't enough—for it to be useful, we need to distribute it. I'll cover the details of gem distribution in the next chapter.

CHAPTER 35

■■■

Distributing Gems

In this chapter you'll learn how you can distribute gems you've created. Typically, you'd either add your gem to an existing gem server or create your own. Either way, your gem will be available to other users.

By default, when you use the gem command, it searches the RubyForge repository. You can add your gems to the RubyForge repository; that will allow anyone anywhere to use the gem install command to install your gem. The gem command lets you specify a custom gem server, so I'll cover setting one up; this can be useful to speed up gem downloads for, say, an entire office.

Distribution Methods

The first and simplest way to distribute a gem is via direct HTTP or FTP download. You simply place the gem file on a Web or FTP server, and your users download the file as they would any downloadable file. They can then install the gem using the full name of the gem file, as you saw in the previous chapter.

For example, if you visited http://practicalrubygems.com and downloaded the TrackTime-1.0.0.gem file, you could install it as follows:

```
cd /path/to/downloaded/gem/file
gem install TrackTime-1.0.0.gem
```

This method involves virtually no setup, and it's very high-performance. You can upload the gem in the same manner you'd update your website—typically via an FTP client. However, using this method involves extra steps for the end user—it's simpler to use the gem install command to download the gem directly. You can do that with the rest of the methods that we will examine in this chapter.

If you distribute your gem on RubyForge, as I'll discuss next, your gem will have the widest distribution possible; users will be able to download and install the gem from any Internet-connected computer worldwide. RubyForge lets any user install your gem with the very simplest form of the gem install command, as follows:

```
gem install tracktime
```

The next method is to distribute your gem locally via a gem server—either using the gem_server script or via a Web server such as Apache. You might want to take this route if for some reason using the RubyForge server is undesirable—if your gem isn't open source, for example. However, using the gem-server method results in a more complicated gem install command:

```
gem install tracktime http://yourserver.hostname:yourport/
```

Let's dive into adding your gem to RubyForge and setting up your own gem server.

Adding Gems to RubyForge

RubyForge provides free resources for open source Ruby projects. It's also the repository the gem install command uses by default, so hosting your project on RubyForge will give your gem the most exposure. It will also provide you with a number of other services, including Web hosting, Subversion version control, bug tracking, forums, and more. It's patterned after SourceForge (http://sourceforge.net/), and much like SourceForge, its services are offered free of charge.

Before you can add your gem to RubyForge, you need to create a RubyForge account. You can do that by visiting http://rubyforge.net and clicking the New Account link in the upper-right corner (Figure 35-1). You'll be asked a few questions, and once you're registered and logged in, you can create a new account by clicking the Register Project link.

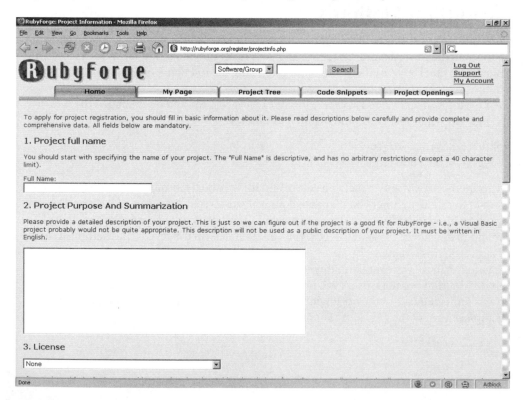

Figure 35-1. *Creating a RubyForge account*

You'll be asked a few questions about your project—the project name, description, license, and so forth. You'll also be asked which license your project will be available under. Different licenses have vastly different impacts on what end users can do with your gem, so choose carefully—the GPL, for example, allows users to redistribute modified versions of a gem under the GPL, whereas a BSD or BSD-like license would let users modify your gem and redistribute it under a proprietary license. There are innumerable other licenses, all of which offer slightly different terms. Figure 35-2 has an example of the kinds of questions RubyForge asks.

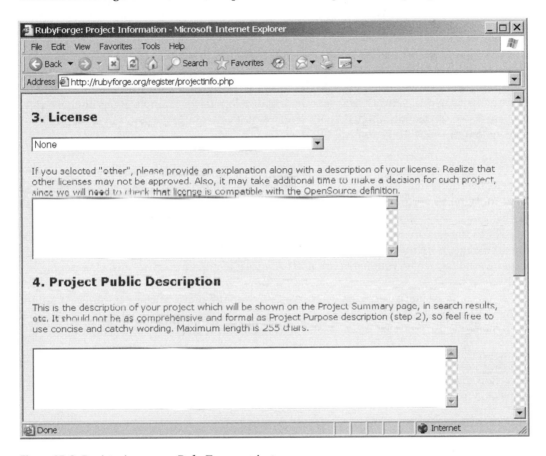

Figure 35-2. *Registering a new RubyForge project*

Note You can also specify a custom license in the event that one of the previously selected options isn't appropriate; simply type in the license terms you prefer. However, this will result in your project's license being reviewed by the RubyForge staff, which will slow down the project's approval. Note that RubyForge accepts only open source projects, so if your license does not meet the *open source* definition provided by the Open Source Institute (http://www.opensource.org/docs/definition.php), it will be rejected.

Once you've created the project, it'll be a few days before it is approved. In some cases, it may not be—for instance, if your project is inappropriate, such as a closed-source project or a project unrelated to Ruby.

Next, you can add files to your project—typically these files are source code, but you can add any type of file associated with your project. If you add a gem file to your project, within a few hours it will be grabbed by an automated process and added to the central gem repository—and then anyone can use the `gem install` command to install it anywhere.

Serving Gems Using gem_server

One easy way to serve gems is using RubyGems' built-in Web server. It can be used on any machine that has RubyGems installed, so it's very simple to get running. Note that the built-in server is low-performance and intended for local use; however, it'll work well if you need to share gems on a local network—for your team of developers, for example. It has not been rigorously tested for security, though, so it's probably not wise to use the gem server on public servers. You can start the gem server like this:

```
gem_server
```

Once you've done that, you can access the server on `localhost:8808`. This serves all of the gems installed on your local machine, so you can use this feature to mirror a number of gems easily.

For example, you could have one machine act as a server for your entire network—install the desired gems on that computer, and then run the `gem_server` command. Because that server would be local to your network—and because it would be used by only a few people—it'd be very fast.

Let's say you'd like to serve the `tracktime` gem from the previous chapter from a computer with the IP address `192.168.0.1`.

First you'd start the gem server on the server machine with the following command:

```
gem_server
```

Then, assuming you have an additional machine you'd install the `tracktime` gem on, you can install it as follows:

```
gem install tracktime --source 192.168.0.1:8808
```

As you can see, it's fairly simple to set up a gem server using the `gem_server` script. The `--source` argument of that command specifies the host name and IP address—in this case, IP address `192.168.0.1` and port 8808.

However, you can also publish your gems using a traditional Web server, such as Apache, LightTPD, or IIS—I'll cover that next.

HOW DOES THE GEM_SERVER SCRIPT WORK?

gem_server starts a tiny Web server that serves pages using WEBrick. WEBrick is a small Web-server-construction framework—it's similar to mongrel, which we covered in Chapter 17. gem_server includes just enough server code to serve gems and no more—it hooks into WEBrick to provide the gem index, which tells the gem install command where the gems can be found, and it provides the gems themselves.

gem_server does a lot of the work for us. Specifically, it provides a tiny Web server and automatically indexes all of our gems. As a result, it's easy to use, but you pay the price in flexibility—you can't serve any content other than gems; additionally, gem_server isn't safe to use on a public server (it hasn't been thoroughly vetted for security) and it's also not particularly fast. It is, however, excellent for use on a private network.

Serving Gems with a Full Web Server

You can also use a regular Web server to serve gems. This gives you all of the advantages of a full Web server such as Apache, IIS, or LightTPD—scalability, performance, and the ability to serve non-gem content. You could, for example, have one subdomain with the documentation for your gem and one with the downloadable gem.

Suppose you had an Apache server installed on a computer. Assuming that your webroot is in /var/www/html, you could create a gem repository served with Apache with the following shell command on Linux or OS X:

```
cd /var/www/html
mkdir gems
cp /path/to/my/gems .
index_gem_repository.rb -d /var/www/html
```

The default webroot for Windows is C:\Program Files\Apache Group\Apache\htdocs, so under Windows you would use the following commands at the command prompt:

```
cd C:\Program Files\Apache Group\Apache\htdocs
mkdir gems
copy C:\path\to\my\gems .
index_gem_repository -d C:\Program Files\Apache Group\Apache\htdocs
```

In both examples, you'd have to replace /path/to/my/gems with the path to the gems you want to serve.

The index_gem_repository command creates an index of the gem directory—it contains all of the information needed to search, locate, and download gems from our repository. Once that command is run, and assuming our Web server is started, our repository can be accessed via the gem command.

Just as we did for the previous example, we can use the --source argument of the gem install command to install the gem. Use the following command to do so:

```
gem install tracktime --source 192.168.0.1:8808
```

As you can see, it's slightly more complicated to use Apache to serve gems than it is to use gem_server, but it's still relatively simple—and since we have access to all of Apache's abilities, we can add other content, such as HTML pages, as desired.

Conclusion

There are a few different ways to distribute gems, and they each fill a different niche. However, between distributing your gems to the world at large using SourceForge, running a small local gem server, and running your own gem-distribution site on a full Web server, you're sure to find a solution that fits your needs.

Index

You Need the Companion eBook

Your purchase of this book entitles you to buy the companion PDF-version eBook for only $10. Take the weightless companion with you anywhere.

We believe this Apress title will prove so indispensable that you'll want to carry it with you everywhere, which is why we are offering the companion eBook (in PDF format) for $10 to customers who purchase this book now. Convenient and fully searchable, the PDF version of any content-rich, page-heavy Apress book makes a valuable addition to your programming library. You can easily find and copy code—or perform examples by quickly toggling between instructions and the application. Even simultaneously tackling a donut, diet soda, and complex code becomes simplified with hands-free eBooks!

Once you purchase your book, getting the $10 companion eBook is simple:

❶ Visit **www.apress.com/promo/tendollars/**.

❷ Complete a basic registration form to receive a randomly generated question about this title.

❸ Answer the question correctly in 60 seconds, and you will receive a promotional code to redeem for the $10.00 eBook.

2560 Ninth Street • Suite 219 • Berkeley, CA 94710

eBookshop

THE EXPERT'S VOICE™

Offer valid through 10/07.

forums.apress.com

FOR PROFESSIONALS BY PROFESSIONALS™

JOIN THE APRESS FORUMS AND BE PART OF OUR COMMUNITY. You'll find discussions that cover topics of interest to IT professionals, programmers, and enthusiasts just like you. If you post a query to one of our forums, you can expect that some of the best minds in the business—especially Apress authors, who all write with *The Expert's Voice*™—will chime in to help you. Why not aim to become one of our most valuable participants (MVPs) and win cool stuff? Here's a sampling of what you'll find:

DATABASES

Data drives everything.

Share information, exchange ideas, and discuss any database programming or administration issues.

INTERNET TECHNOLOGIES AND NETWORKING

Try living without plumbing (and eventually IPv6).

Talk about networking topics including protocols, design, administration, wireless, wired, storage, backup, certifications, trends, and new technologies.

JAVA

We've come a long way from the old Oak tree.

Hang out and discuss Java in whatever flavor you choose: J2SE, J2EE, J2ME, Jakarta, and so on.

MAC OS X

All about the Zen of OS X.

OS X is both the present and the future for Mac apps. Make suggestions, offer up ideas, or boast about your new hardware.

OPEN SOURCE

Source code is good; understanding (open) source is better.

Discuss open source technologies and related topics such as PHP, MySQL, Linux, Perl, Apache, Python, and more.

PROGRAMMING/BUSINESS

Unfortunately, it is.

Talk about the Apress line of books that cover software methodology, best practices, and how programmers interact with the "suits."

WEB DEVELOPMENT/DESIGN

Ugly doesn't cut it anymore, and CGI is absurd.

Help is in sight for your site. Find design solutions for your projects and get ideas for building an interactive Web site.

SECURITY

Lots of bad guys out there—the good guys need help.

Discuss computer and network security issues here. Just don't let anyone else know the answers!

TECHNOLOGY IN ACTION

Cool things. Fun things.

It's after hours. It's time to play. Whether you're into LEGO® MINDSTORMS™ or turning an old PC into a DVR, this is where technology turns into fun.

WINDOWS

No defenestration here.

Ask questions about all aspects of Windows programming, get help on Microsoft technologies covered in Apress books, or provide feedback on any Apress Windows book.

HOW TO PARTICIPATE:

Go to the Apress Forums site at **http://forums.apress.com/**.

Click the New User link.